D0897901

save
every
lamb

books by JESSE STUART

Man with a Bull-Tongue Plow
Head o' W-Hollow
Beyond Dark Hills
Trees of Heaven
Men of the Mountains
Taps for Private Tussie
Mongrel Mettle
Album of Destiny
Foretaste of Glory
Tales from the Plum Grove Hills
The Thread That Runs So True
Hie to the Hunters
Clearing in the Sky
Kentucky Is My Land
The Good Spirit of Laurel Ridge
The Year of My Rebirth
Plowshare in Heaven
God's Oddling
Hold April
A Jesse Stuart Reader
Save Every Lamb

FOR BOYS AND GIRLS

Penny's Worth of Character
The Beatinest Boy
Red Mule
The Rightful Owner
Andy Finds A Way

save every lamb

JESSE STUART

illustrations by
Jean George

McGRAW-HILL BOOK COMPANY
New York   Toronto   London

The author wishes to acknowledge with gratitude the cooperation of
the publishers and publications in whose volumes the material herein
first appeared. "Save Every Lamb!" *Trees of Heaven*, E. P. Dutton &
Co., Inc.; "The Blue Tick Pig," *Esquire*; "Frog-Trouncin' Contest,"
Story; "Turtle Hunt," *The Good Spirit of Laurel Ridge*, McGraw-
Hill Book Company, Inc.; "Sparkie and Did," *Hie to the Hunters*,
McGraw-Hill Book Company, Inc.; "Dawn of Remembered Spring,"
Harper's Bazaar; "King of the Hills," "Saving the Bees," *Esquire*; "To
Market, to Market," *Southern Fireside*; "Soddy," *Chicago*; "Of Yes-
terday," *Southern Literary Messenger*; "Angel in the Pasture," *Esquire*;
"Hot-collared Mule," *Columbia*, under the title "Rock and Rye"; "The
Chase of the Skittish Heifer," *Progressive Farmer*; "The Old Are
Valiant," *Mountain Life and Work*; "Thanksgiving Hunter," *House-
hold*; "Hummingbird," *National Wildlife*; "August," *The Year of My
Rebirth*, McGraw-Hill Book Company, Inc.; "Cities That Vanish
in the Sky," "Night and the Whippoorwill," the *Louisville Courier-
Journal*; "Or They Perish," *American Forests*.

dedication

To "Big" Aaron and "Little" Ed Howard, Cousin Glenn "Penny" Hilton, William (Bill) Collins, Jack Dysard, Aubrey Greene, James Stuart, and Robert "Bob" and William "Bill" Hillman.

contents

introduction, 1

1 Save Every Lamb, 11

save every lamb!, 13
the blue tick pig, 20
wolf boy from walnut ridge, 38
frog-trouncin' contest, 51
turtle hunt, 63
sparkie and did, 72

2 Angel in the Pasture, 93

dawn of remembered spring, 95
king of the hills, 104
saving the bees, 117
another home for the squirrels, 139
to market, to market, 148
soddy, 166
of yesterday, 179
angel in the pasture, 191

3 Night and the Whippoorwill, 195

sir birchfield, 197
old lollipop, 210
hot-collared mule, 216
the chase of the skittish heifer, 227
the old are valiant, 239
thanksgiving hunter, 247
hummingbird, 256
august, 261
cities that vanish in the sky, 266
night and the whippoorwill, 270
or they perish, 274

Oh, singing world, you are too beautiful
Tonight—upon the misty moonlit hill
I hear the plaintive singing whippoorwill,
And down in white-top fields the beetles lull
A drowsy song—and jar-flies sing to rest
The sweaty mules that lie on pine-tree needles.
Oh, world of whippoorwills, jar-flies and beetles!
And now a corn-bird fluting from the nest!
The katydids are singing everywhere—
And down among the trees the night-hawk screams.
The pasture branch is fretting sod-grass seams.
The lazy cows lie under dew-drenched willows
And dream of calving time and better meadows.

—JESSE STUART

from *Man with a Bull-tongue Plow*

introduction

When I was born in W-Hollow, Greenup County, Kentucky, August 1907, this was a wild country. The area was sparsely settled and hills and valleys were filled with quail, grouse, rabbit, possums, ground hog, squirrel, raccoon, weasel, mink, polecat, a few wild turkeys, deer and wildcats. The rivers and streams, then unpolluted, were filled with fish. In the vast timbered areas there were plenty of "bee trees" where the wild honey bees lived and made wild sourwood honey. I was born in this wonderful country, here I grew from boyhood to manhood, and today I live about a mile from where I was born.

Since this was a rural area when I was a boy, every family who lived in the country depended upon the land for its sustenance. No man worked for industry then and got a weekly pay check. We had to "dig our livin' from the hills and valleys." Our fathers were hunters too. They didn't hunt because they had a lust to kill. They hunted to supply our tables with wild meat.

Since this wasn't the day of mechanized farm equipment, we had to use horses and mules on our farms. We had to depend upon our domestic animals for our livelihood and our domestic animals had to depend upon us. Every man who lived among these hills had his mules, horses, cows, hogs, sheep, chickens. No one bought dairy milk in those days. No one bought loaves of bakery baked bread. I was sixteen years old and at Fort Knox, Kentucky, before I ever tasted a loaf of bakery bread.

When I was born, my father was a coal miner. Because he was dissatisfied with the brittle slate roof of his mine and the poor pay, he left the coal mines. We moved from the high ridge down into W-Hollow, where he rented land to farm. We were sharecroppers who moved from farm to farm. We lived on six different farms until my father bought fifty acres on which my grandfather and I built a house. Here we became self-sustaining, like the other families around us. We raised corn which we had ground at the mill for cornbread. We ate cornbread for our noon and evening meals. We raised wheat on hillsides which we cut with cradles, threshed and had ground into flour from which we made biscuits for breakfast. My mother baked loaves for special occasions. We kept from two to eighteen cows. We fattened from two to twelve hogs. We had 500 sheep, a span of horses and two spans of mules. We kept over 300 chickens, raised geese, ducks, turkeys, and guineas. And we kept as many as fifty head of cattle. Our fifty acres didn't support all our livestock. We rented land to farm, land which we have since purchased.

When the 1937 flood flooded this Ohio River Valley and cut us off from the stores in Greenup, Kentucky, we were self-sustaining. We kept a score of refugees in our home until the flood went down. We had most everything, even sorghum and honey to substitute for sugar. But we didn't have coffee. My Uncle Martin Hilton, who lived much the same as we did, wouldn't accept "Red Cross" coffee which was given out to flood victims. We gladly accepted it while Uncle Martin Hilton parched corn and made himself corn-coffee. This was the kind of world in which I grew up, a world that has changed because of more people, industry, and new hard-surfaced roads that now reach all parts of this area.

2

My earliest memories are of our domestic animals and our hunting hounds. Domestic animals and dogs were almost a part of our family. We loved and cared for them as no other people on earth I have ever known. Our hunting hounds and my father's gun kept us supplied with wild meat for our table when I was a small boy, and I followed in his footsteps and carried the rabbits, squirrels, and birds he killed. At night I carried the sack of wild game our possum and coon hounds treed. By the time I was twelve I was hunting with a gun. And often at this age I went into the woods alone on dark autumn nights and hunted all night. I was a good young hunter, an excellent shot with a rifle or gun.

Since this was the life I lived in my youth, it is only natural that I should write about the things I know. Even when I went to high school, one of my best themes, "Nest Egg," was written about a rooster I owned. According to the editors of *Atlantic Monthly*, it turned out to be a short story and was accepted and published twenty years after I wrote it. Every piece in this book, *Save Every Lamb*, is based upon real facts that originated in W-Hollow and the nearby areas surrounding this valley.

"Save Every Lamb" is an excerpt from my first novel, *Trees of Heaven*. And this is the very way my father, mother, brother, sisters, and I saved our lambs. During World War II, when meat was rationed and sheep and cattle were becoming scarce, this excerpt was taken from my novel and was used in Agricultural Colleges and Universities and by the U.S. Department of Agriculture.

Although the first section of this book is devoted to a miscellany of stories about people and animals, these all have their background in the wonderful world of my youth. They are based on my own family with names changed, about my relatives or my close friends. "The Blue Tick Pig," named after a hunting hound my father had once owned, was my pet pig. During a number of my boyhood years, I left school to

3

work to help support our family. First I worked for twenty-five cents a day, later I made fifty cents a day. The man for whom I worked asked me one day if I would rather have the quarter or a little runt pig for my day's work, and naturally I chose the pig. Old Opp Acres, in "Turtle Hunt," was my neighbor and friend who had squatted on my land, and to repay him for this I incorporated him in a novel. I hope I immortalized him in the *The Good Spirit of Laurel Ridge.* He deserves to live forever. Although I, too, had grown up on the land, Opp gave me a college education in wildlife and nature. "Wolf Boy from Walnut Ridge" happened a few miles away from W-Hollow in Greenup County. It shows the true nature of our people, people who love a dog more than they like to work. I simply could not manufacture a story like this, although I have toned it down from the way it happened.

Since readers will not believe the truth, I have had to mix some fiction with my animal, turtle, snake, and bee stories. Now, I have never attended a "Frog-Trouncin' Contest," but my Uncle Jeff, who lived with us more than twenty years, had attended them. "Sparkie and Did" were my boyhood friends, and the reason I know about their hunts and escapades is because I hunted and square-danced with them. Little Did was a good student and city born, and big Sparkie never knew exactly who he was. But it didn't matter, for no man who does know who he is has ever enjoyed life more than Sparkie. Sparkie's mules, Dick and Dinah, are based on two of my father's favorite animals and I didn't even bother to change their names.

The second section, "Angel in the Pasture," is a group of stories connected with the Powderjay family. I didn't do very well trying to hide the identity of the Powderjays. Anyone who has read many of my books and stories long ago guessed that the Powderjays were the Stuarts, that Finn Powderjay was

4

James Stuart and Shan Powderjay was Jesse Stuart. Finn and Shan's parents even have the same names as my parents— Mick and Sall.

In "Dawn of Remembered Spring" I tell of the time I saw a pair of copperheads mating. The place I found them (only time I ever saw this in my life) is less than a hundred yards from where we live today. Since this is one of the farms we rented when I was a boy, we lived here from the time I was nine years old until I was twelve. A family by the name of Deer lived farther down the stream. In those years I probably killed more water snakes than any youth in America, for I worked at killing water snakes for three summers. I think I cleaned them out of W-Hollow and only a very few have ever come back. "King of the Hills" I wrote as an article, but it was accepted and published as a short story. Black Boy was the greatest hunting dog we ever owned. He lived the longest, and at his death we buried him on the top of a cone-shaped hill, the highest on this farm. We put a pile of rocks on his grave so his final resting place, we thought, would always be marked. We had love and great respect for all our hunting dogs.

Today when I read in the papers about our delinquents, I wonder about what I might have been called if the truth had been known in my day and time. When I think of "Saving the Bees" even today I shudder. We believed bees should be left wild among the trees, and we did our best to set all domesticated bees free from their hives, to return to their natural way of life. Yet we barely missed getting shot. And we had a gun shooting back. Every boy in our group was an excellent marksman with a pistol, rifle, and shotgun. "Saving the Bees" isn't a fabricated story; we joyfully lived it. And even after we were grown up, and I was a teacher, we kept our bee-"saving" a guarded secret.

We lived in this house where I am living today when my

grandfather, Nathan Hylton, who lived with us and cut timber, brought the pet squirrels of "Another Home for the
Squirrels" to me. That was when we had our hunting hounds,
Rags and Scout. I made one change in this story, where my
grandfather was dressing up to go to his Church Association.
He was actually dressing up to go see a widow, whom he later
married. She was his third wife and he her fourth husband.
My grandfather had outlived my first two grandmothers. His
new wife outlived her first three husbands, but my grandfather outlived her.

My father used to say that if he kept good bulls and let
his neighbors breed their cows to his bulls, he would be help-
ing the community. He would be getting a better stock of
cattle among our hills. As far back as I can remember he kept
good bulls, but later in his life he wouldn't have a bull unless
he had "the papers" with him. He would pay $500 for a bull,
a suckling calf, when only once in his life had he made more
than $100 per month. Boss was one of these bulls. He was
everything—and more—that I have described in "To Market,
to Market." When the fox hunters teased this bull my father
went back on the ridge at night and tried to catch them. He
could handle and make a pet of any kind of animal. He never
had a bull he had to lead with a ring in his nose. He never
owned a bull that wouldn't follow him like a dog.

Soddy was my calf. And when I owned him we lived here
where we live today. I didn't want him vealed and he wasn't
vealed, because I was determined that he shouldn't be. We
didn't have Don (we often called him Don-Sequal) when we
lived here. We had him much later, after we moved into the
house my Grandfather Hylton and I built on the fifty acres of
land my father bought. Since James is nine years younger
than I am, he had grown up to the age of ten and was now
hunting with a gun. Don-Sequal was really his dog, but all of
us claimed him. We had to feed this dog biscuits and warm
sweet milk. He was a very fragile shepherd and tired easily.

He lived to be only three years old. He was a favorite dog at our house, and we always said then if he had been a person and had gone to school he would have been a real scholar and made top grades. He is mentioned in "Of Yesterday," a dream that I had to write down.

Now, "Angel in the Pasture" is another dream, which happened under entirely different circumstances. It is something I didn't write at all. I dictated this to my wife from my hospital bed in Murray, Kentucky, in October 1954. I had had such a violent heart attack that I wasn't given much chance to live. I couldn't use my hands. The dream was so vivid that I had to get it on paper. And the background of where the dream took place is the home in which we live today. We had lived here from 1915–1918. The cow Gypsy, in "Angel in the Pasture," was the mother of my calf Soddy. And this same strain of cattle goes down to another relative in this book, Lollipop.

In the third section, "Night and the Whippoorwill," are articles and stories that deal with my family, my wife Naomi, and our daughter Jane. "Sir Birchfield," our beloved cocker, sleeps under a pine in the high portion of our yard. Our "Old Lollipop" is now thirty years of age, and is grazing among the stalwart Hereford cattle on a grassy upland slope of our pastures. I saw her less than an hour ago, with her new calf tagging after her.

"Hot-collared Mule" is a story of one of my father's mule trades. This happened when I was a boy and we were living in the little three-room log shack in W-Hollow from which we moved to the house where I now live. "The Chase of the Skittish Heifer" happened here on my father's farm. I wrote this as an article, using real names, but it was taken as a short story. In this instance the truth becomes fiction. "The Old Are Valiant" was written as an article and became a story. My father and I were hoeing potatoes up at the tobacco barn, near Old Opp's cabin, when Jerry-B Boneyard fought

7

the big blacksnake. I wanted to help Jerry-B, as I said in the story, but my father would have none of it. He never liked Jerry-B too well, and I think his sympathies in this fight leaned heavily toward the blacksnake.

"Thanksgiving Hunter" I wrote during dove season in Kentucky after Naomi and I were married, and we had renovated the old house where I had lived when I was nine to twelve and came here in W-Hollow to live. I hadn't posted my land at this time, and hunters came in from everywhere and killed doves that nested in the pines near our barn. They had fed in our barnloft and had picked up the grain our cattle hadn't eaten. Part of this story is fiction. I did find a dove with its eyes shot out and it flew up trying to reach its mate when one called. I knew then there'd never be any more dove hunting on this farm while I owned it. And there hasn't been, either. The dove is one of the most beautiful and innocent birds that flies, and it should never be killed.

When I was brought home from Murray Hospital to my bed here to recover from the heart attack, I had to work my way slowly back to normal life. I had time to think and time to reflect while I was learning to walk again and to get the use of my hands. I made friends with all the wildlife I could. I protected and fed them. And in our yard we planted horsemint so the hummingbirds would come. So I sat and observed the hummingbirds. In our backyard I had time to gather ants and carry them from one ant colony to another and have a battle. After this battle, which took place in August 1956 and is described in "August," I have never had another anthill in the backyard. Other observations were the inspiration for "Cities That Vanish in the Sky" and "Night and the Whippoorwill." I even had time to observe the spiders, insects I had never given much thought to before. When I was recuperating the second year, I used to walk not too far from the house, spread my raincoat on the ground and lie down because I had grown so tired of my bed in the house. Here I

would lie and watch the spiders. And, of course, nights then and now bring the lonesome songs of the whippoorwills—our sacred bird, if we have one.

My world has changed since I was a boy, when everybody in the country lived by digging his livelihood from the ground. No one digs all his livelihood from the soil here any more. Everyone works in industry and drives to and from his work. Men who used to farm and live from the products they grew on their farms now get paid by our Federal government for not farming. This philosophy has changed our country and our people. It has also had a direct bearing on all wildlife. The best example I know is the farm I now own. We used to have twenty-six coveys of quail on this farm. We knew the places where they fed, their cover areas in thickets, and the wild honeysuckle areas where they took refuge at night. Today there is not a covey of quail on these one thousand acres. Since we and others get paid not to grow corn, we leave the land fallow. We do not sow grass for meadows but we cut and bale the grass. Quails used to feed around our corn shocks. Possums, rabbits, and birds ate this corn too. No ripe grass seeds fall from our meadow grasses.

Since we no longer have orchards, but buy imported fruit from our local stores, there are no fallen apples that freeze and lie under the leaves for possums and rabbits. Our wildlife is starving to death. I've seen possums out in my meadows in winter eating dirt. We feed our birds in winter, since we mow our fields and none of the weed patches are left where there used to be weed seed. Today I don't know of a single field of corn grown in this valley. Not only have we stopped planting grain for our wildlife to eat, but the population is growing, and the land where Did and Sparkie used to hunt is now a small sea of houses. Wildlife is shoved back to its last wild refuge stands. These wild areas are dwindling year by year. When wildlife, rabbits, possums, birds and even foxes, are finally starved into submission and try to find feed

9

around houses, they are killed by ruthless young or would-be hunters who kill for the joy of killing. Not half enough has been said in America about what is happening and what will happen to our wildlife if something isn't done in a hurry to preserve those species we have left. My once wonderful world has changed into a world that gives me great unhappiness, and there are not enough of us left to turn the tide of destruction and the starvation of wildlife. This is why I wrote "Or They Perish." Our wildlife, if not fed and protected, will become extinct, and the youth of tomorrow will not have the kind of wonderful world my boyhood friends and I had in which to grow from boyhood to manhood.

1 ❧

Save
Every
Lamb

save every lamb!

Tarvin walks back across the sheep-shanty floor. He puts the gun back in the corner. Subrinea closes the door.

"When air you goin' to feed these lambs, Subrinea?" Tarvin asks.

"Atter while I aim to let their mammies feed 'em."

"Good!"

"It's time now fer more lambs in the barn. Git your boots on and let's go look."

"All right." Tarvin walks back over to the stove. He picks up his boots where he has their tops turned toward the heat from the stove so they will dry. He slips his dried socks into the boots, fastens the straps, sits down on his chair, buckles the straps, and laces the buckskin strings through the eyes and around the hooks.

"Where did you git the water in this pan?"

"I melted snow in the teakettle. That's how I got it."

"I never thought about that."

"Your Pappie said wimmen would know more about lambs than men."

"Yep, he told Ma that. Ma wanted to come out here whether 'r not. Pa wouldn't let 'er. I'm glad she didn't come."

"I am too."

"We jest need one lantern, Honey."

Tarvin and Subrinea walk out to the big barn. They walk side by side in the blustery wind. The skies are coated by frost until they cannot see the moon and stars. They hear the ewes bleating in the barn. They walk through the mist to the barn door, open it and walk down the rows of lambing pens. They look around at the ewes. The ewes look up at them with soft innocent eyes.

"Here's one," says Subrinea. "Look, Tarvin! Ain't he a purty little thing!"

"Dead, ain't he?" Tarvin asks.

"Nope, he's not dead," says Subrinea, bending over the lambing pen and lifting the lifeless lamb in her arms. "It ain't dead. I feel its heart beatin'. It's only cold—the poor little baby is—"

Subrinea takes a pencil from her pocket. She marks a figure 5 on a post in the lambing pen that is near the entry. "Hold this lamb," she says. Tarvin takes the lamb in one arm, holds the lantern with his other hand. Subrinea takes a twine string from her pocket and a piece of paper. She writes "5" on the tag of paper and ties it around the lamb's neck. They walk down the rows of lambing pens on the right side of the entry where they first entered the barn. They do not find another lamb. "Can't tell," says Subrinea; "might be ten lambs born on this side of the barn before mornin'."

Tarvin carries the lamb as they walk over the straw-covered barn floor to the other side of the barn. They walk down one row of lambing pens and up another. "Look," says Subrinea, "look, Tarvin! Here's two, look!"

"Yep," says Tarvin. "One is sucklin' his mammie. We'll leave 'im. Other little fellar is all pooped out."

Subrinea bends her tall thin body over the lambing pen. She picks up the lamb in her arms and holds it as if it were a young baby.

"Can you hold it too, Tarvin," Subrinea asks, "while I

mark the post on this pen?" Subrinea marks "7" on the post.

"Why'd you mark '7'?"

"Because '5' is in your arms and '6' is there with his mammie."

Subrinea takes a tag and puts it around his neck. She takes one lamb from Tarvin's arms, he carries the other lamb and the lantern. They walk toward the sheep-shanty. The shrill wind sweeping over the ridge top blows her golden hair about Subrinea's shoulders and down over the collar of a heavy well-worn frizzled coat.

Tarvin sets the lantern down to open the door. Subrinea dashes into the shanty in a hurry so as to avoid a puff of winter wind that will chill the warm room. She lays the lamb down on the floor. Tarvin hurries into the shanty, puts his lantern on the floor and lays his lamb down beside Subrinea's.

15

"Now let's warm 'em," says Subrinea. She gets the pan of warm water from the stove. She puts her hand into the water to see if it is too warm. "The water is a little warm but it's about right fer these lambs," Subrinea says. "They air very cold. We must hurry." She puts her lamb into the pan of water. She keeps its nose above the water and rubs its legs and back with warm snow-water. The legs begin to move. The lamb begins to show life. "See, it ain't dead," says Subrinea. She is greatly pleased at what the warm water will do. "It ain't goin' to die if I have anything to do with it. I've been where babies were born and I know what to do. I've had to shake breath into a few of these lambs."

Subrinea feels sure of herself with lambs because she has helped with the births of babies among the women of her people. She has learned from her experiences going with her mother. Her mother taught her all she knew and all that was handed down from her grandmother. When it comes to working with the lambs, it is easy for Subrinea. She loves to work with them.

"You can do most anything," Tarvin says. "You'd be a good wife fer a farmer."

"Yes, if I loved 'im."

"A woman must have a strong backbone, nerves solid as a rock cliff, and muscles strong as wild grapevine to go through with all my mother has gone through," Tarvin says, as he watches Subrinea bathe the lambs in the pan of hot water. "There ain't many wimmen that could do it. I jest look at Ma goin' around in shoes without stockin's on her legs. I see the big clumps of blood showin' under the skin in the broken veins. I see the strain of toil on her face. I jest wonder if life is worth livin' when a woman hast to work like Ma has had to work. Ma is still workin' and Pa is still workin'. They have had to pay the price to git a little ahead."

The little lamb baa-baas in the pan. He kicks the warm

water from the pan trying to get on his feet. "Ah, comin' to life, ain't you, Honey—ah, comin' to life!" She lifts the lamb from the pan of water. "Take 'im, Tarvin," she says, "and put 'im under the blanket until he dries. Take 'im away while I bring life back to this 'n."

Tarvin takes the lamb while Subrinea works with the one in the pan, saturating him with warm water, rubbing his feet, legs, and his body. Subrinea's long shapely fingers work over the lamb's body. Tarvin turns back the heavy blanket and puts this lamb with his tag around his neck beside the other lambs. "That's funny, Subrinea, this puttin' lambs to bed," Tarvin laughs. He pulls his pipe from his pocket and loads it with bright burley leaf. He walks over to the stove, takes a stick of kindling and lights his pipe from the blaze in the stove.

"I'm beginnin', Honey, to like to work with sheep fer the first time in my life," Tarvin laughs. "I can't hep it about the weather. Sunshine is bound to come back again. The grass will grow. The trees will leaf. The birds will sing. We'll see lambs on the pasture then and we'll think about this night."

"Yes, Tarvin," says Subrinea. "He's kickin' and baain'! Come and git 'im. Put 'im under the blanket." Subrinea stands up with the lamb in her hands. The water drips from his body to the floor. Subrinea shakes the water from his body and hands the lamb to Tarvin. Tarvin carries him over and puts him across the cot.

A little later, Tarvin lifts one of the dry lambs from the bed. The lamb kicks Tarvin with his long strong legs. He looks at Tarvin with his big innocent eyes. If it had not been for Subrinea he would have been dead. His eyes would have been cold and glaring now and his little body would have been carried out and buried under the snow for the foxes, or it would have lain there until the snow melted and the crows

17

would have stripped his carcass clean. "It's a purty lamb," Tarvin says. He fingers over its dry fluffy body. "You couldn't freeze this lamb to death now."

"Let's take them to their mothers," says Subrinea. "You can carry two lambs and a lantern and I can carry two lambs. Let's take them to their mothers before the milk cakes in their sacks."

"Yes, we'd better."

They carry the lambs to the barn, walk down the entries to the lambing pens with numbers marked on the posts corresponding to the numbers on the tags around the lambs' necks. They put each lamb with its right mother. The ewe knows her lamb by the smell.

"That's funny," Tarvin says, "that in a pasture where there air three hundred yowes and over three hundred lambs, each lamb can find his mother. He smells of a lot of the yowes sometimes before he gits the right one, but he allus gits the right one."

"Look at that mother," says Subrinea, "she won't let number four suckle."

"Yes, she will," says Tarvin. "I'll hold her and you milk a little milk into the lamb's mouth."

Subrinea and Tarvin climb over the rails on the lambing pen. Tarvin catches the ewe by the flanks and holds her. Subrinea milks a few drops from the ewe. She puts the lamb in the right place and in position. She milks tiny streams into his mouth. The lamb starts to suckle his mother. Tarvin holds the ewe and makes her own the lamb. "About one yowe out'n every forty," he says, "won't own her lamb. It's a lot of trouble when a yowe won't own her twins."

Tarvin and Subrinea walk up and down the rows of lambing pens in the darkness of the night amid the sour scent of sheep smell. They carry lambs to the shanty when they chill. They put them in a pan of heated snow-water and warm their bodies back to life. They put them under the

18

warm blanket and dry them. They carry them back to their mothers. They work side by side in the cold blustery night, a night that freezes birds, chickens, pheasants and rabbits to death. Tarvin and Subrinea, with heavy garments clothing their young strong bodies, do not mind the cold. They are happy at their work.

the blue tick pig

Ragweeds are smelly on a hot day. You try pullin'
weeds for the pig and you will know that the hot
sour smell will fill every air sack in your lungs. But
that is what the pig likes. It likes ragweeds, pulsey,
careless and horseweeds. But horseweeds are down
by the river and who's going down there and cut
horseweeds with a butcher knife and carry them
across one's hip and under one's arm one-half mile
for a blue and white spotted pig that looks like a
blue-tick fox hound? One has to think an awful lot
of the pig to do this after one has chopped weeds in
the corn all day. Pulsey and careless are down in
the corn field. A body could pull careless all day
and not have an arm load. Pulsey is too flat on the
ground and it is hard to stoop over and pull it. A
backbone cracks like a broom handle if it would
have to bend over all day and pull pulsey. That is
why it is better to pull the ragweeds from behind
the wellbox for the pig. They have to be cut out of
the yard anyway. Just as well pull them for the
pig.

Pa named him. Called him Blue Tick soon as
I packed him home that day. I worked one day for
Cy Shelton, pullin' tater onions and carried them
to the crib loft to dry. When the sun went down
and I started to go home Cy Shelton said to me,
"Do you want the quarter for your day's work or

would you like to have a pig?" I had never seen the pig, but I says, "I'll take the pig."

So we went out at the pig pen. There was fourteen pigs in a straw bed on the north side of the rail fence in a corner. The sow was fightin' them and they were fightin' the sow. "Here is the pig," Cy said, and he handed me the runt pig by the ears and it was squealin'. The sow jumped up and boo-booed at us two or three times when Cy was balanced on the rail with the pig by the ears. Soon as he straightened up his back and handed me the pig, the sow laid back down on the straw and the thirteen pigs went to nudging her for more milk.

I put the pig in my overall pocket. And Cy said, "Watch and don't smother it. That pig ain't big as a house rat, remember. I been a little afraid a hog-pen rat was goin' to git it sometimes when it got away from the sow. It's the runt. It can't get any milk from the sow. I knowed we'd have to raise it by hand. We don't have time to fool with raisin' a pig like that. The runt usually makes the best hog. It will do it nine times out of every ten. Take care of that pig and you'll have a hog there someday."

W'y of course I'd ruther have Blue Tick as a quarter. A quarter will only buy me two yards of muslin at the store to make me a shirt. It will buy Pa three pokes of Red Horse chewin' tobacco. It will buy three pounds of sugar. A quarter is just what they need at home. They use quarters too often. Now I have the pig. The pig is mine. Someday it will grow to be a hog and then I couldn't put it in my overall pocket. It would rip it then from corner to corner. Think of a big hog in my pocket! I have a rat-sized blue pig with white spots on it. The path is just two miles home. And when I get there I'll give the pig milk. I hope it lives till I get home. If it lives till I get there then it will live to be a hog.

"Less why didn't you take the quarter instead of bringin' that runt pig back here? That is like Cy Shelton to cheat a

child. If he'd fool with me two minutes I'll take that pig back over there and make him eat hair, eyes, blood and all raw as a turnip. Got you over there to work and pammed a pig off on you that is not worth a dime when you was to get a quarter. A runt pig! A day's work gravelin' out tater onions and carryin' them to the crib loft on a hot July day! Takes advantage of my child with a runt pig for a day's work! Come on, let's take that pig back."

"Pa, I wanted the pig. I wanted to raise it. I asked Cy Shelton to take the pig instead of the quarter."

"You did huh! Well, why did you do it?"

"Well, I go out and work for a quarter. I bring it home.

You take the quarter down to the store and you buy salt, sugar, tobacco. I don't get anything. The quarter ain't nothing to me. It is something dead. It is just like a rock. Now I have somethin' that's mine. If it only lives to be a hog. Then look what I'll have. Now it is like a little mouse sleeping here in my pocket."

Pa got over his mad spell. But he wanted the quarter I was to get for my day's work. He wouldn't have the pig. He says it looks like a blue-tick hound did that he used to own. He said the blue-tick hound was a jim-dandy possum dog, the best that this country ever saw. So, Pa, calls my pig, Blue Tick. Pa says, "That Blue Tick pig you got out there at the barn. It takes more time to feed it than it is worth."

23

I tell Pa, "W'y I don't mind runnin' down a goose a-pullin' a tail feather out a quill to fit a bottle stopper for Blue Tick to put his little long rat-like mouth over and draw cow milk from the castor-oil bottle. But I washed the bottle clean. I'd do anything for Blue Tick. I don't mind. When I'm out workin' in the field and the dinner bell rings, I jump over corn rows and furrows and stumps to get down to the house and feed Blue Tick. Murt Hensley told me to keep him on the same cow's milk. And I have done it. I've had him on old Pansy's milk ever since I got him."

Pa saunters out to the little pen I have him in by the wood shed. He stands by the pen and he says, "Someday, and that not before very long, that pig is comin' out of there. Mind what I tell you, them little foot-high boards ain't goin' to hold that pig. W'y it's big as a possum. You feed Blue Tick good or he'd be comin' out of there now. It may be he is too fat. Look at his little belly skin. Tight as a drum, ain't it?"

And I say to Pa: "Pa, he's drinkin' from a bowl now. I can't feed him from the goose quill. He's cut teeth and he bites the goose quills in two after he has drained all the milk through them. He just whales in and bites the quill in two."

Well I'll cut these ragweeds from behind the wellbox for Blue Tick. I won't have to cut them Saturday when we clean the yards. I'll have them cut already. Blue Tick likes ragweeds.

I would go to the river and knife down some horseweeds for Blue Tick, but it is too far and I am too tired. We have worked like mules in the corn today.

Blue Tick ain't tired as I am. But Blue Tick is hungry. He is always hungry. I believe Pa likes Blue Tick now.

I'll bet he wouldn't take a quarter for him. He wanted to take him back to Cy Shelton. But he wouldn't want to take him back now. Pa wants him more than I do.

I know what Pa wants with him. He wants to kill him for meat late next spring about March. That's the idea Pa has

in his head. But I can't stand to see him killed. I'm not goin'
to have Blue Tick killed. The sun is hot. The ragweeds smell.
They go down and open up every air sack in a body's lungs.
The scent is almost strong enough to knock the air sacks out
of a body's lungs.

The potatoes are all dug now. The turnips are pulled.
The corn is cut. Summer has gone. Autumn is here. There is
nothin' growin' now. Everything is dyin'. See how the dead
leaves fall from the trees. The cows have been brought in
from the high hill pasture and turned in on the meadow
weeds that have grown up after the last cuttin'. Nothin' is
growin' now unless it is the meadow weeds. There are a lot of
ragweeds down there and some horseweeds around the edges
in the rich ground. Autumn is here. Nothing but weeds are
growin'. The mules run in the lot, the cows run on the
meadow. The fattenin' hogs have a rail-fence lot. But Blue
Tick is fenced in a plank-fence square.

Since he got bigger I put one plank all the way round his
four-plank pen and made it higher. Now Blue Tick is a shoat
behind planks that will not let him see out and the barn-shed
roof will not let him see up. So I'm going to ask Pa if he will
let me turn Blue Tick out and let Blue Tick see so he will
know more than he does.

Blue Tick was once a pig. He ought to see the stars, for
even a pig likes to look at them. And now he is a shoat. He
ought to eat green ragweeds in the meadow. He ought to
have something besides middlins and cracked corn mixed
with milk in a bowl. He needs to root down in the pasture
where the greenbriers are and find the knots on the greenbrier roots. Shoats like them after they learn to root down
with their noses and get them. Blue Tick is big enough to do
all this and that poor shoat has never seen the stars. W'y he'd
learn to play if he could just get out of that pen. He'd never
even want to go back and look at that pen. He'd learn to

chase a dead leaf as a hound dog chases his tail. He'd learn to
run and play before bad weather comes. He ought to be out
where he can root up greenbrier roots and find chestnuts and
walnuts and pieces of coal and hard slate to munch over.

"You can turn that pig out," says Pa, "but if it starts
rootin' up this yard I'll put ten rings in his nose. You remember that. I won't have my meadow rooted up by that pig. Pigs
are hard on grass when they once get a taste of the sweet roots
that lay a little ways under the ground."

I took the hammer and I hit the planks. The same nails
that I drove in to hold Blue Tick in the pen will screak out of
the little two-by-two willow posts and let Blue Tick go free
again. Hear the hammer hit the planks and hear the nails
loose their holds in the willow wood. Blue Tick goes free
again as he was the day I found him in the lot with his
mother. But he was too little to know he was free then. Now
is the only time in his life he has ever been free. He walks out
of the pen. Then he runs back into it.

Blue Tick is afraid of the wind. He doesn't know it is
something that he can feel and can't see. He is afraid of the
ground. He steps like a person barefooted in stickerweeds.
He is afraid of a cornstalk. Blue Tick is afraid of the shadow
he makes in the autumn sunlight. He sees a tree, but he
cannot tell how far away the tree is when he walks toward the
tree. He hits the tree with his head.

He will learn soon to judge how far away in the wind
the tree is. He looks up at the sky and he grunts. And when
he sees a bright leaf fall from a tree he runs. Blue Tick is
afraid.

Yesterday when the cool wind was messin' with the
greenbrier tops I saw Blue Tick messin' with their roots. He
was goin' down with his nose in the soft new-ground earth. He
must have loved the smell of the soft sweet dirt. I stood
and watched him. And then I said to myself, "I'm glad he's
found the greenbrier roots. I know now that he will not have

to have ten rings in his nose. He won't root up the meadow grass after he has found the brier roots, for the brier roots are sweeter than the grass roots. Shoats like them better too."

I'm glad that Blue Tick has learned how to miss a tree. He walks past them now. He never hits one.

He is no longer afraid to step on the ground. He is not afraid of a leaf. Blue Tick is not afraid of anything. He is a pretty shoat now. His hair is not dirty any more. There is no mud on it. He is clean as the dead leaf because he sleeps with the dead leaves.

Autum is fading into winter. The brown world is changin' to drab. The trees stand leafless in the wind. The cows have been brought from the meadow and turned into the woods pasture. They can browse among the dead leaves. They can sleep under the pines at night. They can sleep among the greenbriers or they can come to the sheds and sleep on the straw. It is up to the cows. The wind sighs among the greenbriers and the bare tree tops.

Blue Tick is growin'. He drinks skimmed milk from a wooden trough now. I made the trough out of a hollow chestnut log. I sawed the ends off and nailed boards over the ends. The milk water-soaked the wood and it is now swollen. There is not a crack for the milk to leak out. Blue Tick knows I feed him. He follows me about over the barnyard. He goes with me when I take the mules to haul a load of fodder. He goes with me to clear ground. He goes with me everywhere I go. He goes like a dog and when Lead goes with me to the field, Blue Tick goes along and trots beside of Lead. But soon Blue Tick pants. He gets tired climbin' hills. And Lead trots along without drawin' a heavy breath. Lead does not like Blue Tick and he snaps at him when he gets close. Blue Tick would be friendly with Lead.

Pa says, "I don't want to get that pig in no bad habits like you have the turkey gobbler and the rooster."

And I say to Pa: "I didn't get that turkey gobbler in no bad habits. He took up that fightin' himself. I didn't teach it to him."

Pa says: "The next time that turkey flogs one of the children I'm going to catch him and put his head across a block of wood and use the ax on his neck. And the very next time that game rooster flies in my face when I go to feed the mules I'm going to break his back with a ear of corn. A body can't feed for having to fight the fowls."

And I say, "I did not get that rooster to fightin' either."

Pa says: "Ain't I seen you go out there 'o a mornin' to feed the hogs and you'd crow and get him started after you all riled up and you'd run and he'd hit you and you'd run and by doin' that you got him so bad we can't live for him tryin' to take the place. Now don't get that shoat Blue Tick to fightin'. If you do, pon-my-words, I'll dash his brains out with a hammer."

When I milk the cows Blue Tick comes up and I milk warm milk from the cows' teats into his mouth. He opens his big mouth and his big white tongue covered with warm sweet milk foam looks like a white ear of corn. Blue Tick likes the milk I milk into his mouth from the cows' teats. I know that I'm not going to have him fightin'. Though he did bow up to Lead the other day when Lead snapped him through the ear and left a tiny hole. Blue Tick follows the cows when he is not with me. He loves the cows nearly as much as he does me. He follows them all day long in their rambles through the winter woods and to the waterin' hole. At first they were afraid of Blue Tick, but anymore they like him and they smell of his nose and snort and he smells of their noses and yawns. I watched them yesterday up on the hill by a chestnut log. The sun come out and the sun rays hit the dead leaves and made them warm. The cows laid down and Blue Tick laid down with them. He got right up close to the cow's spine

28

and just stretched out so lazy-like in the winter sun that a body would a thought him dead. The cows laid there in the winter sun and chewed their cuds and Blue Tick laid right there with them like he was a cow too. When they mooed, he boo-hooed. They all slept there in the sun long as it lasted and when the sun went behind a rift of snow clouds they all got up and came over the hill to the barn.

Winter has gone rapidly. The snow and ice are leavin' the hills now. The hens scratch among the cornstalks in the barn lot. Birds are comin' back. The English sparrows have never left the barn. The house wrens have come back to the rag sack in the smokehouse where they had a nest last year and year before last. Green tips are appearin' on the greenbriers that Blue Tick did not root up with his nose to eat the warts on the greenbrier roots.

Pa says: "Don't believe I'll kill that hog till next fall. Shame to kill him now and him lean as he is. That frame will hold six hundred pounds of meat."

And I'm so glad Pa feels this way about it. But Pa ain't got no right to kill him a-tall. He is my hog. I paid the quarter for him when he was about the size of a mouse. But look at him now! He grows faster than a elephant. His back looks like the winter-colored bluff over there when the sun comes out on the spots of white dead grass. Part of him is bluish like the dirt. Then there are the winter white spots of dead grass in the sunlight.

Now the cows go out to nibble on the greenbrier sprouts. Blue Tick goes with them. He follows them through the woods and sleeps with them under the pines. He is gettin' big like a cow. He comes in with the cows and when I milk them he comes up close for me to squirt milk onto his pretty tongue. He opens his mouth anymore and comes so close I have to soo-soo him back. But I sit on the stool chair and milk the cows and give Blue Tick good warm cow milk and it goes fine for his supper and good for his breakfast on the cool spring mornings.

It's a funny thing. I met Ernie Stubblefield down there this mornin' by the gate and he said his cows had been milked. And our cows had been milked the same mornin'. It is a strange thing. He said that his cows' teats looked like they have been scratched by the briers and my cows' teats was the same way. It is a funny thing. I'll tell Pa about somebody milking our cows. I think I know who it is. Estille Tentress was expelled from school last year for slippin' down in the pasture and milkin' Charlie Pennington's cow. He was caught right in the act. He milked the cow in his dinner bucket and turned the milk right up and drunk it. We was right there hid in the bushes, me and Uncle Urban, and saw him do it. He is the one right now milkin' the cows and I'll tell Pa. Didn't get a pint of milk this morning' from Pansy nor a half pint from Star and Roan put together. He couldn't drink all the milk. He's sellin' it. Estille Tentress is a bad egg around where there is cows. He likes sweet milk and their one cow can't give enough milk for twelve children.

This is Ham Flemington. Here he comes, squat and ducky, black mustache, gorilla-armed, big hands and mushroom face. He comes up the path. He says, "Somebody is milkin' my cow."

And I say: "Somebody is milkin' all three of my cows. Didn't get a quart of strippins from all three cows this mornin'."

"I'd love to know who is doin' it," I say. "I'd like to sprinkle them with shot."

"If I find out I won't sprinkle them with shot. I'll take it to the Law and let the Law sprinkle them with shot."

He passes goin' to town "Fencerail" Isaac Keen. His arms dangle at his side. He comes up and says, "Where is your Pa, son?"

And I says, "Pa is over on the hill clearin' ground."

"Did you know somebody is milkin' my cows? I turned them in the woods pasture that jines your field. Well, somebody got all the milk. There was slobbers all over my cows' teats. They was rough like a brier had scratched them."

Now here comes Pa from the clearin'. "Tin Purvin come over there where I was workin' and said two of his cows that run in the field next to our pasture had been milked and the two cows that run in the northside pasture had not been touched. Tin said this same thing happened once before when he was a boy. But he said Mike McGan found out what it was. He said he watched his cows one whole day and nothin' bothered them. It was the second day round yonder back of that piney pint, the old cow was pickin' up next to a rock cliff and a big cow snake crawled quietly from behind the rock and wound his body up like a corkscrew till he got his mouth over the cow's teat. At first she kicked a little. She mooed and looked at the ground and booed. The she went on pickin' grass and that snake milked every teat she had and then lit right on the other cow and milked her too. And when he got through he was all bloated up and he just rolled up and went to sleep there in the sun. Then Mike said that he shot it with a double-barreled shotgun right between the eyes and made shoe strings out of its hide."

Fain Wimpler comes down the path. He says: "Gentlemen, don't think I'm tellin' you a ghost story, but I went down to the barn last night to milk my cow and somethin' big as a white calf tore out of that barn—bore two planks off and got away. It had my cow tied down and her teats was wet with slobbers. I never saw anythin' like it in my life. I throwed the milk bucket down and whistled for my dogs, but they was both gone after a fox. I was so skeered I couldn't whistle until it had time enough to get over the hill."

Today I take the rifle. Pa takes the shotgun. We go with our cows to the fields. If it is Estille Tentress, we are goin' to

31

find out. If it is a cow snake, we are goin' to get it the first cow he corkscrews up to. Blue Tick goes with us. He roots alongside the cows and eats the blades of sweet grass where he can find them. He roots up the greenbrier wart roots and eats them. He is big like a ram now. He trots along with the cows and Pa says, "Don't reckon it could be that hog suckin' the cows, could it?"

And I says: "Why no, you know it is not Blue Tick when he comes right in with them every night when I milk them. I been around him all the time and I never saw a bad pass out of that hog. Never. Who ever heard tell of a hog suckin' a cow anyway? I never did in my life. Did you?"

"No I never did, and, Son, I'm fifty-six years old. I've heard of cow snakes, but not hogs."

The sweet wind of spring shakes the long blue hairs on Blue Tick's hocks. The leaves, thin, and light-blue green, swish in the pretty spring wind. Flowers grow by the roots of the beech trees. They are wind flowers and bloodroot flowers. But Blue Tick cannot see when a flower is pretty. All he is lookin' for is the taste. He nibbles down the flowers and chops them in his long shoe-like mouth. Then, to think Blue Tick would bother one of the cows. He just don't remember his mother. Maybe he thinks a cow is his mother. I'll bet that is it. Over the winter dead leaves they go and through the little blotches of green grass. They cross the creek and they drink the clear cool creek water. Then up the next bluff and through the wild ferns and the flowers.

All day we follow our cows. The sun is gettin' low in the late March skies. The wind is blowin' among the green grass and the windflowers and the bloodroots. The wind is blowin' through the green pasture leaves and the light green pasture grass. The sky, too, is blue as water-over-June-gravel. The cows trail the path home. Blue Tick trails the cows and we are next in line with gun and rifle.

The stars come out. The whippoorwills call. It is time

for the whippoorwills. It is spring. Blue Tick comes into the barn lot with the cows. Lead comes to the barn lot to lick the old skillet we feed the kittens foam from the fresh milk in. Lead snaps at Blue Tick and Blue Tick bows up his side like a fish as if to say, "Come on, you hound dog, and I'll let you feel one of my tushes." As we are busy milking the cows, Blue Tick and Lead begin to quarrel.

Ham comes over and he says, "Followed my cows all day with a shotgun across my shoulder and I never saw a thing." While Ham is still here Isaac comes over. "Followed my cows the God-blessed day. Never saw nothin' but a blowin' viper snake and a couple of crows. Funny thing about the way our cows all got milked one night."

Then comes Tin: "Boys, never saw a thing all day and I followed my cows with a automatic pistol. I aim to light right into it with hot lead if powder will burn and the trigger will squeeze."

Fain Wimpler comes up to the milkgap and says: "Never seen a thing today, boys. Never seen a thing."

Tonight the moon hangs in the sky like a wisp of dead poplar leaves. I can look out from my window to the barn. The ground is light as day. I can see the old dead potato tops from last year's harvest. I can see little green bunches of grass. I can see the stakes where we heated water to kill the hogs. I can wonder about the cows. I see them goin' back up the trail, Pansy in front, then Roan and then Star. Blue Tick is followin' Star up the trail. I don't believe it is Blue Tick suckin' the cows. Surely he doesn't know how. I get up and put on my overalls and shirt. I slip downstairs. The moon is pretty tonight. I go out across the chip yard, past the barn and through the barn lot and alongside the rail pig pen. Then I follow the trail up the hill path, the way Blue Tick followed Pansy, Roan and Star.

And now I come upon them. They do not see me. I watch them lyin' in the moonlight not far in front of me,

beside a dead chestnut tree top. Blue Tick is sleepin' alongside one of the cows. He sleeps beside of Roan. If he is milkin'
the cows I'll see. The moon is comin' down through the thin
leafed spring tree tops. I stretch out flat on my stomach. I do
not make a sound. The wind blows over me and shakes the
thin leaves on the sour-wood sprouts.

And now Blue Tick wakes from sleep. He nudges Roan
like he was a young calf. He is suckin' the cow. It is Blue
Tick. It is Blue Tick. He is a smart hog. He has never done it
before us. I know now what the ghost was Tin saw. I watch
Blue Tick. The cow does not care. The moon shines down on
them. There they are stretched side by side. Blue Tick is big
like a cow. Pa will kill Blue Tick when he finds this out. I
cannot stand to see him killed. Why did I ever milk milk into
his mouth on the cold frosty mornings? Why did I ever, for
even a hog will learn. The turkey learned to fight. The
rooster learned to fight. The hog has learned to take the milk
himself from the cow instead of having it milked for him.

I go down to the barn and get some corn. I come back
and toll Blue Tick away. He goes back to the cows. So I
throw down so many rails and drive the cows through to the
old house under some apple trees. I drive them in the house.
In goes Blue Tick with them. I throw down the ear of corn.
Blue Tick is eatin'. While he is eatin' I drive the cows out of
the house. I bar the door. Blue Tick is in a big hog pen, one
that will hold him. I drive home the cows.

The young rabbits hop across my path. It is early
mornin'—no sign of sun yet. The thin leaves on the trees stir
in the mornin' breeze and the dew of the mornin' hangs to
the leaves. It is early. It is breakfast time. The house is close.
Just one more fence to cross and the old orchard and then the
house. The door is open. Panels have been knocked out. I'll
look for the tracks. Here they are—down the path toward

Liam Galligher's barn—it is just under the hill. And Liam owns the place we live on. My heavens!

Under the pine trees I run. The rabbits can get out of my way or stay in my way. If the rabbit has made the third grade in school he has learned that man desires blood—that man is a killer. Look at Pa wantin' to kill Blue Tick—and he will kill Blue Tick because he sucks the cows at home and the neighbors' cows. I'm running fast. I am afraid that Liam will kill Blue Tick. Listen— Listen! I hear! I hear! Here comes Liam up the path ridin' a sorrel pony with a blazed face. "I caught the thief," he says. "I got him. It is a hog!"

"My hog," I say. "Yes my hog—you didn't kill him did you—?"

"No I didn't, for that is the first time I ever heard of anything like that in my life let alone seein' it— But it is the truth. I went over to the house and got my wife. She said that she's never seen anything like it in all her growin' up and that if ever her Pap did he'd never said anything about it. So I just drove the cow out and worked him through the partition into the log barn and fastened him in a mule stall. That will hold him. I've just started to tell the neighbors that I got the cow snake and he is a hog after the milk that has been milkin' their cows."

"Don't tell Pa. He will kill Blue Tick."

"No, he must not kill a hog like that— He is too smart to kill. We'll take that hog to the Fair over at Turnipseed and get a decent price for him. That is a curiosity that all the people in the country would like to see. We'll crate him up and put him in the spring wagon right now if you want to and take him to the Fair if it would be all right with your Pa— Reckon he'll care?"

"Blue Tick is mine—not Pa's. I raised him from a mouse-sized pig. I don't want him killed."

"It would be a shame to kill him. Get on this pony

behind me. We'll load him up right now and take him to the Fair and tell about him after he is sold. We'll haul him there in the spring wagon."

The crate is made. We put it in the stall where Blue Tick is. We toll him into the crate. We nail up the end. We open the double door and pull his crate with a mule to the shed. Then we hoist him up to the low joist with a four-strand rope pulley and a mule. We shove the spring wagon under the crate. Then we let the crate down in the express. We have Blue Tick ready for the Fair.

The road is dusty and it leads to nowhere. Turns, willows, creeks—horseweeds—curves—ditches—sandpiles. Houses by the side of the road. Willows by the road. Chip yards beside the road. And the village at the end of the road, though the pony does have a load, a hog, a boy and a man. And the end of the road and here is Turnipseed and the Fair grounds.

Mr. Hix the manager says: "That hog won't suck no cow. I been at this game of buyin' three-legged chickens, and two-headed calves and six-legged cows and three-eyed heifers for a long time— But not in all my experiences have I ever seen a hog that would suck a cow. I'll tell you what I got to have is a cow and if that hog sucks that cow I'll give you four fifty-dollar bills for that hog. If he don't suck the cow you get him off these grounds and do it quick."

"It's a go," says Liam.

A boy with a green shirt and a white necktie with tattooed arms brings the cow from a barn. And when we let him out of the crate and put them both in the tent he bows up to her side and boo-boos. Then he starts to milk the cow and she starts to kickin'. But finally she lets him have his way, for he put his head under her flank and there is not much she can do about it for she cannot kick him. "That beats any novelty I've ever seen in my day in the show business. Here, young man, are your four fifty-dollar bills. And here's you a ten smacker, Mr. Galligher, for having sense enough to haul a hog like that to the Fair instead of butchering it. It is the biggest find I have had in many a year. Hang around and watch people flock in at a quarter a whack to see this tonight. I'll have four hundred people in here this night."

And I have four fifty-dollar bills. I can buy pounds of sugar now and calico shirts and overalls and shoes. But I'm not goin' to buy anything like that. They'll go. One thing will stay and that is land. Nothing can change it much or hurt it a great deal. I'm goin' to buy that forty acres of Priam Hamilton. He wants a hundred and seventy-five dollars for it. Then I'll have twenty-five dollars left.

And as I ride back in the spring wagon with Liam and the moon comes down above our heads and falls on the little pretty green willow leaves alongside the creek—I think of the land I'll own and the willow trees I'll have on my place. Trees will be mine and the wind will be mine that passes over my place. The moonlight that falls on it will be mine. I'll own the big trees and little trees and I can own ducks and chickens and turkeys on my place. The sky above it will be mine while it floats above my place.

And then Blue Tick was gettin' so big and would have made so much meat for us— But how in the green world of spring could I stand to see them boil water to scald Blue Tick with—shoot him between the eyes with a rifle and scald off his hair and scrape him like a turnip! Then hang him up and slit him open with a knife— How could I stand to see it after I raised him on a bottle, to go and look at his big pretty white, clean, sweet-smellin' body when he was hangin' to a gallows with a stick run between the leaders under his hind legs and fastened over the gallows and red blood dripping from the end of his nose.

wolf boy from walnut ridge

"Look what I see," Uncle Jake said as he stopped in the path under the sugar maple tree. "Yonder's a whole army of people comin' up the valley."

"It's not blackberry pickin' time yet, is it?" Pete asked.

"No, I don't see a bucket in the crowd," Uncle Jake said as we stood still in the path behind him and waited. "Everybody's carryin' a chain and a collar."

I had never heard such a noise. There was more noise in the valley now than there had been since the year of the locusts.

We stood under the sugar maple waiting for the crowd that was coming toward us.

"Well, if it's not my old friend Ernie Evergood," Uncle Jake said. Ernie was leading the crowd. "What's this all about, Ernie?"

"Haven't you heard, Jake?" Ernie asked. His lips curved in a smile and color rose in his face. "Haven't you heard what was goin' on?" There were patches on the knees of Ernie's pants, a dog chain in his hand, and a cigar in his mouth.

"I've not heard anything back this way but cow bells ringin' and fox horns blowin'," Uncle Jake said.

"This will open your ears, Jake," Ernie whispered. "There was a man drivin' through these parts who ran into a truck and wrecked his car. He had his wife and dog in the car with him. The little dog was so scared after the wreck that it took to the hills. I believe that dog's hidin' in a cliff someplace. We're out to hunt the dog for the man and his wife who are in the hospital."

While Uncle Jake and Ernie talked I looked over the crowd. My heart fluttered when I saw Effie Stufin among them. I had danced with her at Sandy Falls at the square dances. I'd been with her at bean stringin's on Lower Laurel. I'd sopped foam from the molasses pan with her at Ike Wampler's cane mill on Whetstone Creek. There stood Bollie Beck beside her. Everywhere I'd been with Effie, Bollie had followed talkin' faster than the wind tryin' to take Effie away from me.

"Did you find out where the people who lost their dog was from?" Uncle Jake asked Ernie.

"Sheriff Bradley didn't know," Ernie said. "But he said just to find their little dog would help them more than medicine."

"Then, I'll join to help find their dog," Uncle Jake said. "I want those poor strangers to have their dog."

"Yes, we've always been kind to strangers here," Ernie said. "Look, you'd better join us too, Eif, and bring your boys along. You know a little dog can get close to its owner's heart. Maybe our finding that dog will save their lives."

"It pays to do a kind deed, too," Uncle Jake said. "We can give up a day's work in the tobacco, corn, and cane and never miss it."

It was hard to hear Uncle Jake and Ernie talk for everybody was talking and tramping down the weeds and rattling their dog chains along the path.

"Ernie, just what kind of a dog is it we are lookin' for?" Uncle Jake asked.

"It has a funny name, Jake," Ernie said as he pulled

a paper from his pocket. He spelled the name, "D-a-c-h-s-h-u-n-d."

"I'd call that 'Dashhound,' " Pert Dunn said. "It's a lot easier to say."

"I've heard of Walker, Redbone, Wolfhound, and Bloodhound, I never heard of 'Dashhound' before," Pete said.

"Is it a possum hound or a fox hound?" Turner Whaley asked.

"It's not any good for either one," Ernie said. "'They tell me this dog never saw a fox or possum."

"It must be a vicious dog," Lester Spry said.

"No, it's a timid little dog," Ernie said. "She's afraid of strangers."

"If we're goin' to find that hound, Ernie," Bollie Beck said, "it's time we's movin' along. If you're not goin' to lead this party, I'll lead it. I know this country better than I know my own face."

"You know it well enough then," I said. "And you think a lot of it too!"

Bollie looked at Effie, and she turned to look at me.

"Uncle Jake, I'm goin' to find the 'Dashhound,' " I said.

"Doodle's goin' to find the 'Dashhound,' Effie," Bollie whispered to Effie with his big lips spread in a half-moon grin.

"You bet I will," I said. "I'll be the first to take it to its owners in the Auckland Hospital!"

"Yep, Doodlebug is goin' to find this dog!"

"I'll join the crowd too," Uncle Jake said.

"There's some catch to it," Pete said. "You know people wouldn't own a dog that's not good to tree possums or chase a fox. What kind of a dog is it? Such a dog is not worth huntin' for. But I'll do my best to find it to help the strangers in our Auckland Hospital."

Pete went up the mountainside as we started up the

creek. I walked on one side of Effie and Bollie walked on the other. Bollie tried to do all the talking to Effie. He was dressed in his best Sunday clothes. He pulled his black bow tie out with his big fingers and let it fly back against his white shirt. He was trying to make Effie notice him. Bollie was trying to find the dog. He was trying to get Effie.

Uncle Jake and Ernie walked at the head of the procession and talked about the "Dashhound." This was like a Fourth of July celebration at Greenwood. I had never seen our neighbors so happy since I could remember. Everybody was talking, laughing, and going someplace.

If that "Dashhound" is timid, afraid of foxes, possums, and strangers, I thought, I'll have to talk kind to it. I'll talk just like I used to talk to a doodlebug to make it come from its hole. The kinder I'd talk to the doodlebug the quicker it would come from its den. Old Bollie will never get the dog because he can't talk kind to anybody. Then, he never cares whether he makes people happy or sad. He doesn't care for the strangers in the hospital grieving over their little dog.

"If I find the 'Dashhound' will you go away and never bother Effie and me again, Bollie?" I asked.

"You and Effie again," he repeated with his big half-moon grin. "It's not you and Effie anymore. It's me and Effie. Will you go away and never bother us again if I find the 'Dashhound'?"

"I'll make this agreement with you," I said. "If I find it first, you're never to bother us again!"

"I'll agree if it's all right with you, Darlin'," he said, turning to Effie.

But Effie turned to me. I never saw her prettier in my life. Her hair was golden corn-silk color below her sunbonnet and on her shoulders. Her eyes were blue as the deep pools of mountain water. In one of her pretty hands she carried a little chain and a collar and in the other she carried a stick to

41

protect herself from a poisonous snake should she suddenly come upon one.

"I won't have anything to do with the agreement," she said. "It must be between you."

"That collar you are carryin' in your hand, Effie," I said, "will go around that little 'Dashhound's' neck and that chain you have will lead it home. You and I, Effie, will take it to the Auckland Hospital and make two people very happy."

"You've made your plan all right," Bollie grumbled. "I'll take you up on that propostion. If you find the dog, I'll leave you and Effie alone. If I find it, you be sure to leave us alone."

"Bollie, I can smell a groundhog, possum, or a fox in a hole," I told him. "I can smell a dog, too. If I can bring a doodlebug from its den with my kind words, you know I can bring a dog from a rock cliff that way. See, I've trained myself to use my eyes, ears, and nose. I can use all my senses."

Bollie thought what I said was so funny that he laughed louder than the wind among the leaves. He shook all over like the wind shook a leafy-topped tree.

"If you can smell like that, you're part varmint," Bollie screamed with laughter as he flipped his bow tie on his bull neck. "Effie, he's part varmint. He can smell like a dog. He must be a wolf boy like I've been readin' about over there in India. I'll bet you got claws instead of toenails there in them brogan shoes! Pull 'em off so we can see your claws!"

"Now everybody to the bluffs," Ernie shouted above Bollie's laughter. "This is Deer Creek, and there's a lot of rock cliffs here. This is a good place for a dog to be hidin'. This is one place where people have not been lookin' for the 'Dashhound.' "

We crossed Deer Creek where we began to scatter among the cliffs around the bluff. We could see crowds of people over on Laurel Creek. We could hear people as far away as Short Branch for the whole countryside was filled with people. They had put their hoes and plows away because they loved dogs and each wanted to find this little dog for its masters.

Bollie, Effie, and I stayed together. We passed Uncle Jake and Ernie, who were down on their knees looking back under a big rock cliff.

"Ernie, that dog's right in there," Uncle Jake said. "I nearly know it's in there! Look how slick that hole's worn."

Uncle Jake stood with Ernie's mattock in one hand and with the other he twisted a long black horn of his mustache. Ernie smoked his cigar and looked at the slick hole worn back under the cliff.

"I'll see if it's in there, Uncle Jake," I said. "I might save you a lot of digging."

I put my head at the entrance of the rock cliff and I sniffed a couple of times.

"No dog in that hole, Uncle Jake," I said. "Don't waste your time digging under that big cliff. It's not under there."

"When did you get to be a dog?" Uncle Jake asked.

"That's just what I asked old Doodle, Mr. Seagraves," Bollie said, bending over and slapping his knees with his big hands while he screamed with laughter.

"Who are you to ask anybody anything?" Uncle Jake said. "If you fool with me, I'll shut your trap with this mattock handle."

Bollie didn't say any more to Uncle Jake. Somebody got Uncle Jake's sweet apples each summer. Since he didn't have teeth he baked these apples for his breakfast. Uncle Jake lived alone and he didn't like Bollie.

"That 'Dashhound' is in this rock cliff and we'll dig her out, won't we, Ernie?"

"It's goin' to be a tough job," Ernie warned. "We're not sure it's under this cliff."

"I about know it is," Uncle Jake said.

"Uncle Jake, you'd better listen to Ernie," I said.

"My, my, Doodle," Uncle Jake sighed. "Your senses are so well developed, if you find the 'Dashhound' with your nose, I'll give you my farm. If I find the 'Dashhound,' you give me your interest in the cane field."

"It's a bargain," I said. "Now, I'll really use my nose."

Effie turned to me and started laughing. She didn't think I could use my nose either.

Uncle Jake was digging with a mattock and Ernie was shoveling dirt behind him when we left the cliff. Bollie was laughing louder than the wind. We found a rock cliff around the bluff where several had been. They had tramped the weeds down around the cliff where I kneeled and sniffed the scent from the dark hole that went under the rock.

"Something in there, Wolf Boy?" Bollie asked.

"Yes, but it is only a possum," I said.

"Haw, haw, haw," Bollie laughed, shaking all over. "Old Wolf Boy says it's a possum. If you find the 'Dashhound' with your nose, I'm naming you 'Wolf Boy.' If you win with your nose, you get Effie's good will, a farm, and a good name, Wolf Boy. If you don't win with your nose, look what you'll lose. But, I'll give you the name of 'Wolf Boy,' win or lose!"

We walked around the bluff where we found another cliff and I got down on my knees, stuck my nose in the hole, and sniffed like a dog.

"What's in thar?" Bollie asked, laughing again. "A panther?"

"No, no, just a friendly old ground hog," I told him.

Bollie slapped his knees again with his big hands and laughed louder than before.

"Effie, you ought to get Wolf Boy to pull off his brogan shoes and show you his claws," Bollie said. "What will your poppie and mommie think of you datin' a varmint?"

"What's the matter with you?" I asked Bollie. "Are you going to hunt for the 'Dashhound'? Do you remember we made a bargain?"

"I will not forget that bargain," Bollie said. "But you ain't goin' to find that dog. You're pretending to smell a possum, ground hog, fox, or dog. You want Effie to think you are somethin' special! She must think the same about you that I think!"

"What do you think?" I asked him. "I think I know. But I want to hear you say it!"

"I don't mind sayin' what I think," Bollie said, seriously. All the grin was gone from his face now. "I think you are teched. Yes, teched, Wolf Boy, teched in the head."

As we walked around the bluff and across the hollows, I held Effie by one arm and carried her dog chain and collar. Bollie held her by the other arm and carried her stick to protect her from snakes.

On Little Deer Creek we found another cliff. I smelled in the hole under the cliff.

"Let's don't stop here," I said.

"Why?" Effie asked. "A wolf in that hole?"

"No, none of my relatives there," I said, laughing. "They're Bollie's. I can smell a den of polecats."

Bollie didn't laugh at my joke but Effie screamed with laughter this time as we walked away up Little Deer Creek where there was another cliff upon the bluff above the road. This was about two miles from where the strangers had wrecked their car.

"That looks like a good place for a dog to be hiding," Effie said.

"I agree with you," I said.

"But a hundred people have been there already!" Bollie said. "Look how they've tramped the weeds down!"

"Let me see if there's a dog under that rock," I said.

"If a dog was under this cliff somebody would have found it, Doodle," Effie said.

"But it's a timid dog," I said. "Big-mouthed people like Bollie are everywhere around here today. They can't find a

45

dog. It won't come from under a cliff for men like Uncle Jake and Bollie."

"Now, lissen to that talk, won't you," Bollie said. "Lissen to old Wolf Boy! Gee, that's funny talk. Afraid of big-mouthed Bollie, huh? Well, I like that!"

I got on my knees and sniffed in the deep dark hole.

"What's in there now, Wolf Boy?" Bollie asked. "Your kinfolks or mine?"

"Neither," I said, sniffing louder like a dog. "It smells like dog to me!"

Bollie laughed and laughed as I lay flat on my stummick with my head back under the cliff as far as there was light, sniffing the scent.

"Just like a dog," Bollie told Effie. "I believe old Doodle is half wolf. I'd like to see his toes. He has fingernails, but I'll bet he ain't got toenails. He's got claws down there under his brogans!"

"The 'Dashhound' is in there," I said.

Now, Bollie really laughed for us. He slapped his knees with his big hands and gave a laugh like a horse snicker. His big mouth looked like a half-moon spread across his face from ear to ear. He showed all of his big stained teeth. I thought a good name for him would have been "Old Horse Mouth." That went through my mind but I wouldn't call him that. I was never much for calling people names. My real name was Alfred, and not Doodle, but I got that name by calling doodlebugs from their holes when I went after the cows. Now, I wanted the dog. I knew it was in here.

"What's the dog's name, Effie?" I asked.

"I don't know," she said.

"Let us call her Queenie!"

"That's a nice name," Effie said, looking doubtfully at me. "But don't waste our time, Doodle!"

"Come Queenie, come Queenie." I spoke softly. I patted

the dirt at the mouth of the hole with my hand just like I used to do in the pasture when I called the doodlebugs from their dens. But Queenie didn't come. Yet, I knew there was a dog under this cliff.

"You're wasting your time, Wolf Boy," Bollie said. "You're green as the sap in a pussy willow in March."

"You're a big soft toadstool," I said. "You're about as smart as a copperhead that won't run from a forest fire, but strikes at the flames until they consume him!"

Bollie laughed and laughed again for he thought he was making me hot under the collar. He wouldn't keep quiet while I was trying to call the "Dashhound" from under the cliff.

"Come Queenie! Come Queenie!" I called softly. "Come Queenie! Come Queenie! I'll take you to your owners. They're in the hospital! They will be happy to see you. They love you. They need you. Come Queenie! Come Queenie! I'll take you to your owners!"

I saw two eyes back in the dark hole and they were as bright as two firebrands.

"Effie, put your little hands over Bollie's big mouth," I said. "Keep it closed until I get this dog. Your two hands might be large enough to close his soundbox!"

"Be quiet, Bollie," Effie whispered. "Let's give Doodle a chance to see if he is telling the truth! Maybe he has found something!"

When Effie said this, Bollie stopped laughing. Now we could hear voices all over the surrounding hills and down in the valleys.

"Come on, Queenie," I whispered, patting the ground with my hands. "Come pretty little doggie! Come to me! I won't hurt you! I'll take you to your owners!"

The little "Dashhound" walked out into my arms. It was the strangest looking dog I'd ever seen. It had short legs, a long body, long ears, and short black hair. She knew I was her friend and she missed her owners and was glad to have me for a friend.

"Here she is," I said as I held her in my arms. "Now, Bollie, you'll believe I can smell, won't you?"

Bollie stood there as silent as a dead oak above the cliff. He didn't speak. He stood as rigid and as quiet as a person paralyzed.

"Put the collar around her neck, Effie," I said. "Put it on her and you and I will narrate to the people we have found that 'Dashhound,' and we'll take her to Auckland together and make her owners happy. Maybe we'll cause them to get well. They'll be happy. Queenie will be happy and we'll be happy too, won't we, Effie? Just think, you and I!"

Effie put the collar around Queenie's neck and snapped the chain to the collar while I looked at Bollie's clouded face.

"Oh, my farm," Uncle Jake wailed as he came up the hill with Ernie behind him. "Doodle's got the 'Dashhound.' He's found it under the cliff where we were an hour ago! *He can smell, too!*"

"He's part wolf," Bollie said, unthawing from his freeze until he could speak. "I didn't believe it at first, but I believe it now."

"How foolish to bargain my farm against a couple of acres of cane," Uncle Jake said.

"Uncle Jake, I don't want your farm," I said. "I won't take it. I was only jokin' with you because I've been planning to give you my cane anyway. Haven't we, Effie?"

Uncle Jake was the happiest man I'd ever seen. Effie was happy too.

"He's part wolf, Ernie," Bollie shouted. "I know he is. I thought it was a joke about his smellin' varmints in holes. But it's not a joke! He can smell! Watch him! He's dangerous!

He's got claws on his feet. I call him Wolf Boy and he's from Walnut Ridge!"

"And you promised to stay away from Effie and me if I found the dog," I said, as I stroked little Queenie's head. "Now, this promise holds!"

"I sure did, and I'll be as good as my word," Bollie said.

"Doodle, you're the kind of Wolf Boy I can appreciate," Effie said. "First named after cow pasture doodlebugs, and now a wolf, because you can smell! I wish I could develop my nose the way you have!"

"I wouldn't think about that if I were you," I said. "Too many unpleasant smells in this world. A dog has a tougher life than you think!"

Uncle Jake and Ernie laughed at what I said, but Bollie didn't. He stood there like a big green tree swaying idly to and fro in the wind.

"Wish I could use my nose like you," Bollie said. "I wouldn't mind all the unpleasant smells. If I could have smelled this mornin', things might have been different with you and me and Effie."

Later, I planned to tell Effie the truth. I wouldn't do it now. I'd keep old Bollie, Uncle Jake, and Ernie guessing. Everybody would be guessing too about me finding the "Dashhound" with my nose. I couldn't smell any better than Bollie, Uncle Jake, Ernie, Effie, or anybody else. I was human. I had toenails like Bollie, but I wouldn't let him see my feet.

I learned to look inside the holes in the soft dirt or the dry sand for tracks. They're always just inside the hole. And I'd spent years in the woods, beside the streams, in mud and snow, looking inside holes to examine tracks. I knew about every track in the woods. I certainly knew a dog's tracks. I found dog tracks in this hole under the cliff. They'd gone in this hole but hadn't come out again, so I knew the dog was under this cliff. And my kind words had brought her out to me and into my arms. She had made up with me because I was fond of her.

"Come, Effie, let's go to the Auckland Hospital with her," I said. "Let's make two people happy. We might make them well again. A reward of happiness is the greatest of all rewards!"

"Four people, Doodle Wolf Boy," she said softly as we started down the cliff. "Four people and a dog! The strangers, you and I, and little Queenie, all will be very, very happy!"

I looked back once to see Bollie, who was still standing there like a big green tree with his mouth open and his body trembling like green leaves shining in a soft summer breeze.

frog-trouncin' contest

We hadn't finished choppin' the sour-wood sprouts from our new-ground corn when Uncle Andy dropped his big sproutin' hoe and crossed my corn balk to Young Andy's row. He stood lookin' at Young Andy a minute. Then he said, "Andy, you'll make one of the greatest frog-trouncers ever to come from these parts. I've been a-watchin' ye ever since we've been choppin' in this corn. Ye air built fer a frog-trouncer. Fer twenty-five years I've been the champion trouncer of Ennis County. This year ye can take my place."

Uncle Andy is a-braggin' on Young Andy because he's his namesake, I thought. He wants to make a great frog-trouncer out'n him because he's got too old and stiff to trounce frogs. He wants the champion still to be Andy Blevins. And then I thought, I can cut more sprouts from the corn and cut them cleaner than Young Andy.

Young Andy laid his lightweight shop hoe across a corn balk where the new-ground loam was hot enough to fry an egg as Uncle Andy felt of the muscles in his short thick arms. "Ye've got th' muscles thar," Uncle Andy said. "Muscles might' nigh hard as mine. Nigh hard as rocks. Ye can take my place this year and hold hit fer the next twenty-five years. I'll larn ye th' secrets."

I looked at Young Andy's hair. It was red as Uncle

Andy's whiskers. Uncle Andy didn't have hair growin' on his head any longer—his hairless sun-tanned head was the color of a ripe October pumpkin and tanned brownish-red as a frost-bitten persimmon. Since Uncle Andy didn't have hair on his head, he let hair grow on his face until it was bushy and red as a ripe saw-brier cluster.

I don't have hair the color of Young Andy and Uncle Andy, I thought. That's another reason why Uncle Andy's not interested in me. My hair's the color of a ripe chestnut-burr and the hair on my head is about as coarse and stands straight up like the fine stickers on the chestnut-burr. I stood leanin' on my hoe handle watchin' Uncle Andy examine Young Andy. He was havin' 'im to draw his arms back to see how much muscles he had in his arms. And then he looked at his shoulders and the calves of his legs.

"Ye air a young man built just like I was when I was made the champion frog-trouncer of Ennis County," Uncle Andy said, wipin' sweat from his flamin' crow's nest of red beard with his big calloused hand. "I'll be proud of ye, Young Andy, this September."

Young Andy grinned just like he was already the champion. He looked at me as if to say: "What can you do, Chuck? You're not the well-made man that I am. You'll never make a frog-trouncer." He didn't exactly say these words to me but I could tell by the way he looked that he thought them. I didn't say anything to Young Andy but thoughts were a-runnin' through my head too. I may not have arms as big as yours, Young Andy, I thought. I may not have shoulders as broad and legs like yours with big bulgin' calves of muscles but I take the lower row and keep well ahead of you. And if Uncle Andy can make a frog-trouncer out'n you, I'll do my best to beat you in September.

As I chopped the smelly sour-wood sprouts from around the new ground stumps and the wilted spindly corn, I thought about how much better Uncle Andy was to Young Andy than

52

he was to me. I found myself workin' faster and faster until I was rakin' the sprouts down on Uncle Andy.

"What's come over ye, Chuck?" Uncle Andy asked me as he stopped under the July sun and leaned on his hoe handle. "I've never seen ye work like this before."

"Not anything's come over me," I said.

"Then I must be a-slowin' down," Uncle Andy said.

I looked back to see where Young Andy was. He was in the middle of the new ground and we were nearly to the end.

"If Young Andy can't trounce frogs any better than he can chop sprouts he'll never make a champion," I said.

Uncle Andy didn't answer me. He pulled a sweat-soaked red-faded bandanna from his hip overall pocket, wiped sweat from his eyes and started cuttin' sprouts fast as he could to keep his row ahead of me. But it was all he could do. I didn't haf to work as hard as he did. Once I thought I'd tell him that because he was the champion frog-trouncer of Ennis County for twenty-five years didn't make him the champion sprout cutter. But he was my uncle and he was a lot older than I was and I didn't tell him. Uncle Andy would never let me take the bottom row. All afternoon I crowded him until streams of sweat ran from his beard. Young Andy, with all of his bulgin' muscles, and his barrel chest, followed us through the field.

Next day Uncle Andy sent me to a field in the head of the creek to chop crab grass from the corn by myself. He and Young Andy worked together in the new ground. I knew why he did it. I was too tough for him and Young Andy. I don't have the right color of hair, I thought, and I don't have the right name, the barrel chest, big shoulders, and the bulgin' muscles in my legs and arms but I'll be in the Dysard Grove on September Frog-Trouncin' Day.

Then I thought about the yearlin' bulls Uncle Andy won every year for twenty-five years. "I allus git my beef

53

free," Uncle Andy would brag to Pa and all the other men that had entered the contest. "I let the other fellars take home the turkey gobblers and the roosters." As I worked and thought of the way I had been treated, I'd strike sparks of fire from my hoe when it hit a rock. And I didn't keep account of the hills of corn I cut down. I worked like I thought I'd be trouncin' frogs in September, the day when I'd get to trounce against my first cousin, Young Andy Blevins.

When I quit the crab-grass corn field the sun was down. I thought I'd come by the new ground to see how Young Andy had got along. I didn't hear their hoes swishin' the sprouts before I reached the field. I hurried up the steep slope to see if they had finished the field. It wasn't nigh finished. Then I wondered what they had been doin'. I stood listenin' for their voices. I heard 'em on the other hill across the hollow.

"That's the way to do hit," I heard Uncle Andy say.

They're a-practicin' for the big frog-trouncin', I thought. I'll see what they're doin'.

The last part of the way, I crawled on my belly like I was slippin' on a crow to shoot 'im from a tree-top. I crawled over and under briars, sprouts and weeds until I could watch Uncle Andy and Young Andy. Sure enough he was a-trainin' Young Andy to trounce. They had a basket of toad frogs and a trouncer. I watched Young Andy swing his mallet and I had to laugh for I knew I could do better. Uncle Andy would show 'm how to stand and how to swing to get more power with his mallet.

"Do ye reckon Chuck'll ever make a trouncer, Uncle Andy?" Young Andy asked.

"He don't have the muscles, son," Uncle Andy said. "He hasn't got what it takes to make a champion."

"But he'll try for the bull," Young Andy said.

"He won't even git a rooster," Uncle Andy said, then he laughed a big horselaugh and slapped his knees with his big hands. "Hit takes a Blevins to make a champion. And hit takes me to train a champion. I could still be th' champion but I want to step aside and let a younger man have it. I've had enough beef."

I watched Young Andy train until the sun went down and it had started gettin' dark. I left them standin' by the trouncer talkin' after they'd used up all their frogs. I crawled back on my belly to the road and then I ran for home.

When I reached home, I told Pa about what Uncle Andy and Young Andy were doin'.

"Never mind, Son," Pa said. "I never made a champion trouncer. I tried as hard as any man all my young days but I never got as much as a rooster. I tried to git a yearlin' bull. But I know how this trouncin' is done and I'll help ye all I can. Maybe, if Young Andy can git the bull, ye can git the turkey gobbler or the rooster!"

"But I don't want a second or third place," I said. "I want first place."

"That's the way to feel, Son," Pa said. "My people air just as tough as yer Ma's people. The Hornbuckles air just as tough as the Blevinses. And I hope ye can git the bull. I'll hep ye all I can. I'll make yer trouncin' mallet. Leave that to me. I know how to make one."

I got so mad at Uncle Andy that I quit workin' in the corn for 'im. I went to work for Pa's brother, Uncle Kim Hornbuckle. I wouldn't work any longer for Uncle Andy when he made me do all the work while he took Young Andy out in a secret place to train 'im to trounce. But they weren't the only ones a-trainin'——nearly every man in Ennis County had been a frog-trouncer in his younger days for that was the greatest game in Ennis County—and now these men were a-trainin' their sons or their nephews to trounce. Each man wanted his son to be the champion trouncer and walk from the grove with the yearlin' bull. It was a sort of a disgrace to come away with a turkey and it was a disgrace to come away

55

with a squawkin' rooster under your arm. But you were a
hero if you went away leadin' the bull.

In late July everybody had quit his corn fields and
about all the work a man did was wormin' and suckerin' his
terbacker. Uncle Andy didn't raise terbacker and all he did
was to train Young Andy to trounce. You'd think that men
were a-cuttin' timber everyplace if you'd stand on a hilltop
on a day when the wind wasn't a-blowin' and listen to the
mallets.

Pa cut a tough-butted white oak and sawed the toughest
part from the butt-end for my mallet. He bored into the
middle with an inch auger and filled it with buckshot to
make it heavier. Then he whittled a glut of white oak and
drove into the auger hole to hold the buckshot. He sawed the
glut off smooth with the end of the mallet.

"Son, if ye can swing this mallet, ye'll win the Frog-
Trouncin'," Pa said. "There'll not be another mallet like this
'n in Dysard Grove. Practice with hit until ye can swing it
overhanded and let hit come down square on yer trouncer.
And as ye swing down, jump up and put all yer weight on the
handle. This handle'll hold ye; hit's made of yaller locust."

All through August I practiced trouncin'. Sometimes, Pa
would go with me and show me what he knew about trouncin'.
But most of the time, I went alone. I practiced swingin' my
hammer just as Pa had told me. I got so I could swing it
easy as I could swing a seven-pound ax. And once, when I
was out gatherin' me a basket of toad-frogs, Amos Johnson
slipped up on the hill with a rifle.

"Lay that toad-frog down, Chuck Hornbuckle," he said.
"Put hit down right where ye picked it up. Dump all the
frogs ye have in that basket out on the ground and don't ye
ever pick up another toad-frog on my farm!"

"But frogs are a-gettin' scarce over on our farm, Mr.
Johnson," I said. "I'm learnin' to trounce and I need 'em!"

"That's just hit," Amos Johnson said, "I'm a religious man but I could shoot a man betwixt the eyes free as I ever et a bit of grub 'r prayed a prayer. Hit's the meanest thing I ever heard of—this trouncin'—this trouncin' o' th' poor little frogs. They ketch the flies, bugs and worms and what air the farmers in Ennis County a-goin' to do if young men keep up this crazy trouncin'. Thar won't be a toad-frog left in Ennis County."

I laid the frog down and poured the toads from my basket. I got off Amos Johnson's farm soon as I could.

"Old Andy Blevins has kilt more frogs than any man that's ever lived," I heard Amos Johnson say as I hurried toward home. "If I ever get to the Kentucky Legislature, I'll make a law agin' hit."

But I managed to find frogs on Pa's farm so I could practice trouncin' until September. And durin' the early days of September, I just practiced swingin' my mallet down on the trouncer. I could hardly wait for the last day in September.

Pa went with me. He carried my mallet. Just on ahead of us, we saw Uncle Andy with Young Andy and most all the Blevinses. They looked like a small army of boys, young men and old men and there were many women among them. There were young couples—boys with their arms around girls, and the girls, not to be outdone since they too were Blevinses, had their arms around the boys. And when we reached the Dysard Grove, we found it filled with people. Many had walked to the grove; many had ridden mules, horses—they had come in wagons, buggies and surreys. I'd never seen as many people at the Frog-Trouncin' in my life. Pa said he'd never seen so many at a political rally, Children's Day, footwashin' or a Baptist Association.

When we walked into the grove, we saw several boys lookin' at the turkey gobbler. He was in a crate and the boys would whistle to make him gobble and strut. Very few were around the crate that held the rooster. But men shoved each other to get close to the yearlin' bull.

"Hit's the best bull I've seen here in twenty-five years," Uncle Andy said. Then he bent over and whispered something in Young Andy's ear. I thought I heard 'im say, though I couldn't tell since there was so much noise, "Son, that bull will be yourn. Jist trounce as I've larned ye."

While the old men, young men and boys stood around the tree admirin' the bull, big Sam Akers stood in a wagon-bed and yelled for the crowd to keep quiet while he read the names of the men who would enter the Frog-Trouncin'. When he read Young Andy Blevins' name, Uncle Andy slapped Young Andy on the shoulder and all the men looked at Young Andy. And when Sam read my name from the list, Young Andy looked at me and said, "Chuck, I'm a-goin' to take the bull; I hope ye git the rooster."

"Many a man has trounced twenty years and never got a rooster," I said.

Then Young Andy looked at Uncle Andy and laughed.

"Now the Frog-Trouncin' is ready to start," Sam Akers said. "Come to the trouncer when I call yer name. Ye git three tries. If ye don't send the frog above the tree-tops in one of yer tries, ye're disqualified. Ye've lost. Three judges will make the decisions."

The frog-trouncer was a heavy plank balanced on a wooden horse like a teeter-totter. On one end the toad frog was placed and was tied there, so it couldn't jump, with a white thread. The man trouncin' the frog, hit the other end of the trouncer with his mallet and it sent the frog toward the sky and when the frog fell to the ground it was dead as four o'clock. One had to hit the trouncer exactly right to send the frog straight into the air; if he didn't hit it right, the frog would go sidewise.

"Who are the judges, Pa?" I asked.

"Flem Spry, Harvey Tuttle and Willie Whittlecomb," Pa said. "See 'em a-sittin' upon the hill."

"I see 'em," I said.

"They're all right," Pa said. "Same jedges we had last year. All can see good."

They were sittin' side by side on a log upon the hillside where they could see the frog if the trouncer sent 'im above the tree-tops. There was a clearin' around the trouncer so the frogs would have a chance to trounce toward the sky without hittin' the tree limbs.

"Bill Adams," Sam Akers called.

Then Sam took a frog and threaded 'im to the trouncer. Maybe Bill was scared. He was shakin' mightily—and when he hit the trouncer everybody watched for the frog. It didn't go halfway to the tops of the trees around the trouncer. But it fell back dead as four o'clock and everybody laughed and took swigs from their jugs.

"Two more tries," Sam said as he threaded another frog and everybody tried to crowd over everybody else to be the closest to the frog-trouncer.

Bill swung his mallet over his shoulder with a twist and hit the trouncer on one corner. The frog sailed like a quail just over the tops of the lot of heads and hit a tree.

"One more trial," Sam said, takin' another frog from one of the big willow-baskets and threadin' it to the trouncer.

Bill braced his feet and struck at the trouncer. The frog didn't quite reach the tree-tops.

"Ye'll haf to try again next year," Sam said.

"See, I told ye a lot o' 'em couldn't even qualify," Uncle Andy told Young Andy.

"Young Andy Blevins," Sam Akers called.

"Show 'em, Young Andy," Uncle Andy said, slappin' Young Andy on his broad shoulder.

Soon as Sam had the frog threaded, Young Andy was

ready. He came over with a wallop that sent the frog far above the tree-tops as straight toward the sky as it could go.

"Qualified," Flem Spry yelled.

"Who is that boy?" Harvey Tuttle asked.

"Young Andy Blevins," Uncle Andy yelled. "He'll be yer next champion. I can see 'im a-leadin' the bull away!"

"You've got another nephew to trounce yet and his name is Hornbuckle, not Blevins," I told Uncle Andy. "He's the one that raked the sprouts down on you and Young Andy in the new ground."

"Stay with 'em, Hornbuckle," a beardy-faced man yelled from the crowd as he lifted his jug to his lips. "Don't let a Blevins git the bull every year. Hit isn't fair!"

Bill Cates qualified on the third trounce. Henry Crum, Bill Dugan and Willie Fultz failed to qualify. Dorsey Gardner qualified on the second trounce and Horace Garvey didn't qualify.

"Chuck Hornbuckle," Sam Akers yelled.

While he threaded the frog, Pa whispered to me, "Don't do yer best. Just send the frog above the tree-tops."

"All right, Pa," I said.

On my first trounce, I swung my heavy mallet over but didn't bear on the handle as I brought it down.

"Qualified," Flem Spry yelled.

"Hit's the second-best trounce," Willie Whittlecomb said. "Only Young Andy Blevins' trounce has it bested."

"Ye may git the turkey gobbler, Chuck," Uncle Andy said.

Then Uncle Andy laughed. But Young Andy didn't laugh. He looked surprised when he saw me hit the trouncer with so much ease.

After the sixty men had tried out only eighteen had sent the frogs above the tree-tops. Now we had to fight for first, second and third places. We were ready for round two.

Young Andy trounced his frog far above the tree-tops the first lick.

"Haint seen a frog go outten sight yet," Flem Spry yelled.

"Ye'll see one go outten sight in round three," Uncle Andy said.

Well, everybody cheered, yelled, cussed and carried on so, you couldn't hear your mallet hit the trouncer. We had used two willow baskets of frogs and was ready to start on the third one when we started round three. Ten men were dropped in round two by the judges because they couldn't send the frogs ten feet above the tree-tops. Eight men were in the finish; Young Andy was leadin' and I was second.

"Now fer the last trounce, men," Sam Akers said, raisin' the lid on the fourth basket of frogs. "Do yer level best this time."

Soon as Sam had threaded the frog, Young Andy walked out to the trouncer. He braced his feet, swung a few times in practice and then he came over with a wallop that sent the frog high into the air.

"Not outten sight," Flem Spry said. "I can still see hit."

"I can see hit too," Harvey Tuttle said.

"Boys, I can't see hit," Willie Whittlecomb said.

Then it was my time to trounce. I walked out, didn't swing in practice but I came over with my heavy mallet with all I had.

"Outten sight," Flem Spry said.

"Where did ye send that frog?" Harvey Tuttle said.

"Never did see hit," Willie Whittlecomb said.

And the whole crowd cheered but Uncle Andy and Young Andy. Men and boys swigged from their jugs in my honor. Everybody tried to rush closest to the trouncer.

We had finished the last round and Flem Spry announced: "Chuck Hornbuckle is first, Young Andy Blevins is second and Dorsey Gardner is third."

"Ye didn't pick the right nephew, Andy," Bill Wheeler said.

And while the crowd roared and Pa started after the bull, men grabbed me and carried me on their shoulders from the grove because I'd beaten the first Blevins in twenty-five years. And as they carried me a few circles under the grove before they took me to the road, I saw Young Andy and Uncle Andy leavin' the grove together and Young Andy a-carryin' his turkey gobbler under his arm while small boys followed them hissin' to make the turkey gobbler gobble.

turtle hunt

"Yep, now's the time, Alf," Op said proudly. "The turtle season is on. I'm hungry fer turtle meat!"

The two men were barefooted and their pants were rolled above their knees. Alf's feet were tender and he looked down at the path and chose the smooth places to step. He walked as if he were stepping on eggs.

"Ouch, I stepped on a rock," he fretted, holding up his white, tender foot.

"Put yer feet down and get ust to it," Op growled. "Grit yer teeth together and tell yerself it don't hurt to step on a little rock barefooted."

"But I'd be lying to myself. It does hurt."

"The water will be soft," Op said, "when we get into the creek. There will be soft mud on the bottom and it will be like a-walkin' on cool winter moss."

Theopolis carried his hunting knife in a sheath on his hip. That was all he took with him for hunting turtles. When the two men walked from the well-worn path that led to the spring onto the narrow path down to the hole where they bathed, Op stopped beside a little hickory. He took the knife from the sheath, reached high above his head and peeled down a strip of hickory bark to the ground. Then he peeled another strip down the same width and length and then a third and fourth.

"What are you peeling that tree for, Op?"

"Look on now and larn later." The man was always askin' questions. He never jist watched and larned for himself.

Op used his knife and peeled away the coarse bark, exposing the long thongs of inner hickory bark which was both durable and pliable. He wound these around his elbow and between his thumb and forefinger into a little bundle.

"That's neat work," Alf told him.

"I ought to be able to do it neatly," he said. "I've peeled enough hickory bark in my day to bottom chairs and use fer ropes. I've tried about everythin'. But a body can't get anythin' to tie with he can trust like hickory bark."

Then Op said: "Here's where the creek really begins, where I jump in. Carry the bark."

He jumped into the deep hole where the water came up to his navel. Alf fidgeted nervously along the edge of the bank while Op waded around in the pool and fingered under the bank with his bare hands. Where the water had splashed against the dirt walls it had left overhanging turf matted with the roots of ferns and wild snowballs. Op circled the pool, putting his hand back into every crevice.

"You mean you catch turtles with your hands?" Alf said. "And there's a possibility of finding one where we've been bathing?"

"Yep," Op replied as he fingered under the turf. "We might find one here."

"Won't a turtle bite?"

"Yep, they'll bite all right."

"Ever have one bite you?"

"Nope, never have." He fingered another spot. "Never want one to bite me either. A turtle is like an old stud terrapin. When one grabs a body it won't let loose till it thunders. If it don't thunder, he'll let go when the sun does down."

"Aren't you afraid one will grab you by the hand?"

"Nope," Op grunted. "When I want turtle meat I go ketch me a mess of turtles. A body hast to eat. And up here if a body don't go after his grub, he won't eat. That's the way it's allus been with me. It's a lot of fun to ketch turtles but I don't do it exactly fer fun. I do it to eat."

Op jumped up from the hole and onto the bank, the cold blue water streaming from his clothes. "No turtle in there."

"I should hope not," Alf sounded relieved. "Not after jumping in there naked and taking a bath."

"Now a turtle won't come out jist to bite ye, Alf," Op grumbled. "Ye've got to do somethin' to a turtle! Don't be so skeery."

Below the bathing hole, the stream was shallow. It trickled over the rocks leaving little clear pools, fringed by the ferns here and there, and then it flowed away again, tumbling and splashing over the rocks. Op waded into each still pool and fingered around the brink into each little crevice, between the rocks and under the ferns.

"Aren't you afraid you'll put your hand in on a water moccasin?" Alf asked him.

"Not at all," he replied. "Water moccasins stretch out on rocks and dead logs in spots of sun this time of day and year. When one hides in a hole, he goes back into one too small fer a turtle. Turtles and water moccasins won't have anythin' to do with each other. What could a water moccasin get outta bitin' a turtle's hard shell? But I think if a turtle was a-mind to, he could clamp down with his iron jaws on a water moccasin's thin body and cut it smack in two. See, Alf, wild things in nature get along better'n most human folks. They know their enemies and keep outten their way. And they know their friends a lot better'n we do. The turtle can't eat the water moccasin and the water moccasin can't eat the turtle. So they're not atter one another and they make purty good neighbors. Now the water moccasins do swaller the little minners—I-gollies, there's one now!"

Alf looked up in time to see what appeared to be a thick piece of rope drop from a sunlit poplar branch into the water below.

"I'd never put my big toe up to a thing like that," Alf said. He looked down at his own white toes apprehensively.

"We'll get 'im." Op found a club a little longer than a baseball bat and not as large around. He stirred the sand in the bottom of the pool and made the water muddy.

"You mean *you'll* get him," Alf said, backing away.

"Be real quiet," Op whispered. "He'll stick his head up from the muddy water and I'll let 'im have this club right over the bean!"

Op and Alf stood quietly above the muddied water.

When there were some little bubbles, Op trained his eye on the spot. The thick, hard, iron-rimmed mouth rose first and then the lidless eyes came above the surface just as Op came down with his club. There was splashing and writhing and a cream-colored substance spread over the surface of the muddy water. Op lifted the dying snake from the pool with his club. He tossed it writhing upon the bank and finished killing it with a few more strokes of his club.

"See, it didn't try to bite us," Op said. "It tried to hide. But I kill every kind of a snake. I can't say I like a-one. I've never larned why the Master put the water moccasin here unless it's to thin out the minners."

Then they started down the stream.

"I'm not surprised we didn't get a turtle in Red Bird Crick," Op said. "When we git down here where it empties into Little White Oak, then we're a-gettin' into the turtle country. Turtles love sand and more sunshine than a body will find up here under these tall poplars!"

Op fingered around in the pools where the two streams joined.

"I found one," he said. "The shell feels like a rock, only it's smoother. Come outten there!"

The undercurrent of water had washed away the land and left a little room where it was dark and cool. Op pulled the turtle from his resting place.

"Ye're too small, ye little devil," he said, holding it up for Alf to see.

The turtle wasn't as large as a saucer. His four legs stuck out from under his shell, clawing against the wind. His head was out too, moving this way and that on his long, scaly, black neck. "Ye grow up and I'll be back in a couple of years and get ye," Op laughed, throwing the kicking turtle into the stream.

"I wouldn't want to handle a little turtle, let alone a big

one," Alf muttered. He watched the turtle swim over the water and crawl up the other side of the creek bank and hide under the overlapping turf.

"Ye won't be afraid atter ye handle one," Op told him.

They started down the stream again, Alf lifting his cold blue feet quickly from the water whenever he stepped on the little sharp upturned slate rocks. His teeth rattled from the cold water. They came to a bed of sand, and a cloud of butterflies flew up, frightened. The butterflies had been drinking warm water from the sand where the sunlight filtered through the sycamore and willow leaves.

"There's a good place fer a turtle," Op said, looking the place over carefully. He got down on his knees in the water. He put his hands back in a hole under the roots of a waterbirch. He reached back to his elbow. Then he pulled and grunted and finally fell backward in the water.

"He was pullin' one way and I was pullin' another," Op grunted, holding on to a turtle large as a four-gallon crock. "He's a big booger and he's heavy."

The turtle was snapping at the wind. His head was thrust out on his scaly neck, which was larger around than a hoe handle. His legs were pulling and his toes were scratching the air. Op held grimly to the turtle while he lay in the hole of water on his back with his head sticking up.

"Help me, Alf. I can't get up with this load!"

"How can I help you?" Alf said sharply. "I'm afraid of that thing!"

"Take this turtle," Op commanded. "Take 'im before he takes me."

"I can't do it! I won't touch it."

"Take a thong of the hickory bark then, and tie a loop in it," Op instructed Alf as he lay there in the water. "Put the loop over the turtle's head. Ye can do that, can't ye?"

"Yes, I guess so," Alf admitted as he took a thong from the bundle. He tied a loop in the bark and ran the end of the thong through the loop. Then he dropped it over the turtle's head.

"Now pull on the thong," Op said. "Don't be afraid of chokin' it. Ye can't choke a turtle. And one's head is jist enough bigger'n the neck to make the loop hold good."

Alf pulled on the pliable, strong hickory bark and it tightened around the turtle's neck.

"Hold 'im now, Alf," Op shouted. "I'm lettin' 'im loose."

"I'll try." Alf braced his white feet against the bank.

Op turned the turtle loose on the sand, and Alf held to the hickory thong. Op got up, and the muddy water streamed from his clothes.

"Take it, Op," Alf grunted, as the big turtle dug his feet into the sand and started pulling away.

"Lift 'im up and get his feet offen the ground. Ye can tote 'im then."

"It's a heavy thing," Alf said as he lifted the turtle by the neck. "He'll weigh thirty pounds!"

Alf followed Op down the stream, swaying to and fro under the weight of the turtle.

"Is this a mock turtle, Op?" Alf asked.

"I don't know what ye're a-talkin about, Alf!"

"You know, Op, the kind in mock turtle soup!"

"Mock turtle soup?" Op retorted, training his good eye on Alf. "Shucks, I never heard of a mock turtle in my life."

"Op, you've never been anyplace but around here," Alf said. "I used to have mock turtle soup for my lunch sometimes at Wright Airfield."

"We're not a-ketchin' 'em fer soup, I can tell ye that. We're atter turtles fer meat and eggs. Lutie knows how to cook 'em. I've larned her. But I never heard tell of mock turtle soup! Say," Op said, looking straight at Alf, "jist what is a mock turtle? We've only got hard-shell and soft-shell turtles around here."

"I don't know the different breeds," Alf said irritably as he held the big turtle's open jaws as far away as he could. "I'm afraid it's going to bite me."

"That's an old stud turtle," Op said. "That's what makes 'im so mean."

"How do you know he's a stud?"

"By his shell," Op replied. "The stud has a harder-lookin' shell and it has more color in it! Now let's look around here close and we'll find his mate! The old she-turtle is allus close to the stud. Turtles are never nervous."

"Look up there on the bank," Alf said. "Look!"

"That's 'er," Op shouted with joy. "She's started to lay 'er eggs in the sand, I-gollies."

When the turtle saw Alf and Op, she started back for the water. But Op ran up the bank to meet her, reached down, and picked her up.

"We've got turtle aplenty now," Op said. "And we'll have anywhere from a dozen to two dozen turtle eggs too. The eggs are wonderful but not any better'n turtle meat. Yessir! A body can taste seven different kinds of wild meat in a turtle. Pheasant, quail, rabbit, possum, coon, chicken hawk, and squirrel. All in turtle meat!"

"I don't believe I can carry this turtle all the way to the ridge," Alf sighed. At that moment he was more interested in the weight than the taste.

"Well, I'm not a-goin' to carry both turtles and let ye carry jist yerself. That load'll warm ye up!"

As Alf walked up the stream with his turtle, the sun filtered through the leafy treetops enough to warm his legs. His teeth stopped rattling and sweat broke out on his face. When he and Op reached the cabin, it was late afternoon. Op took the turtles directly to the chopblock where he laid their necks over the block and cut their heads off with his double-bitted ax.

Lucretia had a tub of hot water ready, and Op dropped the turtles in.

"A few minutes," he said, "and we'll pull the shells offen 'em and cut 'em up like ye cut a chicken. I'll show ye some of the purtiest, whitest, cleanest meat ye ever saw in yer life!"

"Look at this, Julia"—Alf turned to his wife. He had never left the wood block. He held the ax handle up to the turtle's mouth and it snapped at it although the body and head were severed. "Ever see anything like this?"

"I never did," Julia said, shuddering. "How can its jaws work when it no longer has a body?"

"It'll keep on a-doin' that till the sun goes down," Op said.

"Op picked up these turtles with his hands," Alf told Lucretia and Julia. "He reaches back under the creek banks and gets them. I wouldn't put my hand in one of those holes for all the tea in China."

Op looked up sharply from the tub of water. "What's tea an' China got to do with huntin' turtles?"

"Nothing." Alf laughed briefly. "Absolutely nothing." He walked toward the cabin on his sore bare feet. He looked bent over, as if he thought he was still carrying the turtle.

sparkie and did

"It's time to git up, Did," Sparkie said, shaking Did's shoulder. "Hear the roosters crowin'!"

While Sparkie stood over Did, stretching his arms above his head and yawning, Shooting Star whined and kissed Did's face.

"Git up, Did," Sparkie said. "I see Peg comin' with the lantern!"

"Shooting Star, that's enough!"

Did arose from beside the dog, sat up, rubbed his eyes, and yawned.

"Did you sleep warm last night?"

"I dreamed of picking peaches on a hot day in July," Did said. "I must've got awfully warm in the night. Shooting Star's a real bedfellow."

"Now, did the fleas bother you?"

"If they did, I didn't know anything about it!"

"I told ye a dog flea wouldn't bite a body!"

The lantern moved through the morning darkness from the house to the barn. While Did sat on the hay beside Shooting Star, he thought about what Sparkie had told him about his going to get Peg an artificial limb so he could wear a shoe, when he made enough money.

"Are ye boys awake?" Peg yelled up to the barn loft.

When Peg's lantern came to the barn at this hour and his wooden leg sounded against the frozen ground, every living thing around the barn awakened. Did heard, above the music of the roosters, Dick and Dinah stand up in their stalls and bray. He heard the popping of knee joints as the cattle arose in their stalls. The hungry fattening hogs spoke to Peg with wheezing grunts. Even Shooting Star and Lightning spoke with pleasant whines and Fleet and Thunderbolt answered them from their kennels.

"Roll out," Peg shouted again. "Yer breakfast'll git cold if ye don't."

"We're up, Peg," Sparkie answered. "We're a-comin' right down!"

Sparkie and Did went down the scuttle-hole with Shooting Star and Lightning following them. They took the dogs to their kennels, snapped their chains in their collars, and left them whining to go free.

"Jest a minute, boys," Peg said.

Peg was on his way to the hog pen with a feed basket of corn in his hand. He came over where Sparkie and Did were caressing the hounds.

"I've jest been thinkin' ye'd better set yer trap line today," Peg said, stopping before them, smoothing down his long, wind-ruffled beard with his free hand. "Won't be long till Christmas, and ye'll be needing some spare change."

"Ye're right, Peg," Sparkie agreed. "The weather's a-gittin' cold enough fer the pelts to look bright when they cure."

"How much of a trap line do ye plan to set this year?" Peg asked.

"From twenty to twenty-five miles," Sparkie said. "Want to set it from Buzzard Roost to the Reeves Pond, then down with the Little Sandy River to Shackle Run."

"That's a good twenty-five miles. Ye'll have to ride the mules around the circuit."

"That's wonderful, Peg."

"Jest as soon as ye eat yer breakfast, the mules'll be

through with their corn and hay," Peg told them. "Saddle and bridle the mules and ride!"

"Ye ever ride a mule, Did?"

"No, I never did, Sparkie."

"Then here's where ye larn."

"Ever set a trap line, Did?"

"No, never."

"Then, here's where ye larn that too."

After Sparkie and Did had eaten breakfast, they went to the corncrib, where they put a hundred steel traps, of various sizes, in each coffee sack. After they had sacked their steel traps, they went into the barn and Sparkie showed Did how to use a currycomb and brush on Dick, who was more gentle than Dinah. While Did combed and brushed Dick until his hair looked fluffy and bright, Sparkie made impatient Dinah stand long enough to be groomed for the long ride. Then Sparkie showed Did how to bridle and saddle a mule.

"Pull the girth strap as tight as ye can pull it," he told Did. "Ye can't git it too tight. The mule draws in a big breath and expands when ye start tightenin' the girth."

"That's as tight as I can draw it, Sparkie!"

"But it's not tight enough. Let me show ye."

Sparkie took hold of the girth and pulled it two notches tighter.

"See, if ye don't have it tight, yer saddle will roll," Sparkie said. "Ye're liable to roll off. Remember we're ridin' over rough roads!"

They took the mules from their stalls and while Did held their bridle reins, Sparkie carried the sacks of steel traps and tied one behind each saddle to the saddle rings.

"Wait jest a minute longer, Did. There's somethin' else we want to take along!"

Did watched Sparkie go down to the barn and run his hand back into a hollow barn log and bring out a long bright shiny pistol. Then he reached back and fetched out another one. Holding the two pistols in one hand, he brought out two holsters.

"I don't mind ye a-knowin' where I keep my belongin's, Did," Sparkie said. "I keep 'em in that log."

"I've stood beside that log many times, but I never dreamed you used it for a secret hiding place."

"I've used it fer years," Sparkie said, putting the pistols in the leather holsters. "It would be a sight to see the different things I've kept in that log."

"Will the mules be scared if we shoot these pistols?"

"They're ust to my ridin' 'em and shootin'," Sparkie said. "Here's the .25 automatic fer yerself. I'll take the .38 Special."

"Is it safe?"

"When the safety's on," Sparkie said, showing Did the safety. "Now when ye want to shoot, pull this safety back and let go!"

"When must I shoot?"

"Any time ye're ridin' along and feel like it."

"Sparkie buckled his holster around him so his pistol would be on his right hip and easy to draw at a second's notice.

"If we see a wildcat, he's a goner," Sparkie said.

"Do we have wildcats around here?"

"Several of 'em around the old coal mines. They plunder the farmers' hen houses and sheep barns. They'll carry off a lamb or a pig."

Sparkie held his hand for Did to step on before he mounted the tall mule, filling the seat of the small cowboy saddle. Sparkie pulled a big burley leaf from his pocket and crammed it into his mouth, put his foot into the stirrup, left the ground, flinging his leg over Dinah's back, and landed squarely on the big saddle.

"We're off," Sparkie said. "Let Dick follow Dinah."

A blanket of white frost lay over the land, rock cliffs, and trees. Where the mules' steel shoes hit the frozen earth, they chipped pieces of frozen dirt, leaving little holes in the white carpet of frost. Dinah wanted to run, but Sparkie held her down with a tight rein while they crossed the pasture field. Dick didn't try to run ahead but was content to follow Dinah.

When Sparkie rode to the drawbars enclosing Peg's pasture field, he slackened Dinah's bridle reins and she cleared the drawbars with a wild leap. Did slackened his bridle reins to let Dick follow Dinah. Just as Sparkie looked back, he saw Did bounce high from his saddle, pitch forward over the mule's shoulder, and hit the frozen ground on his face with his legs and arms sprawled.

"Are ye hurt, Did?"

Sparkie reined Dinah back to Did.

"Just knocked the breath out of me," Did grunted, getting up.

"Bruised yer face a little is all," Sparkie said.

"I've never done any muleback riding," Did said, walking over where Dick was standing, getting ready to mount him again.

"All ye got to do is sit easy, Did," Sparkie told him. "Jest think ye're a-sittin' in a rockin' chear."

Sparkie helped Did mount, then mounted Dinah and they were off. Now they were on the old coal-wagon road and Sparkie slackened his reins so Dinah could gallop. She leaped the rut-washed ditches and threw back a shower of frozen clumps of dirt from her hind feet. While Sparkie rocked easily in the saddle with one hand on the reins, he pulled his .38 from his hip holster and held it into the air, emptying it. Did pulled his automatic from the holster, turned the safety off, braced himself, and pulled the trigger back.

"Ain't this wonderful, Did?" Sparkie said, turning his head back as Dinah raced on.

"G-great!" Did said, trying to get his smoking pistol back in the holster and stick on the mule at the same time.

They rode full speed along the wagon road until they came to the dilapidated coal tipple of a worked-out mine. Here the wagon road ended.

"We haf to take a path from here," Sparkie said.

Great streams of breath were flying from Dinah's nostrils like clouds of fog when she exhaled. They expanded and thinned to nothingness on the clear blue morning air. Her sides were working in and out like a bee smoker.

"Let's wind the mules a minute," Sparkie said. "Then we'll start up this mountain."

"I thought it would rest me to ride a mule," Did laughed. "But I'm gettin' my breath about as fast as Dick. It was hard for me to stick in the saddle! And I thought Dick was goin' to fall several times."

"Don't worry about Dick a-fallin'," Sparkie said. "Mules are shore-footed things. That's why we use 'em among these hills. Ye watch 'em climb this mountain path!"

Sparkie reined Dinah around the coal tipple, past a slate dump, then he turned left onto a narrow path bordered on each side by scrub pines. Often Sparkie had to stop Dinah and break a wild grapevine between the pines on each side of the road to keep them from jerking him from the saddle. But he rode slowly in front and made a way for Did. They rode along a narrow rim of path, barely room enough for a mule to climb. Did trembled in his saddle when he looked on either side at a deep sunken coal mine.

"It's good country fer wildcats and foxes, Did. When they mined this coal out, it left warm caves fer the animals. The only way a body can git one is by trappin'."

"This is a wild country all right," Did agreed.

"Not wild to me," Sparkie laughed.

When Sparkie reached the ridgetop, he stopped his mule.

"That's the Buzzard Roost country," Sparkie said, pointing down to the valley below.

77

"Why is it called that?"

"Buzzards ust to roost in these rock cliffs. They laid eggs here and hatched their young."

Did reined Dick up beside Dinah and looked over.

"What a country," he said. "Look at the cliffs."

"Cliffs and coal mines," Sparkie said. "And plenty of furbearin' animals!"

"But why didn't we set some traps back at the first coal mines?" Did asked.

"Too close to civil-i-zation," Sparkie said. "Animals like a wild country. Here's where they live! Here's where we'll set the big traps fer foxes and wildcats!"

Sparkie dismounted, unsnapped one side of his bridle rein, and tied it to a tree. Did rolled off Dick, stretched and yawned. He did what he had seen Sparkie do; he fastened his mule to the limb of a nearby white oak while Sparkie untied a sack of steel traps from the saddle.

"Do you know where we're going to set them, Sparkie?"

"I shore do," Sparkie said, starting down a path with the sack of steel traps on his shoulder. "Ye follow me. Remember this path, fer ye may haf to come to the traps by yerself sometime."

When they came to a cliff with a hole worn slick between a split in the rock, Sparkie stopped and threw the sack of traps from his shoulder. He pulled off a few loose hairs from the sides of the rock, held them up, and looked carefully at them.

"Gray foxes," Sparkie said.

Did watched Sparkie take gloves from his pocket, shove his hands into them and scoop out a bit of earth big enough to place a trap at the mouth of the hole so the jaws would be even with the ground. He threw the loose dirt he had scooped up into his gloves over the cliff. Then he took a trap from the sack, mashed the spring with his foot, and set the trigger. He put it in the groove neatly.

"Git some dry leaves from back under the cliff, Did," he said. "Be shore ye have yer gloves on."

While Did went after the leaves, Sparkie took a hatchet from his hunting coat and hacked down a small sapling. He cut a stake and sharpened one end. He drove this down into the solid earth in front of the cliff, put the loop on the trap chain over it, and drove the little spike attached to the chain into the stake.

"It takes somethin' to hold a fox," Sparkie said.

Then he took the dry leaves Did had gathered and covered the trap.

"He can't see the trap now," Did said.

"And he can't smell our hands."

"Won't a dog get in that trap?"

"No, it's set too fur back in the hole! I always see to that. I ust to set deadfalls and I ketched two dogs. That larned me somethin', Did. Larned me how to set traps."

Sparkie picked up the sack of traps, swung it over his shoulder, and they moved on to another cliff where there was a big opening.

"Looks like wildcats dennin' here," Sparkie said. "We'll haf to set eight or ten traps to kiver the hole."

Did carried the leaves while Sparkie set the traps and cut the stakes to hold them. After they had set these traps, they went down to another cliff and set traps for red foxes. Sparkie knew where the different animals denned. He would stop at a cliff, scent the wind from back in the hole like a sniffing hound dog, and then he would look around until he found a hair on one of the rocks and he would examine it carefully.

"You know a lot about setting traps for different animals, Sparkie!"

"I ought to know a little fer I've trapped enough!"

After they had set over half of the traps among these cliffs at Buzzard Roost, they climbed back up a little fox path to the ridge road, where they untied their mules, mounted, and rode around the ridge path, facing the red ball of an early sunrise.

The ridge road was wide and Did and Sparkie could ride their mules side by side. They could look down to their right and see the valley where their shack was and they could look from their left down into a valley that was a wild country, where there wasn't a shack to be seen but where there were deep wooded hollows and palisades of high cliffs. This country was the home of the foxes and wildcats.

"I've been a-comin' to Buzzard Roost since I've been big enough to follow the hounds. There's not a high knoll along this ridge road where I ain't listened to my hounds drive home the fox!"

"You don't mean you stayed out winter nights along this ridge where the wind blows so cold?"

"See this little ash pile here?" Sparkie asked, pointing to a pile of firebrands with charred ends. "I carried wood up from the slopes and built that fire on a night last January. It was zero weather and I laid by that fire. One side of me burned while the other froze."

"You can hear hound dogs running here for miles, can't you?"

"Ye shore can. This ridge road is the home of the fox hunters. Here's where we come to hear the chases. Ye can come here at night and listen to the hounds after the fox, ye can listen to horns blowin' all over these mountains. I know about every hunter's fox horn soon as I hear it blow. I know about every rock cliff in this country. I know where to set traps and I know the cliffs where if a fox hunter finds my traps he'll take 'em up and break 'em. I know it 'cause it's my country."

Did noticed that Sparkie never bounced in his saddle. He rode as easily when his mule jumped over the trees that the wind had blown across the ridge road as if he were glued

80

to the saddle. And as he rode along, he took his pistol from his hip holster.

"What do ye say we ride and shoot again," Sparkie said. "I like to ride and shoot when I'm this close to the sky!"

Sparkie started off in a gallop, his pistol high in the air over his head. He began shooting. Did followed him out the straight stretch of ridge road, his pistol barking so fast he couldn't count the times. Now it was a race to see which mule could get ahead. Their mules leaped over entire treetops that lay in their path. Once Dick barely cleared a tree, his hind foot just grazing a limb. He stumbled but didn't fall, and Did held to the saddle horn to keep from pitching forward over his head. Dick kept beside Dinah as they ran toward the morning sun. A cool mountain wind was hitting the boys' faces, a wind so strong they could hardly get their breaths.

"Here's where we stop," Sparkie said, with a grunting breath. "We turn to our right again here! We got to go down a long ridge path!"

"Where are we headin' for now, Sparkie?"

"Polecat country."

"Where's that?"

"It's a lot of fields betwixt here and the Reeves Pond. It's really the polecat country."

Sparkie led the way down the mountain to a broom-sedge-covered field where there were dirt holes under the steep bluffs that fringed these old deserted, worn-out tobacco lands. In each one of these holes they set from one to three small steel traps. They found holes under a few cliffs where they set traps, holes where Sparkie had set traps in other trapping seasons.

"Ye know, Did," Sparkie said, "polecat pelts is where a body makes the money. If we can only git some solid black hides or some narrow stripes! They fetch from seven to nine dollars apiece! That money ain't to be sneezed at!"

They rode across the old deserted fields, Sparkie leading the way. They rode along a cow path through pawpaw and persimmon thickets where the fruit lay in heaps, frost-ripened and mellow, under the trees and under the carpet of leaves.

"See, this is a good possum country too," Sparkie said. "Over in the next hollow the possums den under the cliffs, and we'll set some traps there."

When they reached the next hollow, their mules needed a rest. They reined them to oak trees, took an armload of traps, and went up the hollow to find the cliffs and the slick-worn dirt holes where they set their traps.

After they had set their traps in Possum Hollow, they mounted their mules and rode toward Reeves Pond. It was a long ride over Tunnel Hill and down Nicholl's Hollow and then they came to the Little Sandy River bottoms where they dashed across open corn fields, where often the mules sunk down over their hoofs in the mud. The sun had thawed the frozen ground.

"There are minks and weasels around that pond. Maybe muskrats." Sparkie pointed to a pond out midway of the big bottom.

They rode across the bottom to the pond, dismounted, and tied their mules to clumps of wild snowball bushes. They walked around the pond inspecting the slick-worn holes in the soft bottom earth. Where the holes were used, they set their traps, staking them and placing dead leaves from the wild pond lilies to conceal the jaws and triggers.

"Ye'll see this is the place to git muskrats," Sparkie said as they untied their mules from the wild snowball bushes, mounted them, and rode toward the Little Sandy River.

Where the Reeves Knoll sloped down toward the river were many cliffs, and here they stopped their tired mules and set more traps. At the Putt Off Ford, where the Sandy River bottoms stretched across Hungry Valley, they found more muskrat holes where they set traps.

"We've only got a few traps left, Sparkie," Did said. "When we started with two hundred traps this morning, I wondered where we'd set 'em all."

"We could set another hundred traps if we had 'em," Sparkie said. "Shucks, we ain't visited half the rock-cliff dens and the slick-worn holes that I know among the mountains and hollows! We're jest a-comin' into the good possum country now and we don't have over fifteen traps to set!"

They rode along beside the Sandy River where the tall sycamores grew along the river bank and leaned out over the small winding river.

"I'm a-gittin' mighty hungry, Did," Sparkie said. "I'd like to sit down to a table of good grub. I feel as empty as a hollow beech tree. How do you feel?"

"I feel about the same way, Sparkie!"

They reached the Shackle Run valley where the apple orchards were on the south hillside slopes.

"See, right down here along these bluffs next to the creek are the possum holes," Sparkie said. "The ground hogs dug the holes and the possums took 'em. I know where there are a hundred more dens the possums use. We'll set what few traps we have left."

Did reined Dick to a water-birch beside Shackle Run and Sparkie tied Dinah to a low branch of a sycamore nearby. They took the last traps they had and set out along the steep bluff alongside the creek. They set them in the slick-worn possum dens and returned to their mules, mounted, and rode up Shackle Run toward home.

"We'll ketch somethin' in some of these traps," Sparkie said.

"How often will we have to look about these traps?"

"One will haf to ride the trap line Monday. Would ye like to?"

"I'd love to!"

"Sunshine, rain, or deep snow?"

"It doesn't matter."

The mules were as wet with sweat as if they had swum Sandy River. They rode past a cold ash heap that had once been Tid Barney's barn. Sparkie and Did whistled as they rode slowly toward home.

Did let Dick trot slowly over the rutty road until he came to the coal mine tipple. He went over and over Sparkie's instructions, one at a time. He rode around the tipple, up the path that led to the mountain, along the narrow trail between the sunken mines, and up the mountain between pine groves on each side of the path. He let Dick walk, for the greenbriers and wildgrape vines slapped at his face. With one hand he shoved the briers and vines aside without having his mule stop, and with the other he reined the mule to this or that side of the path until he had reached the mountaintop. When he looked over the cliffs into the Buzzard Roost country, he dismounted and tied his reins to a white-oak limb. With two sacks, rope, his hunting knife, and pistol, he went down the path the way he had gone with Sparkie to set the traps.

When he looked down at the rock cliff where Sparkie had set the steel trap in the groove, he saw what he thought to be a friendly dog sitting out in front of the rock cliff. Did stopped, looked a minute while it looked at him, and then the dog tried to get away, but the trap held it by the left foreleg. When it tried to squeeze back into the groove, Did grabbed it by the hind leg and pulled it out, standing between it and the rock.

It's a pretty fox, Did thought as he pulled his pistol and waited to get a chance to shoot it between the eyes. But the fox wouldn't turn its head toward him. Then he aimed at the side of its head, behind the ear, fired, and the fox fell over, its body quivering, a little red stream of blood trickling from the bullet hole in its head to the slick-worn ground. Did stood watching its gaunt sides work up and down, a little less each time as it inhaled and exhaled, for its life was quickly going.

"First thing I've ever killed," he mumbled to himself, looking proudly at the fox. Then he looked at the trap hanging to its foot. It didn't have a chance, he thought. I shot it with its foot held in a trap.

He put the big fox, warm and limber, into a coffee sack and threw it across his shoulder. But something disturbed him when he looked at the rugged hills where the fox had run free at night and had outwitted a pack of hounds, where it had chased across these mountains with its mate, maybe with its young, enjoying this wild country as he, Did, was enjoying it now. He thought how much the fox had wanted to live and how it had struggled to get away and how it had feared man and death.

Then he walked down to the cliff where Sparkie had set the cluster of traps. Before he reached the traps, something looked up at him and snarled. It showed its teeth like a wolf and snapped and snarled. But it couldn't move, for three of its feet were in traps.

"Another fox," Did mumbled to himself. "It's in pain. I want to get it out of its misery as soon as I can."

While the helpless fox snarled, barked, and looked at Did with its wild beady eyes squinting at the light, Did aimed at the center of its forehead, squeezed the trigger, and it toppled over on the leaves Sparkie had spread over the traps.

It's an unfair way to kill, but it's out of its misery, he thought, looking at its feet that were cut by trap jaws. Did watched the fox's beautiful gray body quiver while its life slowly ebbed away. He wondered what was wrong with himself when he wished that he had not had to kill this fox, he who had always wanted to be a hunter. A few dollars for this hide that some woman would wear. The hide is worth more to the fox, he thought.

When he got the trap loose, he found that one of its legs was broken. He put the big gray fox into the coffee sack, swung the sack over his shoulder, and walked slowly up the fox path toward the other traps.

I hope I don't find anything more, he thought, pulling up the path by holding to sassafras sprouts with his free hand.

He was glad when he came to the cliff where Sparkie had told him he caught something every time he set traps here. Did threw down his sack and walked up under the roof of the cliff. The traps were just as they had been set; they hadn't been molested. Then he walked happily away, picked up his foxes, and went to the next cliff. The traps were empty. He was under the ridge road, walking toward the mule, and had only one more cluster of traps to inspect in a cliff just above him. This was the cliff where Sparkie had told him he never had any luck trapping. Did wasn't thinking about these traps. He was thinking about the foxes he had killed and the way he had stood at close range and blasted their life forever from them.

Gr-r-r- . . .

The cat jumped the length of the trap chain, its mouth open, showing long yellowish teeth, its wild eyes wide and glaring and filled with madness. Its long claws on its front foot sliced Did's overall pants leg as if it had been sliced with a razor. Did jumped back, losing his balance, and tumbled down the steep hill, losing his sack that rolled against a clump of sourwood sprouts. He rolled into a greenbrier cluster that tangled in his overall jumper and hair, and he lay there until he was able to regain his breath. He lay there, untangled the greenbriers from his hair, pulled a few briers from his hands; then he unwrapped them from about his legs, got up, and put his cap back on his head. He drew his pistol from the holster and his hunting knife from the sheath. He went toward the cliff, watching for the wildcat to charge again.

When the cat dashed again, Did fired at it without taking aim, hitting its shoulder. He stopped the cat's advance. It pulled wildly against the trap trying to free itself to get to him, and Did thought he saw the stake give under its weight. Before the cat could do much pulling at the chain, he fired again at its ribs thinking he might hit its heart. This time the cat quivered ... but didn't go down. It stood facing him, snarling, showing its long yellow teeth. Then Did aimed and hit it squarely between the eyes. It toppled over as the foxes had done. Its long ugly body lay there quivering as its feet moved up and down and its toes contracted. It struggled for breath. Did watched the last breath go as the cat straightened its long body and lay perfectly still. Its unexpected attack had angered him at first. Now he wasn't angry. He didn't blame the cat for fighting for its life. Maybe the jaws of the trap were paining its right hind leg, for they had cut deeply, burying the trap jaws in its flesh.

Did put the hunting knife back in the sheath and refilled the chamber of his .38 while a thin stream of cold smoke slowly oozed from its long barrel. Soon as he'd reloaded his pistol, he put it in the holster and walked up to the cat. He pushed down the trap spring with his foot, pulled the buried jaws from the flesh, and released its leg. Then he held it up by the hind legs and its nose came to his ankles. It was much bigger than either of the foxes. It was almost as large as Did. And it was heavy to lift. Did laid it back on the ground, looked at its dangerous claws, felt its muscled legs, and opened its mouth wider to look at its long sharp teeth. He carried the cat up to his mule and stretched it on the ground; then he went back down the mountain and fetched the sack with the foxes.

He wondered how he would carry them on the mule at

first. After thinking it over, he roped the foxes' hind legs together, then he roped the cat's legs together, weaving the rope between the wildcat's legs and the foxes' legs until they were tied securely. He used the sack for a pad across Dick's back and laid the wildcat on one side of the saddle, the foxes on the other to balance the cat. Then he tied them tight to the saddle. He untied the mule, fastened the rein, mounted and rode away, looking back at the game across his mule as it trotted along the ridge path.

He rode until he came to the knoll, where he turned to his right down the long path to the polecat country, the old worn-out tobacco fields now dotted with persimmon and pawpaw groves. Did tied his sweaty mule to a persimmon tree and set out across the broom-sedge wasteland to the cliff that skirted the field where the traps were set.

When Did came to one of the holes, he got down, stuck his face up to the hole to look. One of the trap chains was twisted and he pulled it out with his hand. There was a leg in it.

"Poor polecat," Did said to himself. "He must have wanted his freedom awful bad to gnaw his leg off."

When Did stuck his face up to another hole, a big possum, with his leg in the trap, was lying there asleep. He did what Sparkie told him. He caught the possum by the tail, pressed his foot on the trap spring and freed the possum and put him down into a coffee sack. He had the feeling that he had rescued a living possum from the steel jaws of a trap and he felt good about it. Did found a rabbit in another trap before he reached the end of the bluff and he hit it across the head with a little stick, killing it easily. He put it down in the sack with the possum. Now that he had looked at all the traps along this bluff, he crossed a ravine to the little hill where they had set traps along some rock cliffs.

At the first one Did stopped and put his face down to look in the hole. Something hit him . . . his face and eyes . . .

88

stinging his eyes like a wasp sting planted in each one. . . . He fell backward, dropped his sacks, and rolled to the ground as he had heard hound dogs did when they attacked a skunk. Did never had butterflies walking in the pit of his stomach before, but they were there now as he rolled, wiped his eyes with his hands, and cried. He sat down and waited for the spell to wear off. He would never stick his head in a hole again. When he got up, he approached the hole carefully.

When the polecat backed from the hole toward Did, he stepped sidewise and shot it through the side of the head. Now that he was already covered with the scent, he didn't mind picking it up by the leg and dropping it into the empty sack.

With much caution he approached the remaining traps set in the polecat country, finding two more polecats and another possum. He shot the polecats when they started backing toward him. He freed the possum and put it in the possum sack. He tied more game behind his saddle and, mounting the mule, rode across the sedge grass land toward Possum Hollow.

Where the path forded the creek, Did looked down to see something black beside the water. Dismounting, he found a dead polecat with three legs.

Thirst from the loss of blood after it lost its leg, Did thought. It came down here and gorged on water. Sparkie had told him about this sort of thing.

It was black as midnight. Did untied the polecat sack and dropped it inside. He retied the sack and fastened it securely to the saddle ring. Then he mounted his sweaty mule and rode to Possum Hollow, where again he tied Dick to a pawpaw bush.

He felt a tiredness in his legs as he hurried from trap to trap. The bright carpet of autumn leaves rustled under his feet now that the sun directly overhead had melted the frost and dried away the mists. Did took three more possums from the traps, two large ones and a small midnight possum. He sacked them, hurried to his mule, and was soon on his way over Tunnel Hill, then down Nicholl's Hollow, and across the open river bottoms to Reeves Pond.

Did found two muskrats' legs in the first two traps. He killed a weasel by hitting it over the head with a wild snowball stick. When he examined the last trap, he found a big animal with pretty brown fur with dark rings across it. It was much larger than the kind of mink Sparkie had told him about and when he went near the trap, it stood on its hind feet, lifting the trap that held its front paw. It was a pretty animal and Did hated to kill it. But I'm a hunter now, and I have to, he thought.

While the animal stood looking Did over, Did's right hand fumbled to his hip for his revolver. At close range he leveled at a spot between its eyes, but the animal remained on its hind feet looking at him curiously. At the crack of the revolver, it slumped over, blood trickling from the tiny hole in its head. Did couldn't pick it up as long as it drew its hind legs up and down and as long as it struggled for breath. He waited for its body to become still while the wind played across the open Sandy River, rustling the fine fur, bending it up and down. When it had ceased to move, he freed its foreleg from the trap. He examined this animal and found a collar around its neck. Wonder what it is I've killed? he thought, as he sacked it in the last empty sack.

Did rode along the river until he came to the Reeves Knoll. Here he picked up three more possums and a skunk from the traps. He'd bagged so many skunks he had forgotten how much he smelled of that first one. At Putt Off Ford were six more muskrat legs in the traps. At the last trap he found a rabbit, tapped it on the head with his pistol barrel, and put it in the sack with the strange animal he could not identify. Then he moved on toward Shackle Run, the last lap of his journey. The sun was moving over toward the west and

Did felt hunger gnawing at his stomach as he rode the sweaty mule across the soft bottom loaded with the game he'd trapped.

It's a good thing I didn't get all the muskrats that lost their legs in the traps, he tried to make himself believe, as he thought about the polecat that had lost its leg in a trap. He couldn't stop thinking about how hard a time a four-legged animal had making its way in the woods, and how much harder it would be with three legs.

He tied his mule to an apple tree when he went along the Shackle Run line of traps set in the ground hog holes that possums had taken over. He took four more possums, a weasel, skunk, and rabbit from these traps and he was glad when he had sacked them. He had a load on Dick, and his mule was tired and sweaty. Did loosened his bridle reins, and Dick moved rapidly toward home despite his load. Since Did was tired, he sat in the saddle as if he had grown there, relaxed, and let Dick choose the parts of the road he liked best as he bore him and the game toward the shack. He remembered the way the animals looked at him with their legs held in the vise of steel jaws, with hurt and pain in their eyes, and how he had shot them when they didn't have a chance. The only one he couldn't feel sad about was the wildcat that had fought back. Yet that was something he would have done, he thought, if he had been trapped. He sat thinking, while Dick trotted up the creek, splashing blue water up in sprays that shone like silver in the sun.

2 ❧

Angel in the Pasture

dawn of remembered spring

"Be careful, Shan," Mom said. "I'm afraid if you wade that creek that a water moccasin will bite you."

"All right, Mom."

"You know what happened to Roy Deer last Sunday!"

"Yes, Mom!"

"He's nigh at the point of death," she said. "I'm going over there now to see him. His leg's swelled hard as a rock and it's turned black as black-oak bark. They're not looking for Roy to live until midnight tonight."

"All water moccasins ought to be killed, hadn't they, Mom?"

"Yes, they're pizen things, but you can't kill them," Mom said. "They're in all these creeks around here. There's so many of them we can't kill 'em all."

Mom stood at the foot-log that crossed the creek in front of our house. Her white apron was starched stiff; I heard it rustle when Mom put her hand in the little pocket in the right upper corner to get tobacco crumbs for her pipe. Mom wore her slat bonnet that shaded her sun-tanned face—a bonnet with strings that came under her chin and tied in a bowknot.

"I feel uneasy," Mom said as she filled her long-stemmed clay-stone pipe with bright burley crumbs, tamped them down with her index finger, and struck a match on the rough bark of an apple tree that grew on the creek bank by the foot-log.

"Don't feel uneasy about me," I said.

"But I do," Mom said. "Your Pa out ground hog huntin' and I'll be away at Deers'—nobody at home but you, and so many pizen snakes around this house."

Mom blew a cloud of blue smoke from her pipe. She walked across the foot-log—her long clean dress sweeping the weed stubble where Pa had mown the weeds along the path with a scythe so we could leave the house without getting our legs wet by the dew-covered weeds.

When Mom walked out of sight around the turn of the pasture hill and the trail of smoke that she left behind her had disappeared into the light blue April air, I crossed the garden fence at the wild-plum thicket.

Everybody gone, I thought. I am left alone. I'll do as I please. A water moccasin bit Roy Deer but a water moccasin will never bite me. I'll get me a club from this wild-plum thicket and I'll wade up the creek killing water moccasins.

There was a dead wild-plum sprout standing among the thicket of living sprouts. It was about the size of a tobacco stick. I stepped out of my path into the wild-plum thicket. Barefooted, I walked among the wild-plum thorns. I up-rooted the dead wild-plum sprout. There was a bulge on it where roots had once been—now the roots had rotted in the earth. It was like a maul with this big bulge on the end of it. It would be good to hit water moccasins with.

The mules played in the pasture. It was Sunday—their day of rest. And the mules knew it. This was Sunday and it was my day of rest. It was my one day of freedom, too, when Mom and Pa were gone and I was left alone. I would like to be a man now, I thought. I'd love to plow the mules, run a farm, and kill snakes. A water moccasin bit Roy Deer but one would never bite me.

The bright sunlight of April played over the green Kentucky hills. Sunlight fell onto the creek of blue water that twisted like a crawling snake around the high bluffs and between the high rocks. In many places dwarf willows, horseweeds, ironweeds, and wild grapevines shut away the sunlight and the creek waters stood in quiet cool puddles. These little puddles under the shade of weeds, vines, and willows were the places where the water moccasins lived.

I rolled my overall legs above my knees so I wouldn't wet them and Mom wouldn't know I'd been wading the creek. I started wading up the creek toward the head of the hollow. I carried my wild-plum club across my shoulder with both hands gripped tightly around the small end of it. I was ready to maul the first water moccasion I saw.

"One of you old water moccasins bit Roy Deer," I said bravely, clinching my grip tighter around my club, "but you won't bite me."

As I waded the cool creek waters, my bare feet touched gravel on the creek bottom. When I touched a wet watersoaked stick on the bottom of the creek bed, I'd think it was a snake and I'd jump. I'd wade into banks of quicksand. I'd sink into the sand above my knees. It was hard to pull my legs out of this quicksand and when I pulled them out they'd be covered with thin quicky mud that the next puddle of water would wash away.

"A water moccasin," I said to myself. I was scared to look at him. He was wrapped around a willow that was bent over the creek. He was sleeping in the sun. I slipped toward him quietly—step by step—with my club drawn over my shoulder. Soon as I got close enough to reach him, I came over my shoulder with the club. I hit the water moccasin a powerful blow that mashed its head flat against the willow. It fell dead into the water. I picked it up by the tail and threw it upon the bank.

"One gone," I said to myself.

97

The water was warm around my feet and legs. The sharp-edged gravels hurt the bottoms of my feet but the soft sand soothed them. Butterflies swarmed over my head and around me—alighting on the wild pink phlox that grew in clusters along the creek bank. Wild honeybees, bumblebees, and butterflies worked on the elder blossoms, the shoemake blossoms and the beet-red finger-long blossoms of the ironweed and the whitish pink-covered smartweed blossoms. Birds sang among the willows and flew up and down the creek with four-winged snakefeeders in their bills.

This is what I like to do, I thought. I love to kill snakes. I'm not afraid of snakes. I laughed to think how afraid of snakes Mom was—how she struck a potato-digger tine through a big rusty-golden copperhead's skin just enough to pin him to the earth and hold him so he couldn't get under our floor. He fought the potato-digger handle until Pa came home from work and killed him. Where he'd thrown poison over the ground it killed the weeds and weeds didn't grow on this spot again for four years.

Once when Mom was making my bed upstairs, she heard a noise of something running behind the paper that was pasted over the cracks between the logs—the paper split and a house snake six feet long fell onto the floor with a mouse in his mouth. Mom killed him with a bed slat. She called me once to bring her a goose-neck hoe upstairs quickly. I ran upstairs and killed two cow-snakes restin' on the wall plate. And Pa killed twenty-eight copperheads out of a two-acre oat field in the hollow above the house one spring season.

"Snakes—snakes," Mom used to say, "are goin' to run us out'n this Hollow."

"It's because these woods haven't been burnt out in years," Pa'd always answer. "Back when I's a boy the old people burnt the woods out every spring to kill the snakes.

Got so anymore there isn't enough good timber for a board tree and people have had to quit burning up the good timber. Snakes are about to take the woods again."

I thought about the snakes Pa had killed in the corn field and the tobacco patch and how nearly copperheads had come to biting me and how I'd always seen the snake in time to cut his head off with a hoe or get out of his way. I thought of the times I had heard a rattlesnake's warning and how I'd run when I hadn't seen the snake. As I thought these thoughts, plop a big water moccasin fell from the creek bank into a puddle of water.

"I'll get you," I said. "You can't fool me! You can't stand muddy water."

I stirred the water until it was muddy with my wild-plum club. I waited for the water moccasin to stick his head above the water. Where wild ferns dipped down from the bank's edge and touched the water, I saw the snake's head rise slowly above the water—watchin' me. I swung sidewise with my club like batting at a ball. I couldn't swing over my shoulder, for there were willow limbs above my head.

I surely got him, I thought. I waited to see. Soon, something like milk spread over the water. "I got 'im." I raked in the water with my club and lifted from the bottom of the creek bed a water moccasin long as my club. It was longer than I was tall. I threw him upon the bank and moved slowly up the creek—looking on every drift, stump, log, and sunny spot. I looked for a snake's head along the edges of the creek bank where ferns dipped over and touched the water.

I waded up the creek all day killing water moccasins. If one was asleep on the bank, I slipped upon him quietly as a cat. I mauled him with the big end of my wild-plum club. I killed him in his sleep. He never knew what struck him. If a brush caught the end of my club and caused me to miss and let the snake get into a puddle of water, I muddied the water and waited for him to stick his head above the water. When he stuck his head above the water, I got him. Not one water moccasin got away from me. It was four o'clock when I stepped from the creek onto the bank. I'd killed fifty-three water moccasins.

Water moccasins are not half as dangerous as turtles, I thought. A water moccasin can't bite you under the water for he gets his mouth full of water. A turtle can bite you under water and when one bites you he won't let loose unless you cut his head off. I'd been afraid of turtles all day because I didn't have a knife in my pocket to cut one's head off if it grabbed my foot and held it.

When I left the creek, I was afraid of the snakes I'd killed. I didn't throw my club away. I gripped the club until my hands hurt. I looked below my path, above my path, and in front of me. When I saw a stick on the ground, I thought it was a snake. I eased up to it quietly as a cat trying to catch a bird. I was ready to hit it with my club.

What will Mom think when I tell her I've killed fifty-three water moccasins? I thought. A water moccasin bit Roy Deer but one's not going to bite me. I paid the snakes back for biting him. It was good enough for them. Roy wasn't bothering the water moccasin that bit him. He just was crossing the creek at the foot-log and it jumped from the grass and bit him.

Shadows lengthened from the tall trees. The Hollow was deep and the creek flowed softly in the cool recesses of evening shadows. There was one patch of sunlight. It was upon the steep broom-sedge-covered bluff above the path.

"Snakes," I cried, "snakes a-fightin' and they're not water moccasins! They're copperheads!"

They were wrapped around each other. Their lidless eyes looked into each other's eyes. Their hard lips touched each other's lips. They did not move. They did not pay any attention to me. They looked at one another.

100

I'll kill 'em, I thought, if they don't kill one another in this fight.

I stood in the path with my club ready. I had heard snakes fought each other but I'd never seen them fight.

"What're you lookin' at, Shan?" Uncle Alf Skinner asked. He walked up the path with a cane in his hand.

"Snakes a-fightin'."

"Snakes a-fightin'?"

"Yes."

"I never saw it in my life."

"I'll kill 'em both if they don't finish the fight," I said. "I'll club 'em to death."

"Snakes a-fightin', Shan," he shouted, "you are too young to know! It's snakes in love! Don't kill 'em—just keep your eye on 'em until I bring Martha over here! She's never seen snakes in love!"

Uncle Alf ran around the turn of the hill. He brought Aunt Martha back with him. She was carrying a basket of greens on her arm and the case knife that she'd been cutting greens with in her hand.

"See 'em, Martha," Uncle Alf said. "Look up there in that broom sedge!"

"I'll declare," she said. "I've lived all my life and I never saw this. I've wondered about snakes!"

She stood with a smile on her wrinkled lips. Uncle Alf stood with a wide smile on his deep-lined face. I looked at them and wondered why they looked at these copperheads and smiled. Uncle Alf looked at Aunt Martha. They smiled at each other.

"Shan! Shan!" I heard Mom calling.

"I'm here," I shouted.

"Where've you been?" she asked as she turned around the bend of the hill with a switch in her hand.

"Be quiet, Sall," Uncle Alf said. "Come here and look for yourself!"

"What is it?" Mom asked.

"Snakes in love," Uncle Alf said.

Mom was mad. "Shan, I feel like limbing you," she said. "I've hunted every place for you! Where've you been?"

"Killin' snakes," I answered.

"Roy Deer is dead," she said. "That's how dangerous it is to fool with snakes."

"I paid the snakes back for him," I said. "I've killed fifty-three water moccasins!"

"Look, Sall!"

"Yes, Alf, I see," Mom said.

Mom threw her switch on the ground. Her eyes were wide apart. The frowns left her face.

"It's the first time I ever saw anything like this," Mom said. "Shan, you go tell your Pa to come and look at this."

I was glad to do anything for Mom. I was afraid of her switch. When I brought Pa back to the sunny bank where the copperheads were loving, Art and Sadie Baker were there and Tom and Ethel Riggs—and there were a lot of strangers there. They were looking at the copperheads wrapped around each other with their eyes looking into each other's eyes and their hard lips touching each other's lips.

"You hurry to the house, Shan," Pa said, "and cut your stove wood for tonight."

"I'd like to kill these copperheads," I said.

"Why?" Pa asked.

"Fightin'," I said.

Uncle Alf and Aunt Martha laughed as I walked down the path carrying my club. It was something—I didn't know what—all the crowd watching the snakes were smiling. Their faces were made over new. The snakes had done something to them. Their wrinkled faces were as bright as the spring sunlight on the bluff; their eyes were shiny as the creek was in the noonday sunlight. And they laughed and talked to one another. I heard their laughter grow fainter as I walked down the path toward the house. Their laughter was louder than the wild honeybees I had heard swarming over the shoemake, alderberry, and wild phlox blossoms along the creek.

king of the hills

"Poor Black Boy," Finn said as he stood beneath the pine tree in our front yard and watched Black Boy wallowin' on the pine needles. "His short hair is not black as a crow's wing like it used to be. Black Boy is gettin' old. He's gettin' too old to hunt."

The October harvest moon like a big wagon wheel rolled above the autumn-colored hills. It was one of the prettiest nights I had ever seen for the moonlight on the hills and fields was bright as day.

"Most dogs are in their graves when they get as old as Black Boy," I said. "He'll be nineteen years old tomorrow. Black Boy is older than you are."

"I know it," Finn said. "That's why I hate to see him get so old he can't get up when he lays down."

"That dog taught me to hunt," I said. "I didn't teach him."

"He taught me to hunt too," Finn said. "We ought to try somethin' to make him live longer. Try somethin' that will put pep in him and make him happy."

"You're right, Finn," I said as I watched Black Boy make several tries before he was able to get up from the pine-needle bed and stand on his feet.

"After he gets on his feet, he's all right," Finn

said. "It's just hard for him to get back on his feet after he lays down."

Now Black Boy came up to us and smelled of our pants legs. He put his nose against my hand. The soft tip of his nose rubbed against my arm as he sniffled the familiar scent of me—a scent that he had tracked in the huntin' woods—a scent that he had known all his life. I rubbed Black Boy's head and petted him. After I had petted him, he walked lazily over to Finn and sniffled the scent of his hand—sniffled another old familiar scent that he had known most of his lifetime. Finn patted his head and rubbed his nose. Black Boy was so pleased that he barked to Finn.

"Watch Black Boy strut after he gets up on his feet," Finn said. "You couldn't tell that he was an old dog only by the gray hair around his mouth and on his head. And he's lost all his teeth."

There Black Boy stood between us. He was kickin' the pine needles high in the air with his hind feet. As he kicked the pine needles he growled as if he were still master of the place. He looked like a small black lion except for his gray toothless mouth and his gray head. Black Boy had a big mouth, big neck and his barrel chest rested on strong legs that were set wide apart. His hips were narrow like a lion's hips; his tail was long but he shortened it by carryin' it over his back in two bristlin' curls. Black Boy had been for many years, and was still, the king of the hills. But now age was showin' its marks upon him; still he had never been whipped by any dog.

Now Black Boy stopped kickin' the pine needles high into the air. He just stood and growled. There wasn't anythin' near for him to growl at. Maybe he wanted to hear the importance of his own growl—maybe he growled at the wind.

"You're still king of the hills, Black Boy," Finn said. "But you won't be long. Too stiff to get up after you lay down. You can't last much longer. But you need pep today.

105

You need to have one more glorious huntin' night, Black Boy."

"He needs a spring-herb tonic," I said.

"Say, that makes me think," Finn said. "Pa's got a pint of Honorable Herbs that he keeps in the barnloft for his 'cold remedy.' That ought to be good for Black Boy."

"I'm not givin' Black Boy that moonshine," I said.

"It will be good for him," Finn said. "A hangover won't bother Black Boy."

Finn hurried to the barn fast as his long legs could step. He climbed up the wall of barn logs, placin' his feet and hands in the cracks until he reached the place where hard-pressed hay bulged through a wide crack between the logs. There was a little hole in the hay where Finn ran his hand back and pulled out a bottle. He scurried back down the low-walk and hurried back where Black Boy stood growlin' at the wind hissin' through the pine needles.

"This is the tonic that will make him young again," Finn said.

"It might kill him," I said.

"Wonder if he'll drink it raw," Finn said.

"Finn, let's don't give Black Boy that whiskey," I said.

"Why not?" Finn asked.

"It will be mean of us to give him whiskey."

"Ah, hell," Finn said as he poured the pint of whiskey in a trough where we watered the chickens.

"Here Black Boy," he coaxed.

Black Boy walked up to the trough, smelled of the moonshine, kicked his feet and growled. But he wouldn't drink it.

"He's almost in a notion," Finn said. "And I know what will put him in a notion."

Finn ran to the cellar and came back with a crock of sweet milk. He poured the gallon of sweet milk in the trough to mix with the moonshine. And Black Boy went to the trough growling and kickin' the pine needles with his hind feet. He started drinkin' the milk-and-moonshine. Black Boy gorged himself to hold the gallon of sweet milk and the pint of moonshine whiskey. He licked the trough clean as a pawpaw whistle.

"We're goin to see somethin' happen," Finn said. "I don't know what it will be. But somethin' will happen!"

Black Boy got down on the pine needles and rolled. He opened his big mouth as he looked at us with eyes that sparkled with livin' fire. Black Boy growled as he wallowed on the ground. Then Black Boy jumped to his feet like he was a young pup. He ran circles around us with his tongue out.

"That tonic is workin' on 'im," Finn said. "He's a happy dog. It's doin' 'im good."

Then Black Boy made a beeline toward the barn. He leaped over the gate like a red fox. He took down the path that leads from our barn to the big pasture field. He was out of sight under the trees whose pine needles looked good in the moonlight.

"Where's that dog goin'?" I asked Finn.

"He's goin' to hunt," Finn laughed.

"He's got so he can't smell a track when the ground is damp," I said. "I know he can't carry a track dry as it is now."

We hadn't stood there talkin' five minutes until we heard Black Boy bark treed.

"What did I tell you," Finn said. "Black Boy's got somethin'. Listen to that music won't you!"

"He's barkin' to a bunch of poplar leaves," I said. "That dog's drunk. He doesn't know what he's doin'."

Finn started runnin' toward the sound. I followed Finn out the path by the barn and under the oaks and pines to the far pasture field. We saw Black Boy jumpin' up on a small sourwood at the edge of the pasture field, barkin' every breath.

"Sure he's got somethin' treed," Finn said.

"I believe he has," I said. "I believe he can see it. Probably a house cat."

We ran across the field.

"House cat," Finn laughed as he got to the tree first. "It's the biggest ground hog I've ever seen."

Tall, bean-pole, freckled-faced Finn reached high on the small tree and with his big hand he gave the tree a shake. The ground hog tumbled to the ground. He hadn't more than hit the ground until Black Boy had him. He gummed the ground hog to death with a throat hold.

"Let's take it to the house," I said.

"Hell no," Finn said. "You go to the house and get a mattock and two coffee sacks. Black Boy is runnin' in high gear tonight. Let's stay with him. It may be his last great hunt!"

Before I got back with the mattock and the two sacks I heard Black Boy bark treed. When I reached the pasture field, I saw Finn with the ground hog in his hand, lookin' up the black gum where Black Boy was barkin'. I hurried across the field to the tree.

"He just walked up here and started barkin'," Finn said. "May be somethin' down in the hollow of that tree. I don't know. Can't see anything from the outside."

"Probably nothin' there," I said. "That dog is drunk and you can't trust him."

"Trust hell," Finn said. "I believe there's somethin' in that tree."

Finn pulled off his shoes and climbed the big black gum. He grunted as he climbed for it was a hard tree to climb. When Finn got to the top, he looked down in the tree where the top was broken off.

"Have a surprise for you, Shan," he said. "I'll show you something."

108

"What is it, Finn?" I asked, for I could hardly wait to see.

Now Finn had braced his foot against a black gum limb. He reached down in the hollow top of the black gum carefully. And he pulled a big possum up by the tail.

"Has the drunk dog lied?" Finn asked.

He threw the possum to the ground. Black Boy grabbed it soon as it hit the ground. But I took Black Boy off the possum and put it in a sack.

"That possum had the prettiest bed up in that tree," Finn said soon as he reached the ground. "He was layin' up there asleep."

After Black Boy saw me put the possum in the sack, he went off over the hill like a blowin' wind. He was goin' with his nose high in the air, snifflin' as he went.

"He's after somethin' right now," Finn said. "He's windin' somethin'."

Black Boy hadn't been gone long enough for us to get our sacks and mattock and walk down the hollow when we heard him bark deep in a hollow on the other side of the low ridge.

"He's barkin' in a hole," Finn said as he stopped and listened, holdin' his breath with his hand cupped over his ear to catch the low sound.

I followed Finn as he made his way through the brier thickets over the low ridge and down into the next hollow. Before we reached Black Boy, we heard him kickin' the dirt with his feet. We heard it sprinklin' over the dry leaves below 'im. Then we heard him growlin' as he jerked on a root with his toothless mouth. When we reached him, he had a hole dug big enough to bury himself in by the end of a blackberry brier thicket. The hole was in the soft loamy dirt and he was diggin' fast; he was barkin' like he was close to somethin'. We made our way through the thicket to him. Finn held Black

109

Boy while I struck a few licks with the mattock. Then Finn let Black Boy loose to clean the hole out with his paws. He rammed his head back in the hole and pulled out a polecat that was black as a moonless midnight. I jumped back. I didn't want its scent to settle on me.

"He can't kill it," Finn said. "He doesn't have the teeth."

But he did kill it. He crushed its head with his powerful jaws.

"What a powerful dog he is today," I said. "How can a dog old as he is crush a polecat's head when he doesn't have a tooth in his head?"

We put the skunk in one end of the sack where we had the possum.

"That's the prettiest polecat hide I've ever seen," Finn said. "That will bring a good price."

"Seven or eight dollars," I said.

Now Black Boy was sick. He wallowed on the leaves. He rooted his nose under the dry leaves on top of the ground down to the wet, half-rotten leaves against the ground. He ran his nose down in the fresh dirt that he had dug from the hole.

"The hunt's over," I said. "He's really sick."

"After a dog gets that polecat scent on him he's through," Finn said. "This may end our hunt."

Soon as we had reached the little hollow below us we saw Black Boy standin' to his knees in a hole of clean spring water. Then he left the water and took up the hill as if nothin' had ever happened. He was soon out of sight over the hill where there was a beech grove between our farm and Uncle Mel's farm. And soon as we reached the hilltop, he barked in another hole. Wet with sweat, and tired of keepin' after Black Boy, we hurried down the hill. Black Boy was barkin' in the end of a hollow beech log.

"There's somethin' there, Finn," I said as I took the ax-end of my mattock and started pryin' away rotten slabs from the log.

"We'll soon know," Finn said as he held the dog back so I wouldn't hit his head with the ax-end of my mattock. "I'll bet it's another possum."

"You're right," I said. "Look!"

I pulled off a slab from over the possum's bed of leaves. He stuck his head out to see what was goin' on. Black Boy broke the collar that Finn was holdin' him by and leaped three times his length to the possum. I had to choke him loose before I could free the possum to put it in the sack with the other possum.

"What a possum," Finn said as I put it in the sack. "Did you ever see this dog do any better in your life?"

"Never saw him work this fast," I said.

Black Boy wagged his tail at us. But he didn't hang around for us to pat his head and rub his nose. He was off like a black flash over the brown leaves to the bluff beyond us. We saw him with his head held high in the night wind, go straight to a little rock. We saw him put his head under the rock; we heard him sniffle. Then he barked. Then he started diggin' fast as he could. His hind feet threw sprinkles of loam and wet leaves twenty feet behind him down the steep bluff.

"He's got somethin'," I said, grabbin' the mattock and one of the sacks.

"You damn right he has," Finn said, grabbin' the other sack and followin' me.

Soon as we started up the bluff he brought somethin' from the hole.

"Phew," Finn screamed. "It's a damned polecat sure as the world."

They came rollin' end over end down the steep bluff

111

toward us. And soon as they reached the bottom of the bluff, the polecat's legs stretched out limber. It was dead. Black Boy had crushed its skull with his jaws.

"It's a broad-striped polecat," Finn said, tense with excitement.

Finn put the polecat in the sack while Black Boy rooted his nose down under the dry leaves to the wet half-rotten half-loam leaves. Then Black Boy made for the little fresh spring water creek that flowed from the steep bluffs to drink water. He wallowed in one of the little deep holes against a fern-covered bank.

"Two livin' possums in one end of this sack," Finn laughed. "Two dead polecats in the other. It's gettin' heavy."

"Wonder when the herbs will die in Black Boy," I said.

"When they die in Black Boy," Finn said, "his huntin' will be done for tonight."

"Maybe, forever," I said.

"But this is wonderful," Finn said. "I've never seen anythin' like it."

Now Black Boy left us. He went down the creek toward Ragweed Hollow. And we followed the cattle path down to the fence. We didn't hear from Black Boy. He didn't return to us nor did he bark. Tired of runnin' after him and carryin' the game, we sat down on a beech log to rest. But we didn't rest long. We heard Black Boy bark in a hole on the hill across the hollow. We started runnin' toward him. When we climbed the hill, sweaty, tired and out-of-breath, we found Black Boy in a dirt hole in a little drain.

Finn poked a long stick back in the hole and told me where to dig down to strike the hole. I soon put a hole down for it was shallow down to the hole. Then Finn put the stick back again and told me where to dig. I put down another hole and then another. When Finn put the stick back, he felt a bed of leaves.

"It's a ground hog or a possum," Finn said. "I feel it."

He twisted with his stick; then he pulled it out.

"Red hairs," Finn said examinin' the hairs on the end of the stick in the moonlight.

"Let Black Boy loose before somethin' jumps out," I said.

Soon as Black Boy put his nose to the hole to sniffle, he yelled. Then he started fightin'.

"Somethin' bit 'im," I said.

"A young red fox," Finn roared as Black Boy and the fox tangled.

"What do you know about that," I said. "Who ever dreamed of a fox bein' in a dirt hole?"

"He's found him a rabbit in that hole," Finn said. "He was havin' a good meal when Black Boy found him."

"He's finished the fox," I said.

"We'll just carry it outside the sack," Finn said. "It would take too much room in a sack."

"This will about end our hunt," I said. "Black Boy is gettin' tired. Look at his tongue. It's dropped down like a shoe-tongue."

Finn carried the sack of possums and polecats and the mattock; I carried the fox and the ground hog. It was like carryin' a full-grown hound-dog pup to carry the fox. Now we made our way off the hill. Black Boy walked in front of us. But soon he disappeared.

When we reached the foot of the hill, we started up the Ragweed Hollow jolt-wagon road for home. We were tired now; we were wet with sweat—our clothes looked like we had jumped in the river. And the load of game was gettin' heavier every step we took.

"I hope he won't find anythin' more," I said.

"Listen," Finn said turnin' his head sideways for his ear to catch the sound. "I hear 'im! He's got somethin'!"

We hurried toward the sound. By a log pile at the upper

113

side of the field where Doore's had had tobacco, Black Boy had found another polecat under the log pile. He had it killed when we got there and he was wallowin' on the tobacco-patch dirt. He was rootin' his nose in the ground like a hog.

"It's a narrow-stripe," Finn said. "He's crushed its skull."

"Another damned polecat," I said. "You can put it in the sack or we'll leave it. I don't aim to put my hands on it."

"It's got wonderful fur," Finn said. "Sure, I'll put it in the sack."

Finn opened the sack and put his dead polecat with the other two. He tied the sack and grunted as he swung the sack across his shoulder with one big heave.

"Some load," Finn said. "But there's money in these hides."

"Thank God this hunt's over," I said. "Look at Black Boy. He's sick enough to eat grass."

Black Boy was eatin' stems of dead crab-grass that he found in the tobacco balks.

"You can't tell about Black Boy," Finn said.

And Finn was right. As we were slowly trudgin' toward home, weary under our heavy loads, Black Boy let out a blast of barks that came hard and fast.

"He's treed," Finn screamed. "He can see it! He's close to it!"

Even with our heavy loads, we broke out in a slow run. He was barkin' on Doore's bluff just above the road. We had a good road to get to him.

"Look up there at that ground hog," Finn laughed.

The ground hog was up a little sassafras saplin'. It was bigger than the first ground hog that we had caught. We hurried up the bank to the tree. Black Boy was backin' off

114

and runnin' toward the tree, then leapin' up and barely missin' the ground hog.

"He's got plenty of pep left," Finn said.

Then Black Boy tried to climb the tree but his toenails wouldn't hold in the sassafras bark. Finn shook the sassafras. When the ground hog hit the ground, it hit the ground runnin'. But before it had got many steps Black Boy grabbed it by the throat and choked it to death. It made my load heavier. Two big ground hogs and a fox for me. Three polecats and two possums for Finn. And he carried the mattock. Now we called Black Boy and started home. The October wagon-wheel moon beamed on us; the night wind rustled leaves on the tree dry as oakchips. But now we were goin' home to show Pa the game we had caught with Black Boy before eleven o'clock.

Before we reached home Black Boy barked at somethin' in the bottom.

"You go to him, Finn," I said. "Leave your sack here and I'll watch the game. We can't carry all of this and follow that dog."

Finn walked across the bottom where Black Boy was barkin' on the creek bank. Soon as Finn reached him, I heard him laugh. He came back across the bottom carryin' a big black bug that had pincers.

"Back to his old age," Finn said. "The herbs have died in 'im."

And just as we reached the hog lot bluff, Black Boy barked treed somewhere upon the bluff. I went to him this time and Finn watched the game. Finn heard me laugh when I saw that he was barkin' a cluster of leaves lodged in the forks of a shellbark hickory. The herbs had really died; Black Boy had been livin' in his old world. Now Black Boy was in the world where he was an old dog.

"My God! Black Boy is goin' back to his prime," Pa said

115

as he looked at the pile of game. "That's the way he used to hunt when he's a young dog."

"Thirty dollars worth of hides," Finn said. "And enough ground hog-hide shoestrings to lace our boots for a couple of years."

Black Boy laid down that night soon as we had skinned the game and stretched the hides. Next mornin' at sunrise when we went to feed him he couldn't get up. But he ate a little layin' down. His eyes were not like embers glowin' in the night; his eyes were glassy.

"It's probably a tough hangover," Finn whispered in my ear so Pa wouldn't hear him.

But Black Boy's breath grew shorter; his great panels of ribs didn't heave when he breathed like they always had. And today was his nineteenth birthday. Before the sun had set, Black Boy had gone to the Great Huntin' Ground where there was plenty of game. Pa was up on the barn logs with his hand back in the hay huntin' for his medicine to break his October cold when we told him that Black Boy had finally breathed his last.

saving the bees

Big Aaron called over to me. "I've got something I want to tell you, Shan." I walk over across the creek to a rock cliff. Ennis Shelton, Little Edd Hargis and Dave Caxton are standing beside of Big Aaron Roundtree. Big Aaron is smoking his pipe. Ennis, Little Edd and Dave are smoking home-rolled, hawk-billed cigarettes.

"Now, Shan," says Big Aaron, "we are going to save the honeybees in this country. We are going to try to free them. The honeybees don't have liberty anymore. Look up in your yard! Your Pappie has six stands of them back of the woodyard. Look at the stands of bees my Pappie's got—twenty-six of them over on the bank from the house under the pines! Look at the honeybees that old Willis Dials has! Look at the bees Kenyons have upon the Old Line Special. Look at the bees Uncle Fonse Tillman's got and old Warfield Flaughtery! Boys, we've got to do something about it! Are you willing to jine us, Shan? If you tell anything it won't be good for you! If you are ever caught saving bees and you are whipped because you won't tell on the rest of us—you let them whip you until the blood runs out—and you never tell! Can you be that kind of a soldier?"

"I can," I says. "I'll do all I can to save the bees. We ain't going to take my Pappie's bees, are we?"

"We are going to take your Pappie's bees and my Pappie's bees," says Big Aaron. "We don't have any respect for any person's bees. We are going after all of them. We are going to take the bees back to the woods. We are going to set them free. It is a big job but we can do it. Every man must fight to the last. He can't get cold feet. If he is shot at—he can't let that bother him. He must grab the bee stand and run anyway. The bees must be put back in the woods—let them grow wild again. It's got so in these parts you can't find a wild bee tree anymore. It is a shame to coop bees in boxes

and sawed-off logs and make them work their lives away for a lazy bunch of people. We won't have it!"

The water drips from the roof of the cliff. It drips on my ear and tickles it. The ferns hang over the front of the cliff. There is a pile of ashes on the floor of the cliff with burned-brown rocks around the ashes. There is a wire wrapped around a splinter of rock above and hangs above the ash pile. It has a hook on the end of it to hold a pot. There are chicken feathers around the rocks. Back in one corner of the cliff is a .22 rifle. Beside the .22 rifle is a .32 Smith and Wesson pistol. Beyond the drip of water is a big pile of dry oak leaves.

"Boys, this cliff can be our home," says Big Aaron. "It is our hide-out. We can work from here when we are saving the bees. We can have chicken any time we want chicken. We can have honey any time we want wild honey. We can have Irish taters and sweet taters any time we want them. Show me a house here that ain't got a tater patch beside of it. We have a cup here to catch our water from the drip in this cliff. We have a good oak-leaf bed. All five of us can sleep in the oak leaves with our guns beside of us. This cliff is back from the road and the ferns nearly hide the front of it. It just looks like the green hillside. No one would know that a cliff is here unless he would come over here, push the ferns back and look in. If he ever does that he'll be batted in the face so hard he'll never do it again."

"When will we meet, Big Aaron?" asks Ennis Shelton.

"Be here tonight when you see the moon come above the pines on the Flaughtery hill," says Big Aaron. "You be here, Shan. Don't pick up no stranger and bring 'im along either. You come straight to the cliff. All of you boys be here on time. It is in the light of the moon now and the moon ain't goin' to waste no time nohow gettin' to the top of that pine thicket on the Flaughtery hill."

"We'd all better be gettin' home to get our suppers now," says Dave.

Big Aaron hides the pistol and the rifle in the leaves. He walks under the cliff—pushes back the ferns and sticks his head out. "Everything is clear, boys," he says. He leads the way out. We follow Big Aaron. He is sixteen years old. He has big arms and a big bull-neck. He can pull the plow in the field like a horse. His hands are hard as rocks. He has a heavy beard on his face. He is the stoutest boy among the Plum Grove hills. He can lift 7 x 9 crossties and load them on a jolt wagon. He can shoot a sparrow's head off with the .22 rifle from the top of the highest tree. He says he can save all the bees among the Plum Grove hills.

I leave the boys at the forks of the road. I go up the creek home. I eat my supper, carry in stove wood, kindling—draw up water for the night from the well under the oak tree. I milk two cows and strain the milk into the crocks on the big flat rock on the smokehouse floor. I am ready to go to the cliff. I turn to walk away. "Where are you goin', Shan?" asks Pa.

"Fox huntin'," I says. "I'm goin' out with Big Aaron Roundtree to hear his hound pup run."

"Just like me," says Pa, "when I was your age. I loved to hear hounds. Go out and lay around all night on the cold ground. That's the reason I'm so full of rheumatics today. But you go on and live and learn like I have. I still love to hear the hounds."

I walk down the hollow to the big road. I turn down the

big road—down to the big sycamore. I look up the road and down the road—I cannot see anyone coming. I run across the rocks at the foot of the bluff. I run down behind the trees. I climb up the little path to the cliff. I can hear voices within. I climb up—part the ferns—the boys are all under the cliff. I look toward the Flaughtery hill—the big moon is coming up behind the trees. Its face is red—it is blushing like a young boy that watches things from behind the trees.

"You're here," says Big Aaron. "Now Shan Powderjay —remember if you ever tell anything, the rest of us will down you and cut your tongue out. That is the jail sentence for a tattle-tale among us. We have a job to do and we must do it. You fellars follow me tonight. We're goin' after Willis Dials' bees. I've been past his house today. I know where he keeps his bees. I know a little path that leads up the bank to the bee gums. You fellars just follow me."

We follow Big Aaron down the hollow. We do not go along the road. We follow the creek bed. We wade the water. We come to the big white oak at the forks of the W-Hollow and the Three-mile road. We take to the hill. We follow a fox path over the hill to the Old Line Special railroad tracks. We can see the big log house upon the bank above the railroad track where Willis Dials lives. "See the bee gums in the front yard, boys," says Big Aaron. "There are five of them. There are five of us. The bees ain't working now. Stick little pieces of wood in their holes so they can't come out. Lift them easily. You won't get a sting. I'll get the first bee gum. You just watch me. Do as I do."

Big Aaron slips up the bank. He takes little sticks and stops the two little holes where the bees come out of the gum. Then he lifts the gum to his back. He walks down the bank. No one whispers. Each of us stops the holes where the bees come out with little sticks. We get our bee gums on our backs— We follow Big Aaron up a little path to our left around the Plum Grove hill. After we get away from the yard—a dog comes out and barks. He barks and barks. "Don't be afraid, boys," says Big Aaron. "He ain't no bitin' dog. He's one of them barkin' dogs that never bites. Come on with your bees."

"Lord, but this is a heavy load, Big Aaron," I says. "I don't know whether I can carry it or not. Sweat has popped out all over me."

"You ain't no man," says Big Aaron, "if you can't carry a bee gum loaded with honey and bees." My bee gum is a cut of a hollow log with boards nailed on the top and bottom. It is black gum and it is heavy.

"I'm about all pooped out with my load too," says Dave Caxton. "Sweat is streaming in my eyes until I can't see the path. I'm wet as a river with sweat."

"Follow me," says Big Aaron. "I've got the heaviest bee gum of all you. I got a cut from a hollow beech-log. It's the heaviest wood in the world. I'd hate to think I couldn't carry one cut of a saw-log." We follow Big Aaron down the cow-path and up the Jackson hill. We follow slowly to the top. We are getting our breaths like spans of mules pulling a jolt-wagon load of crossties out of W-Hollow. Big Aaron reaches the top. He sets down his bee gum. "Here's the top, boys," he says. "Now we'll smoke before we go down the other side."

We reach the top of the hill. We put our burdens down. The bees are mad within the gums. If they could get out they would sting us to death. But we have them fastened in behind the little sticks. We roll our cigarettes in brown sugar-poke paper. We fill the papers with crumbled, home-grown tobacco. Dave takes a dry match from his hatband. He strikes it on his teeth. He lights our cigarettes. We stand in the moonlight and pant and blow smoke toward the red-faced moon. The cool wind from the high hilltops hits us. It dries our sweaty clothes. It cools our faces.

"Let's finish our job," says Little Edd Hargis. "How much futter we got to go?"

"Just under the hill," says Big Aaron. "I've got the place picked. It's safe for the bees."

We throw down the stubs of our cigarettes. We twist the fire out'n them with our shoes. We pick up our stands of bees. We walk down the hill behind Big Aaron. We walk down to a locust thicket. There is a ground hog path back under the locusts. Big Aaron bends down and walks back this path. We follow him back to a little open space where he puts the bees down. "Ain't this a safe place for the bees," says Big Aaron. "Look what a purty place for them! See, I got one bee gum here already. I got one of Pap's and brought it here. He ain' missed it yet."

Big Aaron has come already and put rocks down for us to put the bee gums on. He has made foundations for many stands of bees. We place the bee gums solidly on the rocks. "When you get 'em fixed on the rocks," says Big Aaron, "jerk the sticks out and come away and leave them. They'll think they are at home in the morning. They'll work just the same as they've always worked. They are at home out here. They are away from everybody. They have come home to the hills where they used to be."

We place the bee gums on the rocks. We slip the sticks out of the holes. We slip back down the path—over the hill to the hollow. We cross the creek, climb the bluff to the rock cliff. "We are back home," says Big Aaron as he goes under the curtains of ferns to the good leaf bed. Big Aaron sprawls out on the leaves. Little Edd puts the .32 on a shelf of rock. Dave unstraps his rifle. He lays it on the shelf of rocks. We sprawl out for the night. "Our work is done for tonight," says Ennis. "I'm glad it's done too. I looked every minute to see fire flash from a gun when we's getting them bees. It ain't safe where there's a lot of house dogs around."

"Don't talk about it now," says Big Aaron. "You'll get me skeared after it's all over. Forget about it now. Our night's work is done. Go to sleep and dream."

I dreamed that Willis Dials saw me steal his bees. I thought he run me with a corn-cuttin' knife. I was just keeping out of his way. He was just barely touching me with the knife but I would jump out of his reach. His little black eyes looked like balls of fire. He had a pipe in his mouth and his lips were snarled. When he struck—I jumped and the knife just touched me. I could feel blood running from my face and neck.

"Get up all of you," says Dave. "It's Sunday morning—hear the Plum Grove church bells ringing. Get out'n that drip of water, Shan. You've rolled over under the drip. Your shirt is wet." Dave laughs and laughs.

"That made me have bad dreams," I says. "I thought Willis Dials was after me all night. He was cutting at me with a corn knife. I could feel the blood running down my neck and face."

"Well, boys," says Little Edd, "we had a good fox chase last night. Let's all go home to breakfast."

We crawl out of the cliff—walk to the forks of the road. We part at the forks. I walk up by the sweet-tater bottoms to the house.

"Your Ma left breakfast on the table for you," says Pa. "She's gone to Sunday School. Hurry up and eat breakfast and help me do up this work. You can tell me about your fox chase then."

"All right, Pa," I says.

I eat my breakfast. I walk out where Pa is. I help him milk the cows and slop the hogs. I tell Pa about the big fox chase we had. Pa says he must have slept like a log for he didn't hear the hounds and that he always listens for them. I tell him if he didn't hear them it was his own fault for our hounds really put the fox over the hills.

When Mom comes from Sunday School she says: "Mick, did you know somebody took all of Willis Dials' bees last night? Took five stands from him. Said he saw them leaving with them. Said he shot five times. Said they had a wagon over on the road and loaded the bees on the wagon and run two big black horses hard as they could tear up the road with all his bees in the back end of the wagon. Preacher preached this morning about it. People are coming in here and stealing honeybees! Did you ever hear of sicha thing?"

"Must a-been hard up for honey," says Pa. "I never heard of people stealin' honeybees out'n a yard. I've heard o' men findin' bee trees on another farm and slippin' in and cuttin' 'em without permission—but I never heard of thieves brazen enough to walk in a man's yard and carry his bees to a wagon! I don't know what this world's a-comin' to—"

"It ain't comin'," says Mom—"it's goin'—and to the Devil it's goin' fast. We ain't had sicha thing to happen at Plum Grove for years. Betsy Roundtree was talkin' about it as we come back across the hill. She says she puts the fear of God into Big Aaron. I tell her I know that my boy will never steal—never—whatever he does that's onery—stealin' won't be a part of it."

Everybody talks in the community about Willis Dials losing his bees. We hear about how Willis shot at them—how they took to the wagon and drove the big black horses up the road—their feet striking fire from the rocks. We hear all sorts of tales. We do not talk about it. We listen to the others talk. I go to Prayer Meeting on Wednesday night at Plum Grove with Mom. Big Aaron is at Prayer Meeting. He comes to me and says: "We fox-hunt tomorrow night. Be at the cliff by moonrise. We go to Flaughtery's tomorrow night. We got to get his bees. He ain't got but four bee gums. Ain't much but enough to pay us for our trouble."

Thursday night we call our dogs—meet at the crossroads. The dogs take to the hills to start the fox. We go to the cliff. When the hounds are bringing the fox across the hollow by Warfield Flaughtery's house and his dog runs out and barks at the fox hounds, we slip upon the bank back of Warfield's house—we plug the bee gums with sticks. We load them on our backs. We walk away. Little Edd carries the pistol and the rifle. We walk down the creek to the big sycamore, then we turn to our right. We walk up under the pines where the moonlight falls almost as bright as daylight. We put the bee gums down to rest, wipe sweat and smoke. We roll our cigarettes in the brown sugar-poke paper. We smoke and sit silently under the pines in the moonlight. We get up, twist the fire out of our cigarette stubs with our shoes. We move across the hill to the place under the locust thicket where we keep our bees. We place them securely on the foundation rocks— pull the plugs out of the holes. Warfield Flaughtery's bees now have their freedom. We go back to our cliff for rest. Big Aaron gravels some of Warfield's sweet taters from the ridges in the bottom by the sycamore tree. We stick the taters in the ashes under the cliff. We build a fire over them. We lie down on the leaves on the far side of the cliff for a little rest. The fire will burn down—the embers will roast our taters. When we awake, our breakfast will be ready. We'll eat a bite of breakfast and go home. We know our Paps are listening to our hounds bring home the fox.

"Breakfast, boys," says Big Aaron—"wake up to a good sweet-tater breakfast."

I watch Big Aaron rake the roasted sweet taters from the ashes. He peels the bark from one. He eats the golden-colored roasted sweet tater. "Better than honey," he says—"you fellars get up and taste o' one."

I get up from my bed of leaves. Little Edd, Dave and Ennis get up. We get roasted taters from the ashes—peel the bark from them. They are warm and sweet. "I read," says Big Aaron, "where George Washington's soldiers et roasted sweet taters and went barefooted at Valley Forge in the winter time. I'd hate to think I couldn't stand as much as they could stand. People just don't know what good grub George Washington's soldiers had to eat. I ain't gone barefooted in the winter time but I've gone in swimming when I had to cut the ice and that didn't bother me a bit."

"That ain't nothing, Big Aaron," says Ennis—"we've all

done that. Talk about something we ain't done while we're here at the breakfast table."

"We ain't got my Pap's bees and Shan's Pap's bees," says Big Aaron—"but we will get them if we keep our health. Boys, we'll hear a lot about somebody's getting Warfield's bees. Just say we saw that team of black horses goin' out'n the hollow about twelve o'clock— Say we saw the driver slapping the horses with the lines."

"That's it," says Ennis. "He's the man Willis Dials saw gettin' his bees."

"It'll be a joke about how many liars we have at Plum Grove," says Little Edd, "if they ever find our bees. They'll know then about the black horses." Little Edd talks with his mouth filled with sweet tater.

"It's time boys we's getting home," says Dave. "I've got to work in the terbacker field today."

Big Aaron picks up the sweet-tater bark. He puts it in a little pile and covers it over with leaves. "Remember," says Big Aaron, "we meet here Saturday night at seven o'clock— rain or shine or no moon. Now we must all get home and help our Mas and Paps." Big Aaron sticks his head out from under the ferns. He crawls out. We follow him down the bluff—across the creek and up the road. At the forks of the road I leave them. They go up the creek and I go up the Right Fork home.

"Now, Mick," I hear Warfield say, "my bees are all gone. All four stands are gone I tell you. I've found tracks down to the road—a lot of big tracks and little tracks. I can't track 'em no further. I heard dogs barking last night. The fox hounds run the fox right across by my barn. My dog barked and barked. I never thought anything. Now my bees are gone."

"Shan, Warfield lost all his bees last night," says Pa.

"Yes," says Warfield, "I lost my bees. Just keep bees to get honey for Ma and me. We live alone around there and

127

ain't never had anything bothered in the last sixty years. I'll tell you the world is going to hell. I never heard of thieves taking bees before."

"W'y Mr. Flaughtery," I says, "we were back on the ridge last night and we heard a man driving in the hollow. When we walked down to the beech-tree footlog we saw a pair of black horses hitched to a wagon—the driver stood up like a ghost and whipped his horses with the check lines. We saw the fire fly from their hoofs as they left the hollow."

"The same damned thief," says Warfield, "that got poor old Willis Dials' bees. Old Willis wasn't seeing things. He actually saw the thief. I heard that Willis stung him with a few shot. I heard Sol Perkins found blotches of blood on the turnpike. Looks like if that thief got hot lead once he'd be afraid he's going to get it again."

"You can't lock from a thief," says Pa, "and you can't bluff one with bullets. You just haf to get 'im. Put him under the sod is the only cure."

Warfield goes home. I go to the corn field with Pa. I think about when Saturday night comes. "What if someone shoots me? What if someone shoots Big Aaron? I don't want to sleep under no ground. I want to live. Maybe, we'll make it somehow without getting shot."

It is Saturday night. I call Pa's hound dog and my hound pup. I walk down the Right Fork to the hollow. I turn left, walk down the road to the sycamore tree. The dogs leave me and take to the hills. I walk across the creek, climb the bluff up to the cliff. I hear voices. The boys are waiting on me. I crawl under the ferns to the big room under the cliff. The lantern is dimly burning.

"We have a hard piece of work before us tonight, Shan," says Big Aaron. "Uncle Fonse Tillman has one bee gum. He has it around from the house, chained around a big beech tree and the log chain is padlocked. We haf to have that stand of bees. I've brought a cross-cut saw and a meat rind. We'll grease the saw until you can't hear it run—saw the tree off
128

above the bee gum and slip the chain over the stump. We'll fool the old boy. It's a prize bee gum. He ain't robbed it for four years. He's afraid of his bees."

"We ain't afraid," says Little Edd. "I'm beginning to feel like I'm a man if I am shot tonight."

"Let's go," says Big Aaron. "Don't anybody talk. Shan, you help me saw the tree down. You are tall and you can reach above the bee stand and saw and it won't tire you."

We follow Big Aaron out of the cliff. We follow him up across the hill back of the cliff. Big Aaron follows a cow path to the top of the hill. We see the fox hunters' fire on the ridge. Big Aaron cuts down under the hill through the briers and brush—we follow him—we cut back up to the ridge road on beyond the fox hunters' fire. We walk down the point to Uncle Fonse Tillman's little log house. Big Aaron leads us to the beech tree. He runs the meat rind over the saw. We start sawing. The saw slips through the wood like a mouse slips away from a cat. There isn't a sound you can hear ten steps away. "The chain takes up a lot of the sound," says Big Aaron. Our saw eats through the green beech tree. It falls through the night air with a slash—not a dog barks at Uncle Fonse's house. We lift the padded log chain up over the clean smooth-topped stump. Little Edd plugs the bee gum. Big Aaron puts it on his back. We walk back over the hill to Big Aaron's Pap's house. I carry the log chain and the padlock.

"I know Pap's bees," says Big Aaron. "I know where he keeps every stand. We haf to work all night, boys. I'm going to carry two light bee gums at one load. You boys can take one apiece. We can carry all of our bees at five loads."

"You can't carry two stands at one load," says Ennis.

"The hell I can't," says Big Aaron. "You ain't never seed me really put my strength out. I can just about carry three to the top of that hill over yander."

We chain two stands together for Big Aaron. He picks them up with ease. He walks away. We plug our stands of bees. We walk down the hill to the road. We climb the hill under the pines. We rest on the ridge and smoke. We pick up our loads and carry them down under the hill to the locust thicket. We place them securely on the foundation rocks. We take out the plugs. We walk back the little path that leads us to our city of bee gums.

"Now boys," says Big Aaron, "we got four loads to carry from home and a load of bees over at Shan's Pap's place. It will take us all night to do this. We'll haf to work fast. We can't walk across Warfield's tater ridges at the bottom by the sycamore tree. We'll make a path and they'll track us. We'll come up the hill at a different place every time. Let Pap track us down to the road. There's a lot of wagon tracks. He can't go no further."

We follow Big Aaron. We carry the second load. We carry the third load. We carry the last load. We carry away all the bees that Alec Roundtree has. "This will hurt Pap an awful lot," says Big Aaron, "but he has hurt the bees an awful lot. He went into the wild woods and took them from their homes in the trees. Now we take them back and leave them in the wild woods—a place so wild the hoot owls holler in the daytime."

"It's two o'clock in the morning," says Ennis, "and daylight comes soon. Do you suppose we'll have time to carry Powderjay's bees away before daylight?"

"We got two hours," says Big Aaron—"I can carry them away by myself in that time. Come on you fellars. You ain't no tireder than I am. I'm goin' to bring two stands over this time. I'm taking the log chain to wrap around them. Shan you lead us the best way to your bees."

We walk up the hollow with our plugs to stop the holes. Our bees are beside the road. We just walk along—our dogs are running the fox. There is not a dog at the house to bark at us. We plug the bee stands. Big Aaron chains two together —loads them on his back. We get a bee gum apiece and we follow Big Aaron. Little Edd carries the pistol in his hand to shoot if we see somebody coming up the road. "Little Edd, just shoot to skear 'em a little," says Big Aaron. "Put the bullet fairly close and they'll tear out."

We hurry down the road. We cut across the meadow beyond the big sycamore tree. We take to the pine woods on the hill. The moon is down, down. The way is dark. We follow Big Aaron up the hill. He sweats and groans beneath his load. We reach the top of the hill. We are wet with sweat. We are tired out. "Last time tonight," says Big Aaron. "Let us have a good smoke."

"Who—who who are you?" says a voice near by. We never move. We do not speak.

"Who—who who are you?" says the same voice.

The wings of a big owl swoop over us. We can feel the cool air from its wings.

"Did you ever hear a hoot owl speak that plain?" says Big Aaron. "My heart was in my mouth. I thought it was Pap. I thought we's goners. Lord, but how thankful I am. Let's get the bees over and put them with the rest of the bees. This will make us forty-two stands of bees." We pick up our loads again. We walk over the hill to the locust thicket. We place them securely on the foundation rocks. We unplug the stands and walk down the little path we have worn under locust trees.

"Let's all go home and go to bed," says Big Aaron. "Remember we saw that team of horses about twelve o'clock again last night when we followed the fox hounds from the Flaughtery Ridge to the Powderjay Ridge. All tell the same tale. We're going to hear about this and not from Sunday School. Pap will be one mad man in the morning."

I leave the boys at the forks of the road. I am so tired I can hardly get home. I worked all day in the terbacker field— I carried bees all night. I am tired. I can sleep all day if there's not too much war going on in the hollow. I walk home—barely crawl to my bed upstairs. I just get my shoes off and fall across the bed. I'm all pooped out. "Lord," I think, "I'm glad I didn't get shot. I'm thankful to the Lord and I would pray to Him but I've been out taking bees and the Lord wouldn't listen to my prayers." I fall asleep.

"I'm robbed, Mick Powderjay," I hear Mr. Roundtree say. "They got my bees last night. Seventy-five gallons of honey stole from me last night. Lord, how I'll miss that seventy-five dollars! Took every bee gum I had—stripped me clean."

"Well I'll be damned," says Pa—"I never noticed that. All my bees are gone too. Look up there won't you! I'm robbed too! My God—look won't you! Thieves have come right inside my yard and took my bees!"

I get up—put on my clothes and go down. I walk out where Pa and Mr. Roundtree are standing. "Pa, did you say somebody got our bees last night?" I says.

"Look for yourself," says Pa. "I couldn't believe my eyes when I first saw it. Got all of Alec's bees last night."

"What?" I says.

"Yes," says Alex, "I've got Big Aaron out tracking this morning. Said he saw a span of black horses leave the hollow last night about twelve o'clock. Said the driver was layin' the buckskin to 'em and the fire was flyin' from their hoofs! Said the driver was leaning back and holding the check lines like a tall ghost."

"I saw it with my own eyes too," I says.

Uncle Fonse Tillman comes down the hill. He walks with a cane. He comes down to our yard—just ripping out oaths and cavorting. He waves his cane into the air. "Some thief got my only stand of bees last night," he says. "I had them chained to a beech tree. They cut the tree and slipped the chain over the stump—took chain, padlock and bee gum. I'll kill him if I ever find him. I'll kill all the thieves connected with it." He pulls a long blue forty-four from the holster and twirls it.

"We ought to swing 'em to a limb," says Pa, "if we can get 'em. We'll take the span of horses to pay for the bees."

Pa, Uncle Fonse and Alec Roundtree swear and stomp the ground. Pa puffs a cigar faster than I ever saw him puff one before. "A damn dirty shame," he says. "I've lived here all my life and this has never happened before. Somebody from a-fur has to come in to steal our bees."

Big Aaron comes up the road. "Pa," he says, "I've tracked them to the road. I see fresh wagon tracks. I can't track them no further."

"They're gone," says Alex Roundtree. "All my bees are gone."

"Mine too," says Pa.

"And my bee gum, log chain and padlock's all gone," says Uncle Fonse Tillman.

"I've said," says Pa, "you can't lock against a thief. The best way is to fill his hide so full of lead it won't hold shucks."

I walk out across the yard with Big Aaron. "We meet at the cliff next Tuesday night," says Big Aaron, "to set the last of the bee gums free. We're going up the Old Line Special to Kenyon's place. I've looked the place over. I've got the plans. We'll set them free."

"I'm getting afraid," I says. "Look at these men. Listen to them cuss and watch them stomp their feet!"

"Yes, Pa smiled when he cut down the wild bee trees," says Big Aaron. "He can't remember how the bees stung him trying to keep him from robbing them and taking them out'n the woods. Now Pa cusses around because they have gone back where they belong. Shan, you be ready Tuesday night. All this will blow over—besides, we're goin' beyond the Plum Grove hills to get these bees. We're going up the Old Line Special!"

Tuesday night I walk down to the cliff. Everywhere we go we hear wild tales about people's seeing the bee thieves—dressed in white—driving big black horses. People shooting at them and they were hit by bullets and there was blood along the road. We laugh about it. We know what big lies can get started while we work to save the bees.

"Now boys," says Big Aaron, "we go to Jake Reek's place. He has a handcar beside the Old Line Special. See he is a track man and uses the handcar. He has it padlocked but there's a crowbar there. We can pry the chain off. We can put it on the track and ride up the rails to Kenyon's. They live beside the railroad track. We can put the bees on the handcar—come down to Plum Grove in no time and carry the bees back on the hill."

"That is great," says Ennis. "We'll get to ride the handcar. Won't that be fun!"

"It won't be fun goin' up the Old Line Special," says Dave. "We haf to pull uphill. But comin' back we can coast all the way to Greenupsburg. Just turn the levers loose and let 'em work up and down—just watch that one don't crown you on the head."

Big Aaron leads the way. We follow him to Jake Reek's house. We walk down the path to the railroad. The handcar is settin' beside the railroad track. Big Aaron goes over in the weeds. He comes back with a crowbar. He puts it behind the chain and yanks against it with all of his strength. The lock flies open.

"Let's set 'er on the tracks, boys," he says. "Let's go to Kenyon's place and get the bees. The bees are in the orchard way out in front of the house."

We lift the handcar on the track. Little Edd hunkers down. He takes care of the .22 rifle and the .32 pistol. Big Aaron and I pull on one side—Ennis and Dave pull on the other. The wheels grind against the rails. The cool wind hits our faces. We are off up the two streaks of rust—around the curves hard as we can go—into the Minton Tunnel—through it like a flash—out into the moonlight on the other side.

"Boy, I'd like to own a handcar," says Dave, "and just go

places on it. I like a handcar. It's a lot better than walking over these old hills. I don't mind to free the bees when we can go like this. Come on and let's use more elbow grease."

"Just as you say," says Big Aaron. "Everybody pull and let's travel."

"Ah, where you goin' on the Blue Goose?" a man hollers to us.

"Don't answer him," says Big Aaron. "People over here go on this handcar after the Doctor. He thinks somebody is sick. Just keep pulling."

We don't answer.

"Pow. Pow. Pow. Pow." His gun barks at us. "Pow. Pow. Pow." The bullets wheeze all around us.

"Cut down on 'im Little Edd," says Big Aaron. "He's started this with us."

Little Edd empties the .32 pistol at him. We hear him run to the bushes screaming.

"You's nipping fer 'im Little Edd," says Dave. "Good work, boy. When they start this shooting with us we're ready."

Little Edd holds the rifle ready if he shoots again. I stop pulling the handcar to reload the pistol.

"I'll get 'im with this rifle if he tries that again," says Little Edd. "I'm a dead-eye Dick with a rifle."

Now we pull up to a switch and a big white house on our left.

"Right here," says Big Aaron. "Take it easy now, boys. Get the plugs, Dave, and let's go over and get the bees."

We walk over under the apple trees. We plug the stands. There is not a whisper. Every man knows his duty. He picks up a stand of bees. He carries them to the car.

"Three stands left," says Big Aaron. "Shan, you and Dave come with me to get them."

We walk back under the apple trees. We start to pick up the bees. The house dogs let out a yell. We grab the bees and

135

run to the handcar. We put them on. Kenyon's door flies
open. A man stands in the door—dressed in white. He turns
an automatic shotgun loose at us. The bullets fall like rain.
We crowd on the handcar. We start moving and Little Edd
brings down a dog with the first crack of the rifle. He shoots
at the other dog—he whines, yells and runs to the house.
"Just skint him," says Little Edd. "I'll plug that door the
fellar's just closed."

"Don't do it," says Big Aaron. "This is a gun country—
more than the hollow we're from. Let's go down the track—
pump the handcar even if it is downhill. Go faster than the
Old Line Special's No. 8 ever pulled her passengers."

We turn the handcar loose. You can hear it a mile riding
the two streaks of rust. "Pow. Pow. Pow." Somebody shoots
from the bushes. Little Edd empties our .32 at the sound of
the pistol. We keep moving. A bee stings me on the leg. One
stings Big Aaron. They are stinging all of us. A plug is out of
a hole or a bullet plugged a hole in one of the bee stands.

"We'll be there in a few minutes," says Big Aaron. "Just
keep going until we get in front of Jackson's." Before we get
to Jackson's I get nine bee stings under my pants leg. Big
Aaron gets six, Dave five, Little Edd thirteen and Ennis don't
get a sting. We pull down to Jackson's—put the brakes on—
slide the car forty feet on the rusted rails.

"Off everybody," says Big Aaron. "See the bees coming
out at the side of the bee gum. That fellar back yander put a
hole through the bee gum with a .44. Glad it was the bee
gum and not one of us. We are safe. We'll leave that stand
here and take to the hills with the other seven."

"Dave, you can carry two, can't you?"

"Yes," says Dave. "I'm scared to leave that'n. Rope two
together for me."

Dave takes two stands. Big Aaron takes two. The rest of
us take one each. We go up the Jackson hill. We walk fast in
the moonlight. We walk up the hollow, twist to our right

until we come to the locust thicket. We put the bee stands solidly on the rocks—pull out the plugs and leave the bee city.

"Forty-nine stands now," says Big Aaron. "Just lost one stand. We'll never do nothing with them now. Let's run back to the handcar. We may be able to get the car back to Jake Reek's place. If it wasn't for all the bees on it we'd take a ride tonight on that car. I do love to ride it."

We run through the brush like a pack of fox hounds. We follow Big Aaron. He leaps the briers and brush and we leap them and go under the fences. We go back to the handcar. Big Aaron kicks the stand of bees off. There's not many bees in the stand. They are all over the handcar. We get on the handcar and start back up the track. We pull hard and fast through the tunnel—over to Jake Reek's place. The bees sting us. We do not care. We have the handcar back. We pull it from the railroad track—put it where it was—fix the chain and padlock back just like they were. We walk over the hills home and rub the places where the bees have stung us.

"It's all over now, boys," says Big Aaron, "for we have saved the bees. Any man that tells gets his tongue cut out by the roots. Now go to your homes. We won't meet at the cliff until all this trouble blows over. Now let's all play mouse and go to his own house."

"Shan," says Mom, "did you hear about somebody gettin' the handcar over at Jake Reek's place? Said there was a swarm of bees on it the next morning down around the cogs. Said when the men started to pull it, the bees nearly stung them to death. Said a lot of wild men had the car riding it and shooting at men along the road. Shot Mel Spriggs in the leg. Said he hid in the brush and plugged one or two men as they come back. Went up the road and got all of Kenyon's bees. Said Mr. Kenyon pumped lead at 'em until he's black in the face. Said he really filled 'em with shot but they just kept going."

"Lord," I says, "what else is going to happen around here?"

"I'll tell you what's a-going to happen," says Pa. "We've got the thief. Enic Spradling was squirrel hunting around on the Jackson place the other day. He found forty-nine stands of bees. It tallies all but one stand. We've lost fifty stands. You wouldn't believe old Jackson would take all them bees, would you? Well, he has."

"Why he's a sick man," says Mom. "I heard he had the consumption."

"If he's got any consumption," says Pa, "it's the corn-bread consumption. We can't get him on a bee thieving charge. The Government's got him. Got him for selling moonshine whiskey too. W'y he's a bad man. Old Judge April-May-June (A.M.J.) Canter is going to put the cat on him. He'll be on the next soldier train that goes to Atlanter, Georgia. You're going to have to go over there and get our six stands of bees someway. Alec Roundtree is going to send Big Aaron after his. This has been a hard thing to believe. Old Lonesome just sit over there on the hill and acted like he didn't have a bit of life in him. Look what all he's done. Just turned out bad in the deestrict. Let this be a lesson."

"All right, Pa," I says. "I'll get Big Aaron. We'll go for the bees."

"Don't forget to look for Uncle Fonse Tillman's log chain and padlock either," says Pa.

"I won't," I says. "I think we'll be able to find it."

another home for the squirrels

Grandpa walked slowly up the road with his double-bitted ax across his shoulder and his hat in his hand.

"Wonder why Grandpa's comin' home early?" I asked Mom.

"I don't know," she said, looking down the road toward him. "Pap shuffles his feet like he's tired. And, he may be sick."

But I knew Grandpa wasn't tired and he wasn't sick when he looked at me with a big smile and said, "I'm bringin' you something, Shan."

"Grandpa," I said, running toward him.

Grandpa stopped under the apple tree that was beginning to bloom.

"Look in my hat," he said, soon as I reached him.

"Little squirrels!" I shouted.

Then Mom came up and looked into Grandpa's hat.

"The poor little things," Mom said.

"Six little squirrels," I laughed.

"Where's their mother?" Mom asked.

"I don't know," Grandpa said. "She was away from the big chestnut oak when we cut it. We didn't know there were any squirrels in it until the tree fell and a nest rolled from the top."

"Looks like it would've killed these little squirrels," I said.

"They're alive and well," Grandpa said as the March wind lifted his gray hair. "Watch 'em huntin' for their mother."

"We'd better take the squirrels to the house and feed 'em," Mom said. "Shan, go find a goose quill."

Mom and Grandpa walked toward the house, and I hurried to find a goose quill.

When I got back to the house, Grandpa was sitting in the kitchen holding the hat on his lap. He was talking to Mom while she poured warm milk into the bottle she was going to feed the baby squirrels with.

"Here's the quill," I said.

"They'll be fed now," Mom said, as she put the goose quill through the hole she had made in the stopper. Then Mom put the stopper in the bottle.

Mom lifted one little squirrel at a time from Grandpa's hat and cuddled it in one hand while with the other she held the bottle. She put the goose quill to the squirrel's mouth. The baby squirrel put his forefeet around the quill and held it while he nursed the bottle until Mom had to pull 'im away. And while Mom picked up each squirrel and fed him, Grandpa and I looked on. Grandpa would smile and I would laugh.

"Watch how your mother feeds 'em," Grandpa said. "This will be your job."

After Mom had fed one of the squirrels she put it back in Grandpa's hat.

"Look how full that little fellow is," Mom said, laughing. "He'll want to sleep now."

When Mom had finished feeding the squirrels and put them back in Grandpa's hat they went to sleep.

"They can't live in my hat," Grandpa said. "Shan, we'll have to make 'em a box."

That afternoon Grandpa worked in March wind while the baby squirrels used his hat for a bed. I carried tools and planks to Grandpa while he made me a box for my squirrels. Inside the big box, he made a little box for their bedroom. I carried leaves and put them in the bedroom for their bed. Then Grandpa covered the top of the box with a fine-meshed wire. He fixed a little door for me to take them out at feeding time.

"Now they'll have a nice little house," Grandpa said.

"Thank you, Grandpa."

I brought Grandpa's hat from the kitchen and we lifted the squirrels from it and put them in their bedroom onto the bed of leaves.

We stood watching them crawl close to each other like they were hunting their mother. After they had crawled over the leaves a few minutes, they huddled together in a pile and went to sleep. Then Grandpa carried the box from under the walnut tree by the smokehouse into our front room.

"I want this box to stay in this corner, Sallie," Grandpa said to Mom.

"But Mick won't like it," Mom said.

"I'll talk to Mick," Grandpa said. "Leave that to me."

"I don't see why you got 'em in the house," Pa grumbled soon as he came from the field.

"I told 'im to fetch 'em in here," Grandpa said.

"Then if you told 'im to bring 'em in here that's all right, Dad," Pa said.

I never saw anything grow like my squirrels. Their eyes opened. And when I fed them they would fight over the bottle. So I had to get more bottles and more goose quills and fix each squirrel a bottle. They would hold to the goose quills with their front paws until they drained the bottles. With their little stomachs tight as banjo heads they would stretch out in their bed of leaves and go to sleep. Their tails grew bushy, and they would climb all over the box when I went to feed them.

"Poor little things don't know what a mother is," Mom said one day when I fed them.

It worried me when Pa complained of my squirrels. He said he could smell them. But when I sniffed, I couldn't. And I told Pa I couldn't. He said it was because I nearly lived with them. I knew Pa wanted the squirrels out of the house. So, one day, Grandpa and I carried the box to the smokehouse. Then Pa was pleased.

My squirrels hadn't been in the smokehouse three days until Mom went into the smokehouse to slice a ham. I heard Mom let out a scream, and I ran to the smokehouse. She was holding her thumb with her hand, and I saw one of my squirrels jumping over the meat bench.

"What's the matter, Mom?"

"That squirrel bit me," Mom shouted angrily.

"How'd it get out?"

"I don't know," Mom said. "When I come out here it was sittin' on the meat bench, and I started to pick it up and it bit my thumb!"

"I'm sorry, Mom," I said, as my squirrel leaped from the meat bench onto my shoulder, then it ran up on my head and sat down. "Somebody must've left the door open to the box."

Then I lifted the squirrel from my head and started to put him in his box, but the door was closed. I put him in the box and watched him go down behind the leaves and out at a hole on the other side of the box. The squirrel had gnawed a hole through the thick oak planks.

"Don't tell Pa about it," I said. "He'll make me get rid of my squirrels."

"I won't, just for your sake," Mom said, walking across the yard.

142

While Mom bandaged her thumb, I fixed the hole and carried the box back into our front room. Pa didn't like it when he saw I'd moved my squirrels back. He looked at the squirrel box but he didn't say a word. That evening he was cross with all of us. He went to bed early.

"I told you there'd be trouble," Pa stormed next morning, when he found all six squirrels on top of the house.

"Take it easy, Mick," Grandpa said. "Let Shan have a few pets. He'll never be young to enjoy them but once."

When we went inside the house, I looked at the box and there was a hole just at the edge of the piece of tin.

"I found the place where they got out," I said.

"But how did they get out of this house?" Pa asked. "Windows are down and the doors are closed."

I didn't answer Pa. I went upstairs with Grandpa. When we got to the top of the stairs we saw how they'd got on top the house. They'd cut a hole through the roof as big as the end of a pint cup and as round as if it had been bored with an auger.

"Can you fix that hole, Grandpa?" I asked. "Pa will be mad when he finds this out."

"Shore I can," Grandpa laughed.

When my squirrels heard me talking to Grandpa, they came one at a time through the hole and leaped down on Grandpa's head and shoulders. Grandpa flinched and tried to get out of the way. But the last squirrel's toenails slashed little places on Grandpa's neck just like somebody had done it with a knife. I thought he would be mad, but he wasn't. He was nice about it, though the big smile left his face.

While I took the squirrels downstairs, Grandpa changed shirts so Mom and Pa wouldn't see where he had been scratched. When Grandpa came downstairs, Pa looked at his clean shirt and then he looked at Mom. And I put my squirrels back in the box and nailed tin over the hole they'd cut. Then I hurried upstairs and found that Grandpa had put a

143

piece of shoebox over the hole from the underside. It was fixed so Pa wouldn't find the place. Not until it rained.

"Mick, you ought to let Shan just turn his squirrels out," Grandpa said. "I don't blame the squirrels for wantin' out."

"Wouldn't Shan's squirrels leave, Pap?" Mom asked.

"They'll always come back for their feed," Grandpa said. "Of course a squirrel is a thing with a lot of wild nature in it."

"I think that would be a good idea," Pa said, his face beaming.

Pa thought my squirrels would leave or Rags, our dog, would get them.

"I don't like to do it," I said. "But if I try to keep 'em in the box, I'll have to cover it with tin. I don't have any tin."

Pa smiled as I carried the squirrels outside. And Mom was pleased.

When I put the box down and opened the little door, my squirrels ran outside. They took off toward the smoke-house. Pa came outside to watch them. He thought Rags would make for 'em. But he was asleep in the yard and when my squirrels leaped over him he didn't pay 'em any more attention than he did our cats. And when Pa saw this, his face lost its smile. I was pleased.

But I wasn't pleased that evening when we sat around a small fire and my squirrels came down the stairs, one following the other like six full-grown kittens. They came hunting for their box. I ran outside and carried it back into the house. Grandpa thought it was funny. He laughed until he bent over and slapped his knees with his big hands. Mom looked at Pa. Pa looked at the fire.

That night when I went upstairs to bed, I could look up through six big holes and see the stars in the sky. I finished using Grandpa's paper box to stop the holes.

Pa couldn't help but find out what my squirrels were doing when he went to the smokehouse and looked through the roof. They had gone into the smokehouse through a knothole. Each had cut a hole through the roof and from the smokehouse roof had jumped over into the walnut tree instead of climbing up the big trunk.

"Squirrels are smart things," Pa said, laughing.

I wondered why Pa had changed his attitude about my squirrels. Maybe he thought that a big rain would fall some night and it would come through the holes in the roof and wet Grandpa, since he slept upstairs. For my pets had cut our upstairs roof so full of holes it looked like a big, ugly milk-strainer. They had cut more holes in the smokehouse roof, and they had even cut a hole in the corn crib roof, and had gone from the top down to the corn and had hearted the good seed corn that Pa had shelled. Yet, Pa was kind enough not to say anything. And they didn't come back to their box to sleep. I didn't know where they were sleeping. Grandpa said they were sleeping in the hollow of a big chestnut tree that stood upon the hill above our kitchen. Mom said she was sure they were sleeping in the barn. She said she had seen 'em there many times. Pa said it didn't matter where they slept, since they had gone wild. Then Pa gave a sort of a wild laugh that Grandpa didn't like.

On a Saturday morning in June, Grandpa shaved and trimmed his mustache. He was getting ready to attend a conference of his church. I stood at the bottom of the stairs and watched him go up in a hurry. He was a happy man. I waited downstairs to see Grandpa dressed in his good clothes. When I heard him give a wild yell, I ran upstairs to see what was wrong. He was standing near the clothes press holding his hand. I saw a squirrel run up the wall and through a hole in the roof.

"What's the matter, Grandpa? You're getting blood on your clothes, Grandpa," I said. "Let me tie up your finger."

Grandpa held his hand up while I wrapped a clean handkerchief around his big index finger where the blood was oozing.

While he picked up his clothes from the bed with his

145

other hand, Grandpa's lips trembled until he could hardly speak.

Now I knew where my squirrels had been sleeping. They had cut the lining of his coat and made a big nest there. They had cut a hole in the back of his new coat to go into the nest, and gone up the pant legs and cut a small hole through the seat of his pants.

Ma and Pa came running upstairs after they heard Grandpa holler. Pa was shaking all over, trying to keep from laughing.

"I'm sorry, Pap," Mom said pleasantly, as she looked at his clothes, "that you'll have to miss the conference."

"I won't miss it," Grandpa said. "I'll go if I have to wear overalls."

"But Dad, I've got a nice suit of clothes you can wear if it'll fit you," Pa said. "I've not worn it but twice and I'd like for you . . ."

I didn't hear anymore that was said. I thought of something. I hurried downstairs. I ran out in the yard looking for my squirrels. I looked in the walnut, the chesnut tree and in the smokehouse. And then I went to the corn crib. I found them finishing the last of Pa's seed corn. I hurried back to the house, got their box, took it to the crib and put the squirrels in it. I knew I would solve the problems they had caused. The squirrels would be happy away in the deep Byrne's hollow among the hollow beeches. Everybody at our house would be happier too. I had just carried the box to the house when Grandpa stepped out at the door dressed in Pa's suit on his way to the conference. It was a little tight on Grandpa, but looked much better on him than overalls.

"What are you going to do with the squirrels?" Mom asked.

"I'm takin' 'em away," I said. "I can't stand to see them killed. And I'm takin' 'em to the beech grove in Byrne's hollow where I've seen a lot of wild squirrels."

146

"They'll be much happier there," Pa said. Pa was pleased.

"Then you'll be goin' part of the way with me," Grandpa said.

"Over two miles," I said.

"When you get tired of carryin' that box I'll help you," Grandpa said as we walked away together and Mom and Pa stood on the doorstep, their faces beaming.

to market, to market

"Come, Boss," Pa said affectionately to the bull he had raised from a little calf. "We got to be goin', fellow. The truck's waitin' for us!"

Pa had never had to use a ring in old Boss' nose. He had never had to put a halter on his head and use a rope to lead him. All Pa had to do was speak to Boss. It seemed that old Boss could understand what Pa said. He followed him away from the barn like a dog following a man after he'd asked the dog to come along. That's the way old Boss understood Pa. That's the way Pa understood old Boss. Pa was taking old Boss to the Cannonsgate Livestock Market where he would be sold to the highest bidder. It looked strange to see Pa taking away an animal that he loved.

"I hate to take you, old boy," Pa said, as he walked slowly down the path beneath the pines. "But the time has come when we got to do something."

The time had come when Pa did have to do something, too. Boss was no longer the pretty little white-faced bull calf he once was. It was three years ago that Pa had trained Boss to walk on his hind feet like a dog. He would walk that way around the stall and fold up his short front legs. Then, Pa would open the gate and let Boss leave the stall and go to the pasture. Often Boss would stick his tongue out and look at Pa with dark bullish eyes. He was the only calf out of the hundreds and hundreds we had owned Pa could train to walk on his hind feet.

Maybe this was the reason big Boss would follow little Pa, who weighed only one hundred twenty-four pounds, down the path under the pines toward the truck that was waiting for him. Because Pa had finally decided this was the best thing for him to do. Five farms joined the big range where we kept our cattle. Each of our neighbors kept a bull too. And when one of these bulls bellowed, Boss didn't bother to jump the fence. He pushed it down and went to him. When Boss put his head and shoulders against a wire fence, the wires snapped like shoestrings. That was unless the wire was new. Then Boss pushed up the posts and flattened several panels of fence. Not any fence could hold him when he heard another bull bellow.

Boss had killed one big bull for Jim Pennix. Pa had to pay for him and he had to repair three panels of new barbed-wire fence. Boss had almost killed Lonnie Madden's bull when we got to him. Because Lonnie's bull had a big pair of horns and old Boss was a polled Hereford, he made the mistake of trying to mangle Boss with his horns. Boss had him down trying to crush him between his mighty head and the ground when Pa took Boss off. Jake Thompson's, Albert Thomb's and Alec Reed's bulls were smarter. When they bellowed and Boss went through the fences to get them, each of them took one look at Boss and took off. That was one thing other bulls could do. They could outrun Boss. He was too big to do much running up and down the cowpaths on the wooded hills and up the grassy pasture slopes.

Not so much what Boss would do to our neighbors' bulls worried Pa as the stories we had been hearing about the fox hunters who had brought their hounds to the highest range of hills on our farm to chase the foxes that denned in the Stuartland rocks. The hunters had stood on one side of the

seven-wire fence, one built to hold sheep, and had pawed the
dry leaves with their brogan shoes and had imitated the
sounds of other bulls. They had done this to old Boss, who
was on the other side of the seven-wires, to scare Red Arrington, an old fox hunter who was afraid of bulls. He took one
look at old Boss high on the mountain standing in the moonlight and this was enough. When Red Arrington ran away, as
he did every time the hunters teased Boss, all the hunters
would clap their hands and shout with laughter.

One night Boss walked through the seven-wires to get
them and each hunter took to a tree while Red Arrington ran
as fast as a fox over the mountain despite his seventy years of
age. Pa heard about this and he was afraid Boss was getting
disgusted with men as well as rival bulls. For once when
Charlie Sprouse, a neighbor, came through our barnlot, Boss
tossed his head in many strange ways to let Pa know he didn't
like it. Pa was afraid Boss might hurt some innocent man
walking across our pasture. This was another reason he was
taking him to the market.

I followed behind and watched the big bull follow my
father. There was not any more difference in this big bull's
following him than a shepherd dog's.

Except the bull was so large and Pa was so small that it
made one laugh to watch them. Not if one knew how Pa had
raised old Boss. It gave me a sad feeling to see Pa taking
him away. I felt sad to see this big friendly animal leaving
our farm. He was friendly to us even if he didn't like other
bulls and fox hunters. I knew as I walked behind them that I
was not half as sad as Pa was. For in the distance I could see
the truck backed up against the steep bank where we had
made a fence to use as a loading chute. Cousin Penny Henson
was sitting in the truck waiting to haul old Boss to market.

"You don't mean to tell me, Uncle Mick, that you can
load that big bull without a ring in his nose?" Cousin Penny
said to Pa.

"Watch me, Penny," Pa said. "I'll take old Boss onto the truck."

Pa walked into the little enclosure. Old Boss followed him. Then Pa walked down the little bank, the way we had to drive the cattle onto the truck after we got them inside the enclosure. Boss followed Pa onto the truck bed. Cousin Penny stood behind the truck and soon as Pa and Boss were safely inside he fastened the gate on the truck bed and roped it securely. Pa didn't get down to ride in the truck cab with Cousin Penny and me but he rode standing on the sawdust in the truck bed with old Boss. We were on our way to the market.

I looked back as the truck jolted along to see how Pa and Boss were riding. Boss wasn't used to the truck since it was the first automobile ride he'd ever had. Pa was saying something to him and rubbing his shoulder. Boss seemed to understand all Pa was saying. He braced his feet when the

151

truck slowed and gained speed. Soon, we had reached Route 1. The ride was smooth from now on. Boss didn't have to brace his feet and Pa didn't have to explain. We passed truckloads of cattle going to market. We passed truckloads of hogs and sheep.

"Have you ever been to Cannonsgate Livestock Market?" Penny asked me.

"Never have," I said.

"Wait until you're there today and you'll see why I'm rushin'," Penny said. "I thought we were early. But look at the people on the road. I want to get there and get unloaded soon as I can."

In a few minutes we reached Route 23, the broad national highway that took us directly to Cannonsgate. Cousin Penny stepped on the gas. I looked back to see how Pa was getting along. He was holding his hat with one hand. His other arm was across old Boss' shoulder. Pa was standing close beside Boss. One truckload of hogs passed us and the beardy-faced man sitting on the side next to our truck laughed as he pointed to Pa riding beside his bull. He yelled something that Pa couldn't understand.

In Roston we stopped to get gas. Pa climbed down from the truck bed.

"When we get to Cannonsgate the pinhookers will swarm around this truck," Pa said. "They'll be wantin' to know the price of my bull. What's he worth?"

"Put him on the market, Pa," I said. "Let the cattle buyers bid for 'im."

"That's what I say," Cousin Penny said. "You'll get more for 'im that way."

"But the pinhookers will be wild about this bull," Pa said. "They'll swarm around this truck soon as we get to Cannonsgate. They'll be askin' me my price."

"But you don't want to sell 'im that way do you, Uncle Mick?" Cousin Penny said.

152

"Sure don't," Pa said. "I want to put 'im on the market."

"Then put a price on him you know they won't take," Cousin Penny suggested.

"But, I don't know how cattle are sellin'," Pa said. "I can't read the livestock report in the paper. My radio won't play. I don't know what to ask for 'im."

"Good bulls are sellin' at twenty dollars a hundred," I said. "I heard that yesterday over the radio."

"How much do you think Boss will weigh?" I asked Pa.

"Nineteen hundred pounds," Pa said.

I looked at Cousin Penny and he looked at me. We didn't agree with Pa's calculation.

"What do you think he'll weigh, Penny?" I asked.

"About seventeen hundred," Penny said. "How much do you say?"

"Seventeen-forty," I said.

"He'll weigh more than that," Pa said, shaking his head sadly.

"Say twenty dollars a hundred, Uncle Mick," Penny said, "your bull ought to be worth three hundred sixty dollars!"

"That's an awful price for a bull," Pa said. "The way I've sold cattle all my life! I never sold an animal for that much! Looks impossible to get that much for a bull!"

"But you don't want to sell him, Pa, to the pinhookers?" I said.

"That's right," Pa answered.

"Then I'd ask this much for 'im and the pinhookers won't even bite," Cousin Penny said. "You'll be able to put 'im on the market."

"All right," Pa agreed. "That's business. They'll look at price before they buy!"

Then Pa started climbing back into the truck with Boss.

"Boss, we're goin' to ask a big price for you," Pa said softly as he rubbed the big bull's kinky head.

"Nice bull you got in that truck," said the filling station attendant while Cousin Penny was trying to make the right change so we could be on our way. "How much do you expect to get for 'im?"

"Three hundred sixty dollars," Cousin Penny said.

"Not enough for that animal," said the small palefaced filling station attendant. "A lot of fellows stop here with loads of cattle. I've never seen a prettier bull than that one. That big fine-looking bull for three hundred sixty dollars when a little veal calf sells for sixty-five?"

"We'd better raise the price of the bull, Uncle Mick," Penny said as the filling station attendant went inside. "What do you say we ask three hundred eighty-seven dollars for 'im? You know the pinhookers won't take you up on that price."

"Suits me fine," Pa agreed. "How does it suit you, Boss?" Pa asked, turning to the bull. "Reckon pinhookers won't laugh when we ask that much for you, Boss?"

Cousin Penny climbed in the cab and I beside him while Pa stood in the truck bed with one arm up over old Boss' neck while with his other hand he rubbed his nose. Cousin Penny stepped on the gas.

"It's a funny thing," Cousin Penny laughed, "how fillin' station attendants think they know all about the price of cattle. That bull won't bring three hundred dollars. Wait and see! I've hauled a lot of cattle up here. Uncle Mick thinks he's got a better bull than he actually has. He won't bring the top market price. He's fooled in his weight too. He's over-guessing but I wouldn't tell 'im so. Don't want to hurt his feelings."

When we pulled under the Cannonsgate over-head, there was already a half-mile line of trucks of all makes and descriptions ahead of us. They were loaded with sheep,

154

calves, cows, steers, heifers and hogs. The half-ton truck with one little bull in it, that we pulled in behind, was almost surrounded with pinhookers. When Cousin Penny pulled his two-ton truck in behind it with old Boss standing as erect and pretty as you ever saw a bull stand, all the pinhookers left the half-ton truck and the little bull, and they swarmed around Cousin Penny's truck.

"What will you take fer 'im?" shouted a tall red-beardy-faced man, wearing a big black umbrella hat and with a crook in his hand. He started to punch Boss through an opening in the truck bed to make him stand around.

"Here, don't do that," Pa warned. "You don't have to punch this bull. He won't stand for it."

"How much does he weigh?" asked a short broad-shouldered man, wearing a fur cap with attached earmuffs and carrying a mule whip across his shoulder.

"Is he your bull?" asked a small man wearing brier-scratched boots on his bowed legs.

"Best lookin' bull I've ever seen at this stock market," said a mousey little man that wore boots and spurs and carried a quirt in his hand. "He's a handsome thing! Look at 'im, won't you!"

Boss never looked better to Cousin Penny and me. We were standing behind the pinhookers who were crowding each other to get closer to the truck.

"I guess this bull to weigh nineteen hundred," Pa said.

"He won't weigh eighteen hundred," said the red-beardy-faced man. "But how much will you take fer 'im?"

"Three hundred eighty-seven dollars," Pa said.

"Odd dollars," the red-beardy-faced man mumbled to himself as if he were puzzled.

Then I saw the short broad-shouldered man, who was wearing the fur cap with the earmuffs attached, reach into his pocket. The red-beardy-faced man saw him goin' down in his

155

pocket after his pocketbook. At least he must have thought so for he screamed up to Pa: "Your bull is sold. I want 'im."

Cousin Penny had not stopped his truck over a minute. Pa looked down from the truck at the red-beardy-faced man as he looked up at Pa. There was a strange look on Pa's face. But Pa had stated his price. There wasn't anything he could do since more than twenty men gathered around the truck had heard Pa set the price on old Boss. The man pulled a big billfold from his pocket. Pa came down from the truck. He paid Pa nineteen twenty dollar bills, a five and two ones. Cousin Penny left his truck and he and I started walking toward the market with Pa.

"That's funny," Pa said. "The truck wheels had hardly stopped rollin' before old Boss sold. I believe I'm stung. Damn the pinhookers!"

Then we met Flood Hall, a short broad-shouldered timber-cutter from Greenwood County who had quit cutting timber and had gone into the cattle business.

"Who brought that big fine lookin' bull in here, Mick?" Flood asked us as he started to run past us.

"I brought 'im, Flood," Pa said.

"What'll you take fer 'im, Mick?" Flood asked as he hurried on toward the truck where the men were still standing around talking about old Boss.

"I've sold 'im, Flood," Pa said.

"Oh, Mick, why didn't you let me know," Flood said. "We're old friends."

Flood stopped dead in his tracks. I thought he would sink to the street. He acted like a man that had missed the buy of a lifetime.

"But I set a price, Flood," Pa explained, "that I didn't think anybody would accept. I planned to put old Boss on the market. Raised that bull from a calf. Got the papers right here with 'im!"

"What did you get fer 'im, Mick, if that's a fair question?" Flood asked.

"Three hundred eighty-seven dollars," Pa said.

"Now, I feel better," Flood said. The sad expression left Flood's face and he twirled the quirt he was holding in his big right hand. He was happy. "You got eighty-seven dollars more than that bull is worth. Old Sherm Potter bought that bull. Am I glad to see 'im get a stingin'! He's poured it on me a time or two!"

Now Pa's face changed from an expression of gloom to one of happiness.

"I'm hard to fool on cattle," Pa said to Cousin Penny and me. "I've lived a long time. I've sold a lot of cattle to pinhookers. They've never made much off old Mick!"

Pa had confidence in himself now.

"Well boys," Pa said to Penny and me as Flood Hall walked on toward the truck where the men were standing around admiring old Boss, "I'll do a little pinhookin' now. I'll buy myself a young bull to replace old Boss."

"Here's a nice bull," Pa said as we stopped beside a half-ton truck to look at a young Hereford bull.

"How old is that bull?" Pa asked the driver.

"Six months," he said.

"What will you take for 'im?" Pa asked.

"Two hundred dollars," he said.

"Not for me," Pa said, shaking his head sadly. "That's too high."

"Cattle are high as a cat's back, Mister," the man said very irritably, as if Pa should know.

We followed the line of trucks up to the cattle chutes where they were unloading. We asked the price of all the bulls in all the trucks. The lowest price for a scrub Jersey bull was one hundred fifty dollars. Pa didn't want him. He just wanted to know the price. One Hereford bull about half the size of Boss that interested Pa, sold before our eyes to a pinhooker for two hundred fifty dollars. The owner had papers with him. Pa had papers with old Boss too.

"I'm ruint," Pa said. "I sold too cheap. I don't care what my old friend, Flood Hall, said. He tried to make me feel good by sayin' those kind words. That's all."

We looked over fourteen bulls. Pa wouldn't buy any of them at the prices the men asked. Only one had papers. That was the one that sold for two hundred fifty. The others were scrub bulls of all breeds, descriptions, colors and kinds. They ranged in price from one hundred fifty to three hundred fifty. Pa didn't buy. When we reached the cattle chutes where they were unloading from the trucks we ran into old Professor Wentworth. He had been a rural school teacher in Greenwood County. But he had quit teaching and had gone into the cattle business since he had found it more profitable. Our meeting him was what caused something to happen.

"Mick, I've just seen that fine bull you brought up here," he said, running toward Pa. "He's the finest thing that's ever come to this market. Somebody told me you only got four hundred dollars for 'im."

Pa looked strangely at Professor Wentworth. He didn't tell him how much he got.

"If I could've only seen you first, Mick," Professor Wentworth said as he took a little book and pencil from his inside coatpocket, "I would have bought your bull. See, I don't do any guesswork on this cattle business. I go by facts and figures. How much did the bull weigh, Mick?"

"I guess 'im to weigh nineteen hundred," Pa said.

"Nineteen hundred at twenty-six cents a pound," Professor Wentworth said as he put the figures down and started calculating.

"Twenty-six cents a pound," Pa said.

"That's right, Mick," Professor Wentworth said as he continued to figure. "That bull will bring top price. Wait and see if I'm not right. Say he weighs nineteen hundred.

158

He'll bring four hundred ninety-four dollars on the market."

"Well Sherm Potter will make some money on that deal," Pa said.

"Flood Hall owns 'im now," Professor Wentworth said. "I was right there when he changed hands. I saw him pay four hundred twenty-five dollars to Sherm for the bull."

Pa didn't say another word. He turned and walked away. Professor Wentworth and I stood there watching Pa disappear into the crowd of livestock sellers, buyers and traders.

"I wish I'd never shown your father the figures," Professor Wentworth said, looking at me with sad brown eyes. "He's a sick man over that trade."

I didn't say a word to Professor Wentworth. I took off through the great crowd of men wearing broad-brimmed hats, boots and carrying crooks over their arms and quirts in their hands. I never saw such a crowd of unshaven beardy-faced men. They were talking cattle, sheep and hogs everywhere I hurried to find Pa. These were cattle men, cattle buyers, traders, sellers and pinhookers. I never saw anything like it. I never heard as much trading talk in my life. But I couldn't find my father. I even went to all the cattle pens looking for Pa. I first looked at the pen for yearling bulls. I couldn't find 'im. Then I went to the pens for heavy bulls. Old Boss was in a pen by himself. I asked if he had been weighed.

"Two thousand twenty-five pounds," said one of the group of men still following and admiring the bull.

Then I wondered if Pa had seen Boss in his pen. I wondered if he knew that he'd come the closest of more than fifty men guessing his weight. I knew if Pa had seen Boss in the bull pen with a number pasted on his fat hip he would be sick now. If Pa could have heard the comments I'd heard then he would be sicker. I'd heard no less than forty men say that old Boss was the finest bull that had ever been brought to the Cannonsgate Livestock Market. After listening to the swarm of men gathered around old Boss' pen brag what a fine bull he was, I took off again to hunt for my father. I looked around the heifer pens for him. I looked around the cow pens, I looked around the calf pens and the yearling steer pens. I thought Pa would try to invest some or all of the money he got for old Boss in cattle of some sort to take home. But nowhere could I find Pa. Then I found Cousin Penny hunting through the milling, trading, buying crowd of cattlemen.

"Penny, have you seen Pa?" I asked.

"Nope, I haven't, Shan," he said. "Too bad Uncle Mick lost the way he did on that bull! I feel so guilty I'm not goin' to charge 'im anything for haulin' 'im up here."

"I feel guilty too," I said. "I feel sick. Pa loved that bull. Never knew him to love an animal more. I feel that I'm partly responsible too, Penny."

Then Cousin Penny and I agreed to search for Pa until two o'clock in the afternoon. That was the time they started putting cattle, sheep and hogs over the Cannonsgate Livestock Market. We agreed to meet each other every thirty minutes at the stock-market door and report to each other.

Six times Cousin Penny and I met each other at the door and reported to one another. The reports were always the same. We hadn't seen anything of Pa.

When the bidding started Cousin Penny and I went inside. This was the first time I'd ever been inside of a livestock market where cattle were driven in front of the prospective buyers and the man that bid the highest took the cattle, hogs or sheep. There was a floor about thirty by thirty feet square and it was covered with sawdust and shavings. On each side of the floor, the seats went up like baseball bleachers, only steeper. There was a gate on the south where the cattle were let in and a gate on the north where they were let out after the bidding was over and they had been sold. Cousin Penny went up in the west tier of steep seats and I went up on the east tier of seats. Cousin Penny scanned the tiers of seats on my side with his big brown eyes for Pa. I scanned the tiers of seats on his side. Pa was not inside the livestock market.

We watched them bring the yearling heifers in first. They brought them one at a time and sometimes by groups. They sold them by the head and by the hundred-weight. There was not any certain way they sold them. But I saw something I had never seen before. Cattle buyers lined the wall of the arena below. And when the cattle were turned through the south gate, they started punching them with their crooks and tapping them with the leash on their quirts. They made them keep running so everybody could see them. They even used the stalks of their mule whips to gouge them between the legs and made them kick. If the cattle showed plenty of life the buyers were more interested and the price went higher. I noticed the well-marked cattle fetched big prices too. Cattle marked like old Boss fetched the money. They brought top prices.

Penny and I watched and waited for Pa. We thought he would surely come to watch the bidding. Then I wondered if he'd gone home alone. Cousin Penny and I waited until they started putting the bulls over the market. It was about five o'clock in the afternoon when the first young bulls came through the south gate. Well-dressed men bid on the fat ones. They bid them in for slaughter. I wanted to wait until old Boss came through. I wanted to know the price he fetched.

Bulls coming through the south gate got larger. Soon they were selling the heavy bulls. Many bulls sold for twenty cents a pound. Fewer sold for twenty-one cents a pound. A fewer still sold for twenty-two cents. Not too many sold for twenty-three cents. And a very, very few, sold for twenty-four cents. I saw two bulls sell for twenty-five cents and one bull, the bull for which the owner asked Pa two hundred fifty dollars, sold for twenty-six cents.

Then something happened that brought excitement to

161

the Cannonsgate Livestock Market. Something that will never be forgotten long as any man or woman lives who was there that Friday afternoon on January fourteenth nineteen forty-nine. The gate opened and old Boss came through. He took his time and looked over the people sitting on the steep seats above him. He looked at the line of strange specimens of cattle buyers and traders that admired him more than he admired them. They were looking at Boss and they looked at each other. Every well-dressed man in the crowd stood up. I watched Professor Wentworth. He was watching eagerly. Flood Hall stood near the auctioneer. Sherm Potter was sitting on the bottom rail.

The auctioneer started old Boss at twenty-three cents a pound. And the bidding of the well-dressed men began as they moved in closer along the bottom rails that enclosed the arena. They wanted old Boss for beef. That they were willing to pay for him was an evident fact. Just as the bidding was getting hot and the auctioneer's words and half words went into the loudspeaker like bullets and fragments of bullets, something happened. Red Arrington, who traded in cattle and fox hunted, recognized old Boss. Old Boss recognized him too. Boss started toward him. Red was sitting on the bottom rail.

"It's the Mick Powderjay bull," Red screamed. "I know 'im. He's dangerous!"

Red fell backwards with his feet sticking up in the air. His two feet were about the level of the eyes of the spectators, traders, buyers and sellers sitting on the first row of the steep seats on the opposite side. Just when this happened Boss put his head under the rail. Then something else happened. At this very minute the keeper had opened the north door to let old Boss through since men were gouging him with crooks and hitting him with quirts while Red Arrington was down on his head screaming. Pa walked up to the door. He was

162

weaving like an oriole's nest hanging to a topmost wind-swayed bough.

"Get out of here before you get killed," said the north door keeper to Pa. "You can't come through this door anyhow. Go around!"

"Who said I'd get killed?" Pa said. "Who said I was at the wrong door? I'm coming through."

> "To market, to market
> To sell a fine bull,
> Sherm Potter skinned Mick,
> And now he's full."

Professor Wentworth chuckled in childish glee and everybody laughed.

The keeper grabbed Pa. I knew that something had happened to Pa. He had imbibed of the spirits. This was something my father never did due to his bad heart and high blood pressure. Now he was going around and around with the doorkeeper.

"What do you say, Boss," Pa shouted.

"That's the old man that fellar cheated outten his bull," said a man near me. "Look at 'im now! He's in some shape!"

"I'm comin', Boss," Pa shouted.

"Do something with that bull, men," shouted the auctioneer into the loudspeaker.

"He's a mad bull," men shouted.

The small group of women sitting near me raced to the highest section of seats. They were screaming until I couldn't hear what Pa was saying. Pa tore himself loose from the doorkeeper and came inside. The doorkeeper was left holding Pa's coat. The well-dressed buyers were getting out of the way. Old, experienced cattlemen were running out of the market. They were going through doors and windows. For old Boss with one motion of his big head and giant neck tore

163

the bottom rail away to get to Red Arrington. Pa finally got over to Boss.

He rubbed Boss' neck and his forehead. Boss stopped when Pa touched him but the cattle buyers and traders didn't stop. They kept on trying to get out. The little auctioneer chinned himself up and was sitting on a higher seat.

"Walk like a man," Pa shouted. "Show 'im, Boss, who your master is!"

When Boss rose to his hind feet and folded back his stout forelegs, licked out his long red tongue and walled his big black shining eyes until they looked like living embers in the dark, the auctioneer went to a higher seat. Men poured out the doors and windows fast as they could go. Professor Wentworth ran to the last seat in the bleachers, up among the women, to pacify them. Their screams were frantic. Even Cousin Penny was scared. He was trying to run this way and that and he couldn't because there was always somebody in any direction he started. Flood Hall was trying to get out the door. Old Boss walked a few steps on his hind feet while the people screamed. They thought he was trying to charge. Little Pa, his face flushed ripe-plum red, walked around the circle with Boss.

"Do something with that bull," Flood Hall screamed. "Why didn't you tell me!"

"I'll give you three hundred for 'im, Flood," Pa shouted. "That's what you told me he's worth! I won't buy 'im by the pound. I'll buy old Boss back and take 'im home where he belongs. Won't I, Boss?"

"I've auctioned cattle thirty years and I've never seen anything like that," screamed the auctioneer. "Take three hundred for 'im Mister unless one of the bidders want him at twenty-three cents a pound!"

"The bidders are all gone now," Cousin Penny shouted.

"Get that dangerous bull out'n here," shouted Red Arrington. "Get him out before he turns this house over."

"What do you say, Flood?" Pa said. "You said a while ago Boss was worth that!"

Boss was walking on all four feet now. He drew back his tongue. "Get back up there, Boss," Pa shouted. "Show 'em you can walk like a man! But, Boss, I'm not tellin' you to go after any of these men that hit you with quirts, stabbed you with crooks and with whip stalks. If I did, Boss, you'd get 'em all right."

"You can take 'im for that," Flood Hall screamed. "Get 'im out of here!"

Flood was backed into a corner. He couldn't get out. He was scared of Boss. He was afraid, since Pa was feeling the spirits, that he would tell Boss to charge toward him and Boss would do it. For Boss was walking for the second time on his hind feet. Pa was walking beside him.

"Then you're mine again, Boss," Pa screamed. "Everybody heard me buy you back, Boss, and I got the money here to pay for you. It's the same money I got for you this morning, Boss. I'll have a little money left too, Boss!"

"Get 'im out," shouted the auctioneer. "Get 'im out so we can finish selling these cattle!"

"Come on, Boss," Pa said.

Boss dropped down on all four feet and followed Pa through the north gate. Cousin Penny and I went down from the bleachers as the people started coming back looking strangely at the little red-faced man leading the big two-thousand-pound bull with his hand. Old Boss followed him contentedly.

soddy

I followed my father down a cowpath under the sassafras and pawpaw bushes. "This is the last place in the pasture we have to look. If she's not hiding here I don't know where she is."

Little saw-brier vines raked my bare feet until I couldn't keep up with my father. He walked fast in front of me over the path old Gypsy had made, and after he'd take a few steps, he'd stop and look to his right and then to his left, under the pawpaw and sassafras, to see if Gypsy were hiding there.

"When a cow calves she hunts the best place to hide in the pasture," he said as he stopped in front of me where the path went through a thicket of brush and briers. "Here's the most outlandish place in this pasture for her to hide."

"Look, Pa!" I shouted. "Look behind you on the other side of the path! Gypsy and a pretty little calf. Look, Pa!"

"Now, don't get too excited," he said calmly. "You've seen calves before!"

"But not as pretty as that one," I said as I watched him stand up beside his mother on awkward spindly legs.

"I told you we'd find her in the best place to hide in this pasture," Pa said as he began breaking a path among the sumac, pawpaw, sassafras and stools of saw-briers, that vined among and tied the

bushes in clusters. "This whole pasture is a good place to hide. Not a clear spot for grass on the forty acres. Nothing but brush, briers and trees!"

I set my bare feet down carefully on selected spots of ground to miss the briers as I followed my father from the path to over where old Gypsy was washing her pretty calf. As she washed its face with her long tongue, she mooed gently. She was talking to the calf but it wasn't talking to her. It was standing with big dark bright eyes wide apart, wondering at the world it was born into. And when Pa reached them, Gypsy was not rude, but she wasn't too friendly. The calf smelled of Pa's pant leg to see what it was and then it gave a little snort and jumped back beside its mother.

"I hope it's a heifer," Pa said, looking it over. "It's a purty thing all right. No wonder old Gypsy is so proud of it. It's the color of these clay hills when I turn the sod over with a hillside-turning plow and it bakes in the mornin' sun. It's a soddy-color. But it's not a heifer as your Ma and I hoped it would be so we could raise ourselves another cow."

Pa's expression changed. He was disappointed. My father, a small, thin man with large sky-blue eyes, looked at the calf as he smelled of my overall leg and didn't jump back. I reached down and put my warm hard-callused little hand over his soft nose and he didn't mind that either. I could tell he liked me and I liked him. Old Gypsy must have thought it too. She warned him and warned us too with short loud blasts. Maybe she could tell Pa was disappointed. Maybe she didn't want him to like me. Maybe she was jealous.

"I'm goin' to call him Soddy, Pa," I said. "I like that name."

"No need to name 'im," Pa said. "We can't keep a bull calf."

Old Gypsy was a big bony cow with a pair of horns that curved in and almost met at the tips. She had big wild-looking black eyes that now shone in her excitement like embers

167

in the dark. She was as brown as a shellbark hickory leaf in October after it's bitten by the first frost.

"All right, Shan," Pa said, "let's drive her and the calf in to the calf pen. Let's get 'em out to the path."

Gypsy had had calves before and she knew she couldn't stay hidden. We drove her over to the path and Soddy trailed after her on his frail awkward legs, smelling of the earth, briers and leaves as he toddled along.

"Pa, can I have Soddy?" I said. Gypsy walked along the narrow path she'd made between bushes and the calf followed and Pa walked behind. "I'd love to have him."

"What would you do with 'im if you had 'im?" Pa asked. "Keep and feed 'im a couple of winters and then get a small price for 'im?"

I knew that Pa was going to do as he'd done before. I knew old Gypsy was nine years old. I was nine years old too. Pa and Mom got her, a tiny calf, the August I was born. They raised her by hand so they could have a cow. I never remembered the first calf she had. She had him when she was three years old. But the second, third, fourth, fifth, sixth calves I remembered. And Soddy was the seventh. The three male calves, I could remember, had been sold for veal. The three heifer calves, each we had planned to keep for a cow, were always sold to somebody else for a cow because we always needed the money.

And as Gypsy walked along and talked to Soddy with her plaintive moos, I thought she must know that she wouldn't get to keep him long, either, because he was a boy calf and all her sons had been snatched away from her in infancy and she never saw them again. I followed behind Pa as he walked behind Gypsy and her calf and a lot of thoughts went through my head.

I remembered how I'd taken Gypsy from the pasture to the house for Mom to milk. I'd done it since I was five years old because Pa was always at work on the farm. Each early

168

April, I'd take Gypsy to this pasture which was over a half mile from our house. In the afternoon at about five o'clock I'd go to the pasture, hunt her, loop a little rope over her horns, lead her to the drawbars where I could climb upon her back, and I'd ride her to the house.

I got to know Gypsy as well as my father or mother, our horse, our hound dog Rags and our small flock of chickens. Our chickens were named and I could call any one by its name. We rented Winfield Flaughtery's farm and it was down in a deep hollow surrounded by high hills. The sun crept in at midday. It was a lonely place.

And I thought about Gypsy's calves that I'd wanted to keep and none before had ever been as pretty as Soddy. But Pa and Mom couldn't keep them. And when they vealed one of her calves, Gypsy would follow the fence for three or four days and nights and bawl every two or three minutes, until she'd get so hoarse she couldn't bawl. I always thought she sounded like she was crying. And that's the reason I could never forget when Pa and Mom vealed one of her calves. We kept the heifer calves longer and she never cried so when Pa and Mom sold one of them to a neighbor for a cow.

When we drove Gypsy and Soddy to the milkgap, she stopped beside the gate on the calf pen which Pa had built four years ago when we first moved to the Flaughtery farm. Gypsy knew where to go. I opened the gate and she went inside and Soddy followed her and I closed it behind her.

"Now, keep water in the pan for this calf," Pa told me, "but don't give him any green grass."

"Then you're goin' to veal him!" I said.

Pa didn't say another word as we left Soddy in the pen beside Gypsy and she was talking to him. We walked down the path and up Ragweed Valley for home. And I never said another word to Pa. When we got home Pa went in the kitchen and told Mom Gypsy had a male calf.

"Pa, how much does a veal calf bring?" I asked, breaking the silence at our supper table.

"About twenty-five dollars," he said.

"We never got but nineteen dollars for the one we vealed last year," Mom broke in.

"I know, but this one's a better calf," he said. "It'll fetch every cent of twenty-five dollars. Maybe more."

I didn't say anything more at the table. I think Pa had already told Mom that I liked the calf and wanted to keep him.

After supper I walked back to the milkgap and took Gypsy from the calf pen as I'd done when she'd had calves before. When I drove her outside the pen and closed the gate, Soddy wanted out too. He wanted to be with his mother. He butted his head against the pole fence. But I patted his head and rubbed his neck and shoulders and he was very still. When he smelled of me I rubbed his nose and looked at his big bright innocent eyes that were filled with the wonder of his new world.

I took Gypsy home and Mom milked all the milk Soddy'd not taken, and that was plenty. For Gypsy was a great milk cow. She gave enough milk to fatten two calves the size of Soddy for veal. Mom didn't save the milk for the first nine days after Soddy was born. So for the first nine days I'd turn Gypsy in the pen to Soddy, morning and night, and then I'd take Gypsy home for Mom to finish milking. Then I'd bring her back to the pasture and she'd not got very far away from Soddy's pen all day.

Before I let Gypsy in the pen to Soddy and often after I took her out, I'd go inside to play with him. He'd look at me and shake his head. He'd act like he wanted to butt me. I'd put my head against his head. We'd butt each other—not much—but a little. I thought if he could speak my language and I could speak his, we'd called it playing-heads. He'd run around the pen kicking up his heels and I'd chase him.

Then I'd run around the pen and he'd chase me. But always before I left him, I'd rub his head, shoulders, back and side and feel the softness of his pretty sun-dried-clay-colored hair. And I'd look into his wondering eyes and he'd look up at me. And all the time I played with him, I'd think that he had only eight weeks from the time he was born to live.

After the first nine days I had to stay inside the pen and make Soddy stay on his side of Gypsy. He got exactly half the milk and I took Gypsy home for Mom to milk the other half for us. I always fed Soddy first because he would always be hungry night and morning. I kept a big kettle filled with fresh water from the stream that flowed through the pasture for him to drink. I took good care of Soddy and played with him every minute I could. And after the first nine days I started counting the days my calf had to live.

Soddy was my friend and playmate and the best one I'd ever had. Once I let him out of his little caged-up world and he followed me like a dog over the cowpaths running and playing, and old Gypsy was at our heels bawling something awful. I'd had dogs and loved them. I once had a pet coon that grew up and joined the wild coons in Ragweed Hollow. I had a pet ground hog too that dug a hole under our hearth and slept in it all winter, came out in the spring and got with other ground hogs and left. I had six pet squirrels once and they went back to the wild squirrels in the tall timber. I had two pet crows and they finally flew away and I never saw them again.

But I never had a pet I loved as much as I loved Soddy. He was more company than anything I'd ever known in the long months between January when school was over and August when school started again, except for my brother Finn, of course. I played with the dog, horse and chickens, and was friendly with Gypsy. And our chickens followed the horse and were friendly with him. And in the winter, when the horse wasn't working, and he and Gypsy were in our little

171

barn in separate stalls, they were friendly with each other. Often they whetted noses and stayed close together in our barnlot.

Then I got to thinking of some way to keep Soddy. I couldn't let him die. I couldn't stand to think about it.

"Pa, I want you to keep Soddy," I said one morning at the breakfast table. "He loves me and I love him. We were playmates from the first time we saw one another."

"Now, don't start that again, Shan," he said. "You've been poutin' around about my goin' to veal that calf from the day he was born. He's only a brute. He was born to be of some good to the human race. And all he's good for is to eat. He's a nice calf for veal."

Mom didn't say anything. Not then. She looked across the table at Pa and then she looked at me.

"I remember how Gypsy cried when you vealed her calf last year until you and Mom couldn't sleep," I said.

Tears came to Mom's eyes when I said this. Mom was full of sympathy for Gypsy.

"But that calf will be vealed," he said. "Now don't mention it again."

"I wish there was some way for you to keep him, Shan," Mom said.

"If I had twenty-five dollars I'd pay for 'im," I said. "I'd own him."

"If I had twenty-five dollars," Pa said, "I wouldn't veal him. That's just it. I need twenty-five dollars. I don't make any cash in the summer here except what we get for eggs. I've got to have twenty-five dollars in six more weeks to pay bills I owe in Greenwood."

"I can dig ginseng roots and sell 'em," I said.

"No you can't," Pa said. "Not now. Ginseng roots have to be dried well. You don't have time. Besides if I knew where there was any seng I'd dig it myself."

172

I knew where there was some seng but I wasn't telling Pa.

"How much a pound does it sell for?" I asked.

"Dave Dabney pays over six dollars a pound for it in Greenwood," he said. "But it takes a lot of seng roots to make a pound after they're dry."

Now when I went over the pasture hunting Gypsy, I took a mattock with me. I knew ginseng and I knew the coves where it grew. I'd let Soddy out of the pen and he'd go with me. He wasn't supposed to have anything but milk since he was to be vealed. But I didn't think his eating the green things on the earth would hurt him. Soddy didn't know, as I dug seng and he'd come up behind and butt me, that I was digging roots to save him. When Gypsy would hear him trying to talk to me in his language, she'd come running and we'd all be together.

I dug every four-prong, three-prong and two-prong and little one-prong I could find. I dug all the seng in this forty-acre cow pasture and yet it wouldn't have weighed more than two pounds. I didn't believe I could ever find enough and the days were passing. Soddy had only two more weeks to live when I finished digging all the seng I could find in the cow pasture. I had to think of something else while my seng was drying.

Since there wasn't any place for me to go on Sundays, here is what I did the last two Sundays Soddy had to live. I went to the Seaton Woods, a great wild range of hundreds of acres, and I found more seng. But it was green and the roots were heavy. Dave Dabney wouldn't buy it. Mom had tried to get Pa to let me keep Soddy but he wouldn't. Now I didn't have enough seng to make four pounds when it was dry and Soddy had only three more days to live. I had to do something in a hurry to save Soddy. I took my pole-ax and made another pen for Soddy. It was over the hill from our cow pasture down in a deep hollow where Gypsy couldn't hear him bawl and he couldn't hear her. I made the pen on Mel Shelton's farm. It was under the shade of the giant beeches, over a cool blue stream where Soddy could have all the fresh water he wanted. I cut a gap in Winfield Flaughtery's fence and made a little gate behind a blackberry thicket.

On the last day Soddy was to live I had him in this pen. Instead of taking Gypsy to his pen, for I thought she might give away the secret, I put her in Soddy's old pen and took Soddy to her, that night and morning. But that day when Gypsy walked the fence and cried after she missed Soddy, Pa said, "What's the matter with that cow?"

"I don't know," I said.

The next morning when Joe Tolliver drove up in his huckster wagon he had a long rope to tie Soddy to the slat-sides of his express-wagon bed. He, Pa and I went up to the pen to get Soddy. Gypsy was walking around the fence crying something awful lonesome to hear. When we went to the empty pen, I never saw an expression on anybody's face like Pa's.

"That calf's gone," he said, looking at me. "You know anything about it, Shan?"

"This morning before Mr. Tolliver came Gypsy gave him his breakfast right in that pen!"

"Are you tellin' me the truth?" he said.

"Yes, I am," I said.

"What do you know about this?" Pa said. "Reckon there's a timber wolf in this county?"

"Somebody might've stole 'im, Mick," Joe said.

That morning Joe went away without Soddy. And Pa and I went over the cow pasture hunting for my calf while Gypsy followed the fences and bawled. Mom told Pa it was so ordered for something to happen to the calf since I wanted to keep him for a playmate. But Pa didn't believe in tokens. He laughed at Mom.

174

For four days after Pa and Mom had missed Soddy, night and morning I took Soddy to Gypsy instead of taking her to him. I'd run to Soddy's pen and fetch him to Gypsy in a hurry. I couldn't let Gypsy know where he was. If she had known, she would have broken through the fence to him.

All the spare time I had, I hunted for more ginseng. I found a clump here and one there. I'd dig this seng, take it home and lay it upon our smokehouse roof to dry.

On the fifth day, which was a Saturday, I went to fetch Gypsy from the pasture. Pa had already taken the horse to the field to plow. When I walked up to Gypsy, who was standing by the pen waiting, I saw a light flash in her dark eyes. She saw something and I looked quickly in the direction she was looking. I saw Pa's brown sun-tanned face go down behind a clump of saw-briers. He had followed me. I pretended that I didn't see my father.

"Come on, Gypsy," I said. "I've got to take you home. Too bad, Gypsy, somebody's got Soddy. Maybe a timber wolf got him, Gypsy!"

Gypsy mooed to me. She didn't want to go. She wanted to give Soddy his breakfast. But I took Gypsy home for Mom to milk.

"She's not giving her milk down for some reason," Mom said. "She's not giving half the milk she's been giving."

That morning after I took Gypsy back to the pasture, she walked behind the pasture fence and cried. When Pa came home for dinner, he said, "It's a strange thing that cow has never taken on so until today." Mom didn't say anything and I didn't either. "Tomorrow is Sunday but I'm going to find that calf if he's still alive. I'll find his carcass if he's been killed."

That afternoon while I hoed potatoes in our garden, I thought about poor Soddy. He hadn't had any breakfast. But I knew he had water to drink for a little stream of cool water flowed through his pen. But I hated to think he had to go without breakfast. But then I thought it was better for him to do without his breakfast than to go to a butchershop. That's where he would have been if it hadn't been for me. I'd saved Soddy.

When I went to get Gypsy late that afternoon, Pa had already brought the horse home from the field. He had started to unharness him. When I got around the bend I took off running. I knew Soddy couldn't do without both meals in a day. I ran as fast as I could. I took a nearcut across the pasture to Soddy's pen. He looked lean and hungry and he butted me as I opened the little gate and let him through. He ran as fast as I ever saw him to the gate in our pasture behind the blackberry thicket. I let him through and he took off again. He knew the way to the pen where his mother fed him. And while Gypsy talked to Soddy, I watched the road up the hill to see if Pa was following me.

Sunday morning when I went after Gypsy, I never bothered to fetch Soddy to her. I knew Pa was somewhere in the pasture. He had gone to look for Soddy. When Mom milked Gypsy she wouldn't give her milk down. When I took her back to the pasture she walked around the fence and bawled. But I didn't stay long at the house. I told Mom where I was going and that I wouldn't be back until later afternoon that Sunday. Mom looked strangely at me as I went away with a sack and mattock.

In the Seaton Woods I went from cove to cove. I went down in the deep valleys where the yellow poplars were fifty feet to the first limbs and the dark loamy earth was covered with peavine. Here I found patches of ginseng by old rotted logs and stumps and around the cliffs. I never stopped hunting ginseng all day. I went from one patch to another. And just as the sun started going down behind the tall trees, I'd filled my paper floursack. I knew now, when the roots dried, I might have six, seven or eight pounds. I had enough to pay for Soddy.

When I got home, Pa walked across the yard.

"Where 've you been, Shan?" he asked me.

"To the Seaton Woods," I said. "Look here!"

I showed him what I'd found. He said, "I've never seen anybody find that much seng at one time!"

Mom came out of the house and walked across the yard.

"Did you find Soddy?" she asked Pa.

"I've been everyplace," he said. "I never found that calf. I went around the cliffs and I never saw the carcass of a dead calf. I know that calf was stolen from that pen. Somebody got 'im. I'd like to know who that somebody was."

Then there was silence among us as Mom looked at Pa and then at my ginseng sack.

Mom said, "Old Gypsy walked that fence and bawled most of the day. I've never heard her cry so mournfully as she has today. She cried until about three o'clock. I went inside the house and shut the doors so I couldn't hear her."

Then Mom started smiling as she looked down the valley. I turned and looked in the direction Mom was looking. Pa looked that way too. Gypsy was coming up the valley with Soddy tagging beside her.

"What do you know about that?" Pa said.

Then Pa, Mom and I started to meet Gypsy and Soddy. When we met them, Gypsy and Soddy stopped and we did too. Gypsy looked at us with her big dark eyes and Soddy came up to me and licked my hand with his long sharp tongue. Then, he started butting me. He wanted to play heads.

"What will you do with Soddy now, Mick?" Mom asked.

"He's had green pickings," Pa replied. "We can't veal him."

"Pa, sell 'im to me," I said. "I've got enough ginseng to pay you fer 'im now, I've got over four pounds when it dries out. I might have fifty dollars worth of seng. I'll give it all to you for Soddy!"

Pa was always a man of few words. He had always been a

firm man. When he said anything he meant what he said. But something came over Pa now as he watched Soddy put his head against mine and we butted one another. Maybe it was the first time Pa had ever seen a calf play with a boy.

"Shan, I'll sell that calf to you," Pa said. "But I won't take all your seng. I want what I asked for the calf, twenty-five dollars. If you have fifty dollars worth of seng, you keep the rest of your money. If you don't have twenty-five dollars 'worth you dig more and pay me. I'm a man of my word."

Then I pulled Soddy up close to me and put my arms around his neck while he shook his head and butted at me and licked out his long tongue. Mom looked at me and the calf and then she looked at Pa and smiled. Pa's eyes had a different light in them and his face had a softer expression. Old Gypsy stood there and watched Soddy and me too. She was as contented as I had ever seen her.

of yesterday

I told Bob that I had put away enough wine. He went into the smokehouse to get more. Everybody knows Bob around here. He's been on Tiger River all his life. People ought to know him. His sandy hair is always bobbing up and down on his hatless head. His face is always September oak-leaf red. His teeth are not all there in front. His eyes are blue shining pools of water on the sand. Bob gets around slow as a mule. I like to hear him laugh.

"Where's the wine," said Bob, as he swaggered through the door of his house into the room where the fire was crackling on the wide-open fireplace. Bob laughed. Evelyn nodded for Bob to take the wine out. I remember how he laughed. I remember how the blue-wine beaded in the pitcher. I remember the taste of the blackberry wine, how I held the glass to my lips. I remember how the words came out of my mouth when I asked for more. They were shapeless words and hard to get out past my lips but I got them out.

I could see Evelyn, Bob's wife, as she moved through the dim-lighted room. Evelyn was tall and slender. Her clothes fitted her tight around the waist. Her sleeves were loose at the wrists. Her hair was black. It was wound up like a wad of paper on the back of her head. I remember how she walked through the room. She took my empty glass and the pitcher from the table where Bob and I were sitting. When I looked at Bob he laughed. I remember it.

Evelyn came back through the room. She had grown a foot. She spun around enough to make me dizzy. But I remember Evelyn. She took Marion from the chair—little sandy-haired rascal, he'd been hitting me with a rubber ball. She took him to bed upstairs. He moaned in his sleep. Bob just sat there and laughed. Evelyn looked so tall as she went wagging that boy to bed—the biggest boy I ever saw just to be four years old.

"Don't go to sleep," said Bob pulling at my coat sleeve, "Fred and Roscoe will be here after a while. They're comin' with the dogs and guns. We're goin' to Lost Creek to that good bird country."

"How can we go to Lost Creek when it is dark as tobacco smoke. It is night. Fire lights the room. It is dark as pitch outside. We can't shoot birds when it is dark. Scare them up and shoot them in the moonlight? Get a bird between you and the moon you might shoot it. I'm afraid to hunt in the night with shotguns. I might shoot somebody's cow out grazing for acorns. Acorns will dry the milk up in the cow's udders too."

"Fred and Roscoe are comin'," said Bob, "and they are goin' to bring Fleet. She is the best pointer in these parts. Fred has a pumpgun. Roscoe has that old automatic Smith Fields used to have. It will be fun to see old Fred shoot. He thinks he's in a schoolhouse teachin' youngins. W'y he can't hit the side of a barn. You can beat him, Shan. You can do that. You can shoot a bird when it buzzes like a bumblebee out of the dead grass."

"I can hit a bird in the daytime when it buzzes from the dead grass, Bob. But I can't shoot a bird when the wind is dark. I can't shoot in the night. I can't hunt with a double-barrel shotgun by the light of the stars and the moon. I might shoot Fred. I might shoot Roscoe."

"They are here," said Bob. "They are here. Hear the T Model Ford down by the gate? They have come. Hear them talkin'. Roscoe's all tuned-up to shoot birds I'll bet a dollar."

I heard the voices. I could hear them plain. Bob left the room. He must have gone to get the shells. Evelyn came in through the side door. I could see her as plain as I could see my hand resting on my knee. Evelyn had grown another foot taller. Evelyn was like a corkscrew now. "Here's some good wine, Shan," she said to me. "That wine Bob made is not as good as this. Try it and see for yourself. This is golden wine. I made it from the dandelions that grew behind the smoke-house. I made the wine last April."

Evelyn handed me the glass. I loved Evelyn that minute. Just think she slipped the wine to me. It was good wine—golden wine. I must not love Evelyn. She is Bob's wife. She knows wine. She knows what I like. Bob gave me blackberry wine. Bob has gone out of the room and left me. He has gone after the gun, shells and a hunting coat. It is time for Bob to be back. Roscoe and Fred are at the gate.

Evelyn took the empty glass and walked back through the side door. She was another foot taller. I watched to see if she would get through the door without bumping her head. She made it all right. I'd hate to be that much higher than the rest of the women in this world—higher—yes—higher than the men. Her head was up out of the rain if there was rain falling.

Bob came through the front-room door. "Here is the coat," said Bob as he handed me a coat streaked around the pockets with blood. "Here is Bill Lawson's little twenty-eight-inch double-barrel. I got it for you. You must do some high-powered shootin' or you'll not be able to get a bird with the rest of us fellows today. Here's your coat. Here's your shell-vest."

Good old Bob. He handed them to me. I put on the vest. A shell dropped on the floor. I picked it up and put it back in

181

the hole, the shell emptied when it fell. Bob's a good fellow. He just laughs too much. It spoils his looks when he laughs. He laughs all the time. He laughs when he looks at me. I picked up the gun. It was light—too light if the shells had any kick to them. It would jump all over my shoulder. We had to hurry. Bob opened the door. I saw Fred standing at the chip yard. I saw Roscoe beside of Fred. He was resting his gun on a block of firewood.

"First time in my life I ever went bird huntin' at night," I said to Bob. "We'll get shot. We'll sprinkle each other with shot. We'll get sprinkled with shot. It's dangerous huntin' with a crowd anyway. Four's a crowd. I've always liked to hunt by myself. I never did like to hunt with a crowd. Four men make a crowd. I am afraid."

We walked out of the door. I stepped from the top to the bottom step. I remember. I was afraid the gun would go off and shoot a hole through the roof of Bob's house. It didn't go off. I could see the frost on the ground. I could see Fred standing there. He was talking to Roscoe. I could read the words he said. They spelled out letters on the wind. His breath was white and when he spoke it wrote the words until I could read them.

"We have been waitin' a long time on you," said Fred. His face was chubby and red as a pepperpod. His eyes blinked like two cold stars in the sky. He looked like Santa Claus. He just didn't have a pack—a little short, heavy man with a long blue gun across his shoulder. He was dressed in brown—a heavy fur collar stood up around his neck.

"We've been gettin' ready, boys," said Bob, "we've been slow about findin' the shells. We found them. Shells are things a fellow needs most when he is huntin' birds. A fellow can't do without shells. If you try to shoot wind in a gun barrel you'll come home with your coat empty."

"You are quite right," said Roscoe. His black eyes twinkled. He looked from behind big glasses like an owl and blinked his eyes. "If you shoot wind in a gun barrel you are liable to kill a calf."

"This is a funny huntin' party to me. It's about the funniest I ever saw," I said. "If you don't mind I'll go back to the house and watch the fire burn the wood. We have more fire than matches at Bob's place. The fire might go out. Where would we go to get some fire? We don't have any matches."

"Come along with us," said Fred. "This is goin' to be a real huntin' trip. Up on Lost Creek the birds are thick as grasshoppers. It's a little cold handlin' a gun-barrel in the frost. Watch and don't get your tongue to the steel. It will hold your tongue till it thunders and jars you loose. We need you with the party. You won't get any birds with that double-barrel. We'll sack the quails."

"Turn Fleet loose," said Bob, "and she'll soon have us among the quails. She's the best in these parts." Roscoe unsnapped the chain from the collar with the bright trimmings. Fleet ran toward the hill behind the house. I could see her go. She is a big dog. She has black ears and a brown face. She has a light blue body with black spots over her body. Her tail stands straight out with her backbone when she trots. Long hair hangs down from her tail. Fleet is a pretty dog. I remember how she ran toward the hill.

"We'd better scatter, boys," said Roscoe, "if we want to roust the covey that feeds here at the corn field's edge. There's a covey of fat birds here. I know there is. I shot into them the other day. I got two. Gun clogged on me. I guess the birds were glad o' it."

We scattered as we took to the hill. I went to the left. The white frost glittered on the leaves. The air was the color of tobacco smoke. The moon in the sky might have been the sun, the sun in the sky might have been the moon. A dead leaf in the wind might have been a bird. A bird might have been a dead leaf.

I remember old Fred as he waddled up the hill like a fat duck. I could see his gun across his shoulder. It was blue in the smoke-colored wind. It was bluer than smoke. I remember little Roscoe running through the brush and tramping the brush piles to scare out a rabbit. I remember Bob following close to Fleet as he could.

"Pow-pow."

It was Bob's gun barked. "Just a rabbit," said Bob. "Just a rabbit. You take it, Fred. I don't care to kill rabbits when I'm huntin' birds. It was just such a pretty shot I couldn't keep from takin' a pop at it as it topped the bank."

I could hear the guns. I could hear them pow-pow. I never saw a thing to shoot. I tramped the brush pile. I couldn't find a thing. I could hear their guns get further and further away—just a rumbling in the distant broom-sage, the corn fields and the woods. I could still see the blood on the ears of the rabbit Bob killed. I could feel the wind on my face. I could see the dead leaves on the trees. I could see the moon in the sky if it was night. I could see the sun in the sky if it was day. I couldn't find a rabbit. I couldn't see a bird. Bob had Fleet with him. He must be getting plenty of birds the way the guns were popping behind the tumbled hill covered with red-brush and saw-briers.

I sat down on a log. I was tired. Old words came to me. I said them over. I laughed like Bob laughed when I thought of these words:

> "Hunters' luck:
> Wet tail
> Hungry gut."

I saw the weeds shaking. It must have been a rabbit. I put my gun to my shoulder. I saw it coming. It looked like a fox. I took good aim. I looked again. It was a dog. It was Don. It couldn't be Don. He had been dead for three years—my dog that had hunted these hills over and over again with me. It

184

just couldn't be him! But it was Don—the white on the tips of his brown ears. The white spots above his eyes. The long hair on his legs that made him look like he was wearing a pair of rabbit-skin leggins. It was Don. He had a quail in his mouth.

"Good old Don," I said. "Good doggie! Bring me the bird like you used to do, boy!" He just wagged his tail and looked at me. He held the bird in his mouth. He wagged his tail. He was the same thin dog he used to be before the flower-pot fell off the porch and hit him on the head. He afterwards took running fits. Finally he took a fit under the poplar tree in the kitchen yard. He ran round after his tail 'til he tumbled over—quivered and died. This was my dog.

He jumped all over me with his front paws. He held the bird in his mouth. He used to bring the birds to me. I would knock down five out of six shots nearly every time in fair shooting. Don never stopped until he found them all. He would bring them one by one and lay them down by me. He whined and laid the bird at my feet. He jumped up and kissed my face. He barked and he made little circles like he was chasing his tail around through the dead broom-sage. He was the same old Don he used to be. I picked up the bird and put it in my hunting coat. On the other hill I saw the blue smoke swirl from Roscoe's gun. I saw a bird fall. I heard Fred laugh. I heard him shoot. I heard him say: "W'y Bob I can't hit the side of a house. You boys know that. I can't get my gun on the right apex to shoot straight and fast. When I was over in France I did better shootin' than this."

"Pow-pow-pow." I heard them shoot. It sounded like a battle. I saw the birds rise from the broom-sage. I heard the guns. I saw them fall like as if all the life went out of them and each bird was just a rock that was tossed up in a curve and fell straight down to the earth. I heard Bob say: "I got that bird, Roscoe. You can't claim that one."

I knew I was not dreaming. I was not dead. I was not asleep. My gun barrel glistened. The dead leaves fell from

185

the trees. The wind rippled the dead grass. Briers pulled at my pant legs. Crows flew over the fields. Crows swarmed around Alf Pennix's fodder shocks. I thought once I'd shoot into the crows. Then I thought I'd let them have a little of the lost grains of corn and fill their craws up. Winter was coming on and corn was hard to get. Don was here. Everything was real. Same old Don-Sequal. He started for the briers. He wiggled his tail. I'd get the birds now. I knew I would. I had the dog.

I saw Don-Sequal. He had pointed a bird. His paw uplifted. His tail wiggled just a little. I walked up with both barrels cocked. Oh, how I needed a Winchester now. I just had a double-barrel. The birds flew up. I shot both barrels into the covey. I never saw so many birds. They fell like leaves from a tree. It seemed as if they all fell from the bright blue autumn air. It was one of the best shots that I ever made.

"Bring them to me," I said to Don.

He went to work. Once he carried me two birds. Then he went back seven trips and brought me one each time he went back. I got nine birds. Don brought me one. I had ten birds. I had shot twice. What luck! We followed the way the covey flew. We hadn't found where they flew into the brush. I saw them light at the far edge of a corn field in some blackberry briers. They hit the ground running. Don pointed again. I threw out my empty shells. I reloaded. I walked up close to where Don wiggled his tail just a little bit. The quails flew up like a flock of blackbirds. I emptied both barrels into the big covey. They fell from the air like leaves. I couldn't tell how many I had killed. But I had brought them from the air.

"Bring them to me, Don," I said "Bring them to me, boy."

He started carrying the birds to me. I sat down on a rock. He carried one at a time. He brought me twelve loads

of birds. Some of the birds were very pretty. I tried to find
out how many shots I had put into each bird. I looked while
Don fetched them from the broom-sage. I found two that I
had just put one shot into each bird's head and had killed it.
They were not shot to pieces. They would be good birds to
eat. I would get more birds with Don than Roscoe, Fred and
Bob. I could hear their guns pow-pow in the distance. They
were just doing a lot of shooting maybe and that was all.
When Don brought me the last bird he jumped a rabbit from
a clump of bushes. I was reloaded. I shot once. The rabbit
turned over and over. Don ran and fetched me the rabbit.
Twenty-two birds and one rabbit. I would have two coveys to
follow now. Don ran ahead. He hunted the brier thickets at
top speed. I had to remember how I used to have to carry
him home after a day's hunt. He would hunt 'til he fell. He
had never been a strong dog. He would only eat warm biscuit
bread and drink warm sweet milk. He had a bad stomach. We
thought he was going to die several times. But a better dog
never went into the autumn fields for quail. A better dog
never went into the tall walnut timber for squirrels. I remember he sent seventy-seven squirrels to their death in one
season. I had their tails hanging on the gable end of the corn
crib and the mice gnawed the fleshy ends to pieces. On nights
he would tree opossums. There were other dogs better than
Don for opossums, minks and polecats. But he would get his
share of them. He was a vicious dog for all his thin body
could stand. He killed one ground hog that was larger than
he was. He had killed one ground hog a few days before he
died. Now he was back with me and we were getting the
birds.

We crossed a Plum Grove hill. We didn't follow the
coveys to their lighting places. We hunted for new coveys. A
covey used to feed last summer by the big sycamore tree
where the footlog crossed the creek. We went down there. I
kicked the old stumps and the brush piles to scare out a

187

cotton-tail. I never jumped one. But I saw Don down by the sweet apple tree that stands where the road forks to go to the Plum Grove church house. He had found the birds. I saw his paw raised in the bright blue air. He was pointing toward the black-haw bushes. I ran fast as I could. I had both hammers back on my gun. As soon as I got there the birds buzzed right out in front of me over the meadow. It was a pretty shot. I pulled both barrels.

I reloaded and fired again. I think the whole covey fell down upon the close-cut meadow. I saw the tiny birds fluttering on the grass. Don ran out and brought me a bird at a time. He would run under the fence and back to me with a bird. I stayed in the big road and got them as he went under the fence and picked up sixteen birds from Cooper's meadow. I now had thirty-eight birds. My hunting coat was bulging out. I would have to throw the rabbit away if I killed many more birds. I was getting tired of carrying such a heavy load. I hoped he wouldn't find any more birds. I would hunt back toward home. I would cross the Wheelers' field and down over the Collins' hill. I had gone to Lost Creek to hunt but I'd rounded back among my own Plum Grove hills. It's hard to cross Wheelers' fields without finding birds. I saw Don run over in the weed patch where a little branch runs off toward Shackle Run. I saw him stoop down. He pointed. More birds. I walked down over the young green wheat. The birds flew out—right over my head. I fired both barrels among them. They fell fluttering over the green wheat. Only a few buzzed on through the bright blue fall-time air. I helped Don to pick up the birds. We picked up thirteen birds this time. My hunting coat sagged with fifty-one birds. I had three miles to walk home.

We started for the Collins' hill. I talked to Don and kept him with me. I didn't want him to hunt any more. I would have to carry him, a gun, a rabbit, and fifty-one birds and I would have a load. That would be too much. I couldn't make it. I'd started to feel the walk and the load in my legs already as I climbed the hill. Don pointed by a stack of rails. I ran out beside the rail pile. I saw the quails in a huddle. I could have killed them all on the ground. I didn't do it. I let them have a chance for their lives. They flew into the bright air against the sun. I aimed and fired both barrels. The quails fell like leaves from a peach tree after the September frost bites the leaves. Birds fluttered all over the ground. Don picked them up one at a time. I sat down on a rail pile and put them in the hunting coat. I killed nineteen birds. How could I get them all in my hunting coat? I had seventy birds and a rabbit. Don was too tired to hunt more. I was too tired to carry any more birds. I saw a quail come walking up the hill toward me. It was one that I had crippled.

"Get it," I said to Don. He jumped for the bird. It flew at me. It flew in my face, it knocked my hat off. I shot at it when it flew on over my head. I missed it. It flew at my face again. Don-Sequal jumped at it but it was too high for him. It was too close to my head for me to shoot at. I hit at it with my hands. I said "shoo-shoo" to it. But it kept coming. I struck at it 'til my arm got tired. Then my left arm got tired hitting at the wind. I never could hit the quail. I never heard of a quail fighting a man before. This quail was fighting me. I got so tired that I couldn't fight any longer. Don gave out too. I just sat down. I gave up like a sheep. It would fly down and pluck a hair out of my head. It would throw it down and pluck out another. It was making me bald-headed. I couldn't help it. I hollered for Fred and Bob and Roscoe. My head was feeling cool in the wind. I screamed. No one answered.

Marion was pouring water on my head. I was at home. There was Roscoe. He was leaning back in the chair laughing. There was the empty wine bottle.

A cool rain was falling. The leaves had been swept from the trees by the wind. Up on the hill in the mule pasture was Don's grave. The rain was falling on the bright yellow clods.

The rails would be there still if I'd go and look. And the mules couldn't tramp over his mound. I didn't want to go and look. I had been with Don and we had had a long hunt together. We had journeyed back over the Plum Grove hills the same old route we used to take and get the birds. He had kissed my face and my hands and had brought me a bird from the woods. It was good to see Don again. It was good to see his paw lifted in the blue autumn wind. It was good to watch him carry birds to me. We had hunted again together over the hills at home.

angel in the pasture

Shan slowly closed his eyes and entered a beautiful world long past, with sun he could not hold in the sky, flowers he could not keep fresh on their stems and sumac leaves he could not keep from going into an autumn season, coloring and dying and blowing hither and thither in the autumn winds.

The sudden flight of a pheasant from the cluster of saw-briers at his feet startled him. He stopped suddenly to watch the big bird rise up on its whirring wings to go over and down beyond the brush fence that enclosed the pasture field. He'd scared this rooster pheasant up, and often his mate with him, many times before. But he'd never found him in this part of the pasture where there was a grove of pine seedlings. Saw-brier clusters grew among these young pines and he had to be careful where he stepped since he was barefooted.

The sun was getting high in the blue sky and he'd not found the cow yet. Gypsy was hiding. He'd been down in the deep Burns Hollow where the tall beeches grew. He always went there first in the mornings to see the gray squirrels. They fed early and went into their hollow dens in the giant beeches long before the morning sun had dried the dew. Squirrels hunted their breakfast early and long before the old ones had returned he had sat under the den trees and watched the young squirrels come out of the holes and play on the big, leafy branches.

He also knew where the wild birds' nests were, redbird, ground sparrow, song sparrow and thrush. He'd found a whippoorwill's nest once on a big leaf under an oak and he'd found a hummingbird's nest, too. He knew the crows had their nest in a tall pine and the chicken hawks had their nest in the bushy top of a giant white oak.

He could find all these birds' nests and he'd always been able to see snakes before they saw him. But Gypsy was hard to find in this forty-acre pasture. That's why he always came here ahead of his mother. She had her morning housework to do before she could come. There was a place where he always drove Gypsy for his mother to milk. That was the big white oak which was once a shade tree. The old Burns house was deserted now and the big, bushy-topped white oak didn't shade anybody but Gypsy, his mother and himself.

"Shan! Oh, Shan!" his mother called. "What's keepin' you so?"

His mother's voice wasn't so pleasant. He'd know her voice anywhere and any time. He'd been a little slow this morning, watching young squirrels, listening to young hawks and crows when their parents fed them. He liked to stand under the trees and listen to the voices of young crows and hawks. He'd tried to catch the old hummingbird on the nest, but she'd always fly off and whistle through the air like a bullet. Like the whine of a .22 rifle.

"Shan, Shan, do you hear me?" His mother called louder this time. "Answer me, Shan! What are you doing? Have you found the cow?"

"No, Mom," he replied. "Gypsy's hidin' some place. I'll find her in a few minutes. I've been over all the pasture nearly!"

"You've had time enough to have been over all the pasture two or three times," she said. "I'll find the cow myself."

When she said this Shan knew he'd not have time to

throw sailing rocks and arch them up, over and down like the rooster ringneck pheasant had flown. He wouldn't have time now, since his mother had come, to talk to the birds, squirrels, hawks and crows, and pretend he was a brother to them. He talked to everything when he was out in the woods alone.

As he stepped between the saw-brier clusters he touched the small pines with his hands. There were dewdrops on the pine-tree needles. These dewdrops weighted them like little lumps of polished silver until the sun lifted them skyward in white ribbons of mist. There were dewdrops on the red-tinted sand-brier leaves, on the hard stems of the sand-briers, on the milkweed and silkweed leaves that were shaped like stiff hogs' ears, only they were green. And the bright wind above him was filled with streamers of mists.

Shan knew his mother was hunting for Gypsy, too. But he could not help but stand and breathe the fresh wind of June and drink the white mists into his lungs. This pasture field was wonderful! He'd never seen it prettier and he'd been hunting Gypsy here for two springs and summers. He wanted to be among the good wind, songs of the birds, beauty of flower, leaf and brier forever.

If only I could command the sun to stop where it is in the sky and hold all the white mists where they are in the air, Shan thought. *If I could only keep the birds singing like they are singing now, and keep the soft, warm June winds blowing. If I could keep the pasture daisies as white and the wild roses as pink as they are now. If I could keep the saw-briers in clusters with red-tinted leaves and the little pines and sumacs the same size as they are now! If I could make this pasture and this world and time stand still I'd do it!*

His father was thirty-five years old, his mother thirty-three, and they were very old and very wise to him. He was nine years old in 1916, and he loved everything about it.

Shan stepped from the grove of miniature pines which was parented by a tall seedling pine standing in their midst.

At last he stepped into the narrow little path made by Gypsy's tracks. The path made a sharp U-turn where a sweet-apple tree grew. And around this turn stood Gypsy, picking up the blighted sweet apples that had fallen.

"Go on there, Gypsy," Shan yelled loud enough for his mother to hear. "What are you doin' hidin' from me?"

"So you finally found her," Shan's mother said. She had come into the path behind him, and he was surprised to see her pleased and smiling. She was five feet eleven inches tall; her hair was black as the crows' wings, her eyes were gray as the bark on the poplar tree and her teeth were as white as daisy petals.

"Come, Shan," she said. "Let's get the milking done."

While his mother milked, Shan stretched himself out on the ground to look up into the white-oak leaves. When the wind rustled the leaves he could see the blue sky and the changing leaf pictures.

He couldn't keep the pine seedlings from growing into saw-log timber. He couldn't stay the hunters' guns from pheasants, crows, hawks and squirrels. He couldn't hold the wild rose and the blooming daisy beyond their seasons. He couldn't keep the young spring wind blowing over him. He suddenly wanted his mother to finish milking. He listened to hear her say, "Shan, let's be goin'." For he was waking from this dream world he couldn't hold into a world of reality.

Instead of a warm, June wind and green leaves above him there was a clear, cool tent. That wasn't his mother standing there. Reality. His mother no longer milked Gypsy under the white oak. She rested at Plum Grove. This wasn't 1916. Dream world or real world, there was one thing he was certain of: he had been with an angel in that pasture.

3 ❧

Night and The Whippoorwill

sir birchfield

We were delighted when our friends, the Birch-fields, wrote us they had an orphaned pedigreed cocker they would like to give us. They assured us he was a splendid pup and would make a lovable pet.

We never had this type of dog in my father's home. His dogs were always practical—hunting dogs, hounds, shepherds, curs, feists and mixed breeds. They hunted, protected the house, barn and sheep or, like Sir Robert, the shepherd, went to the pasture to fetch home the cows.

When Naomi Deane and I were married, three dogs from my father's home upon the hill followed us the half mile to our house in the valley of W-Hollow. They went back to my father's place every night to climb up a ladder to the barnloft and sleep in the hay. But they spent their days with us, since we fed them. Sir Robert was an old dog even then. And when he died at the age of four-teen, he disappeared. We never found his remains. Then, there was Jerry-B Boneyard, a mongrel. Due to a cancer on his shoulder, we had to have him put to sleep. He was nearly fifteen. And the last of the three to die was delightful Trusty Red Rusty, a pedigreed Irish setter. He lived to be fifteen, but old age caught up with him at last. And now, would a cocker take the place of the rugged dogs we had all our lives? I wondered.

We thought the young cocker would be a nice pet for our daughter Jane. I wrote the Birchfields that we wanted him. Soon after, I received a telegram informing me that the dog had been expressed from Virginia to Ashland, Kentucky. Immediately, Naomi, Jane and I hopped in the car and started out to pick him up. When we got to the Express office, sure enough, we found a wooden crate with as pretty a little white cocker puppy with honey-colored spots over his body and freckles on his nose as we'd ever seen. It was a warm spring day and he'd been put outside where the air was fresh. He had been sick on the journey and now felt lost and bewildered. When we looked through the cracks at him, he barked at us. He had come from a good home, one where he had

been fondled and loved but he didn't know that where he was going he would get equal attention.

After I signed the necessary papers, the Express man helped us open the crate. I took the scared little cocker and put him in Jane's arms. I don't know if Jane, Naomi or I became more attached to this little bob-tailed, long-eared, cocker pup. We loved him. And he loved us from the start.

Jane got into the back seat of our car with her puppy. As we drove along, we discussed names for him. We decided Naomi's idea was best. We would call him Birchfield to remind us of our friends who had given him to us. So, Birchfield it was.

His first night with us, Jane wanted Birchfield to sleep

in his box in her room. During the night, he woke up and cried and Jane did the same. Naomi and I got up and comforted Birchfield. Naomi took him in her arms, and in a few minutes he was fast asleep. He was very tired after his long journey. Now he was among strange people and in a strange house. Since we got up at 5 A.M., Naomi and I were awake before Birchfield. When he heard us walking through the house, he began whining and scratching on the sides of his box. On that first morning, when Naomi, sleepy little Jane and I sat around the breakfast table, we let him run around the dining-room table. We had various kinds of puppydog food we had purchased for him in advance. Naomi experimented to determine the kind he would like best. He ate all four kinds but he preferred one to the others. And he liked milk. He was a greedy little puppy who would eat almost anything, and he would have eaten far too much if Naomi had let him.

After breakfast I took Birchfield out in the yard to show him his domain. Our yard extended to the hillslopes and there were no fences. Land spread out in all directions with no houses close by. He would have over 700 acres on our farm and with other farms adjoining ours, his playground was almost limitless. But we soon learned he wanted to be only in the yard and wherever Jane went. He seemed to understand that she was a child and he a puppy; he acted at first as if he belonged to her. He played with her in the yard and followed me about the house and yard. But when I left the house, walking up or down the W-Hollow road, he would turn and go back. He was a beautiful puppy, a bundle of white and golden fluff running in the April wind over our grass-carpeted yard. He soon learned his name and became housebroken.

At night, when we put Birchfield in his box, he didn't want to go to bed. He would start crying. Then we put him up on Jane's bed. For weeks he slept at the foot of her bed, until Jane unintentionally kicked him off in her sleep one night. He was terribly offended and came into our room crying. I lifted him up into our bed. He slept between Naomi and me. This was the first time in my life I had ever slept with a dog. My father brought us up never to let a dog even come in the house. He said there were houses for people and houses for dogs. They should be friends but live apart. We permitted Jerry-B Boneyard to come in and lie before the open fire. Later, he went back to my father and mother's home and tried to sneak in. My father wondered how he failed in training Jerry-B Boneyard. He learned when he came to our house one morning and caught old Jerry-B napping before our open fire. Now we were permitting Birchfield to live and sleep with us, something we never told my father as long as he lived.

Since I had stopped hunting and posted my land, wild game came into our yard. Birchfield didn't know what wildlife was. When we fed the birds grain on the back yard sidewalk, he discovered that if he ran toward the birds they would fly up, and it gave him a superior feeling to have something else be afraid of him. So we built boxes up high where our birds could feed and Birchfield wouldn't run them away.

In the early part of Birchfield's first summer, he saw a snake for the first time. A fine looking bull black snake crawled down the hill and started across our yard to go to the creek for water. Birchfield ran playfully alongside the snake. The snake stopped, coiled, and struck at him but missed. Birchfield barked as if he had been bitten and came running to me.

Then, there were little ground squirrels that denned behind the rock walls of a stream that flowed under our house. Birchfield soon learned he could chase these little squirrels. We didn't like him to do it and I scolded him. When three of our chickens flew over the woven wire of their acre lot,

Birchfield ran after the big strange birds as fast as his short legs would carry him, while I hollered for him to come back. If he heard me, he didn't pay any attention! When the chickens saw this bouncing fluffy ball coming at them, barking at every breath, they took off in three directions. He followed one up Shinglemill Creek where our pasture fence crossed the valley. The hen got through the fence all right, but Birchfield's long ears caught on the barbed wire. He howled and I went running. He had split one ear and the other had a long four-inch tear. I picked crying Birchfield up in my arms and took him in to the house. Naomi and I drove him to the animal hospital where the veterinarian, Doctor Martin, sewed up his ears.

He made his second mistake when a big male possum came to our back yard expecting us to feed him as we had done for a long time. Birchfield ran up to greet the possum, as though he were another dog. But the possum knew, or thought, all dogs were his enemies. When Birchfield stuck his little freckled nose up to the possum's long sharp nose, the possum opened his mouth and then clamped down on Birchfield's nose, holding it in a vice-like grip. I ran over to them and made the possum let go. When it released Birchfield, he ran toward the house howling. He never had any use for a possum again.

Then, by playing with a wasp on the ground, and having it sting him on the nose, he learned bees weren't suitable playmates either. But, after he'd been with us two years, Birchfield became educated in country lore. He learned who were his friends and who his enemies. He discovered that certain big cattle with horns cared little for a dog. And when I went to look at cattle and Birchfield was with me, I'd pick him up in my arms and hold him. In this position he was very brave and barked and jumped at a cow who stuck her nose up to me in a friendly way.

Each week, spring, summer, fall, or winter, from the

time he had come to us, Birchfield got a bath and had his hair combed. Afterwards he was given a raw egg beaten up in milk—a delicacy. He spent much of his time following the streams, jumping down into the water after minnows and salamanders. In his second summer with us, we took him fishing over on the Tygart River. He ran along the edge of the water, wading out and catching bits of wood or a leaf and retrieving them for me. We fished all afternoon. Jane caught only a little fish, too small to take home, and we threw it back in the river.

When we walked up through Matt Hall's meadow on our way back to the car, a very large shepherd saw us and came running toward Birchfield. Birchfield ran toward the big shepherd, as he had once run toward the chickens in our garden. All my yelling didn't stop him. The shepherd met him with mouth open and teeth bared. Before I could get to them, Birchfield had the shepherd by the neck. The shepherd took off across the meadow into his own yard with our Birchfield still holding his throat, his feet not even touching the ground. And I ran after them to get the two dogs apart. Birchfield's teeth must have been hung in the shepherd's long hair; he had bitten the shepherd's neck and it was bleeding. He was glad to let loose and get into my arms again. When I took Birchfield away, the shepherd slunk off shamefully around the house with his tail between his legs. After this incident I knew Birchfield was no coward. He could whip any dog his size in the whole area.

Some months later, we had to take Birchfield to the hospital again. He had teamed up with some bad company when he joined a female dog and her suitors. The suitors all were larger than Birchfield and they chewed him up and left him for dead. Old Opp Akers found him beside the road and carried him to us. We took him back to Doctor Martin. This time he was in the hospital a week and emerged as good as new.

In the early summer of 1949, Naomi and I took a European tour and Jane stayed with my brother. We left Birchfield at home and had my nephew, Gene Darby, come down to our house and feed him. Naomi and I spent almost three months away. When we returned it was mid-September and Jane was back in school. We stopped by the schoolhouse to take her home. She cried when she saw us, but when Birchfield saw us he cried even more. "He beats any dog I have ever seen," Gene Darby told us. "He never left this house and yard. He's looked for you to return every day since you've been away." Then Gene pointed out the little path he had made across the hill above our house. "See, he gets up there, walks over onto the garage roof and then climbs from the garage roof onto the top of the house. I've seen him sitting up there by the chimney looking up and down this valley for you to come home."

Birchfield loved all the people who came to see us. When our friends wanted to take pictures, he thought he had to be in them too. He soon learned to get close to those whose pictures were being taken instead of the photographer. When Earl Palmer came here to photograph this area, he couldn't get Birchfield out of camera range. He took a picture of Birchfield and me under a walnut tree, which my mother had set when we lived at this place and I was nine years old. How many times this picture of me and Birchfield has been used on bookjackets, in textbooks, magazines and newspapers I cannot estimate.

Birchfield was not separated from us again until I had a heart attack in 1954. I spent nearly two months in the Murray Hospital. Naomi came to Murray and brought Jane. Back home, Birchfield kept vigil from the rooftop of our house, patiently looking down the valley for our familiar car to come up the lane. People who were strangers and passed our way were amazed to see a white dog on our housetop. On a few nights when Birchfield kept a late watch, those who saw him in the darkness got scared, ran away and said they had seen a white ghost.

When I came home and went to bed, Birchfield found my room. I wasn't permitted visitors but I was permitted Birchfield. He seemed to know something was wrong with me and spent half of his time on the bed. The rest of the time he spent with Naomi in the kitchen and running over the house. Birchfield was seven years old then, the average lifetime of a cocker, and in equivalent man-years he was forty-nine. He was beginning to look so dignified, I thought he should have an honorary prefix to his name. I called him Sir Birchfield.

I spent the great part of 1955 in bed. Each morning Sir Birchfield came to my room and hopped upon the bed, wagging his stubby tail faster than I could count. Since I was permitted some hard candy to hold in my mouth I always kept a few pieces in my pajama pocket. Sir Birchfield, who liked candy very much, always checked to see if I had some. If I did, I just gave it all to him, for he wasn't content as long as I had a piece in my pocket. Since he was getting a little older now and wasn't as rowdy and rambunctious as he had been in his youth, he would often put his head on the pillow beside mine, stretch out and fall asleep. And he would snore. Naomi said she often came in my room and found us both fast asleep and snoring.

In early winter of 1956, after spending much time in bed, and taking my daily rest and sleep, I began getting up very early. I went to the kitchen and fixed my breakfast. Then I put on my sport coat and filled all the pockets with feed for the wild birds, squirrels and rabbits. Before the break of day, I was off up W-Hollow. Birchfield went on my early morning walks a few times, but he was very jealous of all the birds, who recognized me as their friend and flew in from the hills for me to feed them. He would chase away my birds, rabbits, ground squirrels and gray squirrels. Now that he was older and slept more soundly and snored louder, I usually tiptoed past the garage where he slept at night without his noticing. But, if I woke him I had to turn around and go back to the house. When I went inside, Sir Birchfield came with me. He woke up Naomi and Jane, insisting that everyone get out of bed and join him. He liked to be near the breakfast table, and sat on the floor while we ate, having his breakfast from a bowl at the same time.

One morning when I went out to the garage to see why Birchfield hadn't got up, I met him on the sidewalk dragging his hindparts by inches. He didn't cry or whimper but looked up at me with asking, sad brown eyes. I picked him up in my arms and carried him into the kitchen. I wondered if somebody had run over him with a car in front of the house or if someone could have shot him. Naomi, Jane and I went over his skin to see if we could find any buckshot wounds. He'd not been shot. So, I put him in the car and took him to the animal hospital. Sir Birchfield had been there many times before and he didn't like to return. We were afraid this could be the end for our affectionate Sir Birchfield.

"This is something that's more prevalent in species of the bird dog family," Doctor Martin said.

"Will he walk again?" I asked.

"Well, he's ten years old now," Doctor Martin said. "He's old for a cocker. I'm not sure that he will. Although one can never tell!"

This time Sir Birchfield spent three weeks in the hospital. When we visited him a couple of times he was delighted to see us and cried when we left. When we brought him home, he was really a happy dog. Doctor Martin warned us about overfeeding him and getting him overweight. He could stand up but he had little use of his hips. Very often he dragged one of his rear feet. And sometimes he'd fall over and we had to lift him up. But by constant trying and exercising his hind legs and hips, he gradually got so he could walk fairly well again by the spring of 1958.

When I was approached to teach at the University of Nevada in Reno, in the summer of 1958, we puzzled about what to do with Sir Birchfield. We knew he was too old to leave alone at home and he wouldn't be happy anyplace else. We were leaving in early June and would not be home until September. My nephew, Gene Darby, was living in W-Hollow with his new bride, Hilde. Since she loved dogs and was especially fond of Sir Birchfield, we asked them if they would live in our home and look after the property and the dog. They agreed.

After our return in the autumn, Sir Birchfield was much better but age was slowing him down. He went with me on walks and on drives. I had firelanes made with a bulldozer that could be used as little roads for a pickup truck. I took Sir Birchfield up on the seat of the truck beside me. And he and I rode every day over the farm. Sir Birchfield looked out like a little man and if I didn't lower his window, he pawed the glass until I did. He became very attached to the pickup truck. Then, Naomi found a green rug he liked very much. Despite his weekly combings he shed white hair all over the house. Now, when we moved from room to room we took his rug with us and he shed only on the green rug that he knew belonged to him.

We left home again in July 1960 for a year of teaching in Cairo, Egypt. We kept in contact with Gene and Hilde, who were again taking care of our home, our dog, and our horses. When we returned Sir Birchfield was as well as could be expected for his age and ailments. He greeted us at the end of the walk and followed us slowly inside the house.

In August we took him back to the hospital. "His heart isn't doing its work now," Doctor Martin told us. "This weight isn't caused by overfeeding. Fluid has gathered." We left him in the hospital for a week and when we brought him home, he looked like himself again. But in a few days he began swelling up again. When Naomi sat down in the house he was always beside her lying on his green rug. When she went outside he followed her. In his last days it was obvious that Naomi appealed to him more than anyone else. In the fall we had him back in the hospital for three weeks. When we went to pick him up, I asked Doctor Martin if there was any diet to hold his weight down and prolong his days. He shook his head. "Give him what he wants."

One afternoon, while I was at Ben Webb's home, Naomi called to say Sir Birchfield was dead. "Sir Birchfield has just died on his green rug at my feet of a heart attack. He rose up, struggled for breath and fell over. He went like that. Come home. I'm terribly upset."

Ben went home with me. I didn't want to see Sir Birchfield lying dead on his green rug. Ben wrapped him up in the rug, carried him to the garage, and placed him in his bed beside the furnace. The next day we had him buried, still in the green rug, under a pine upon the hill in our yard. This was one of his favorite spots. After he was laid to rest, we agreed not to get another dog. His death was like losing one of our family. We thought then and still believe we could never have another dog so devoted to us.

When Naomi and I went around the world on a lecture tour the summer of 1962, we had to provide pictures for advance publicity. I was also asked for pictures of our home and the farm. When we searched among our old photos, we could find very few pictures that didn't include Birchfield.

In Iran we found pictures of our home, of us and Birchfield on bulletin boards at the places where I was to speak. And when a picture of me was used in a newspaper, it was one with Birchfield beside me. When people there, who are curious about anything American, asked me about the things we left behind, they asked me about Birchfield. I knew I couldn't tell them they were old pictures and Sir Birchfield had died nearly a year ago. He had to be a living symbol.

Everybody talked about our beautiful dog, even in Iran, a predominantly Moslem country where dogs are not cherished as they are in America.

Everywhere a picture of me was displayed in Egypt, it included Sir Birchfield. Even in Cairo and Alexandria where homeless dogs sought refuge in the desert, Sir Birchfield occupied a place of honor. In Greece, the Philippines, Formosa, and Korea, it was the same. In West and East Pakistan, where dogs are not popular and are left to forage for their food, our dog drew attention. I realized Sir Birchfield wasn't really dead at all; he was alive, alive on our Journey Around the World.

old lollipop

In Cairo, Egypt, we lived in one of the best residential areas in an apartment overlooking the Nile. We were the only people in the area with a picture of a cow on our mantelpiece. My wife was a little reluctant to have the photograph of Old Lollipop, a Kentucky hill cow, so prominently displayed.

Our Old Lollipop was different from the cows of Egypt. She didn't look anything like one of their water-buffalo cows. She was part or all Guernsey. Maybe it was her magnificent pair of horns that aroused curiosity. In our large color picture, Old Lollipop was standing on the ridgeline of a green Kentucky hill with white clouds in the background. She was a magnificent animal, standing as solid as a stone and looking forward with her jet-black eyes. Her face was half white and half dark brown, and there were white spots on her brisket. Her long horns came out past her forehead and the points of each horn curved in until they almost met.

Old Lollipop wasn't just an ordinary cow. She was unusually wild, and didn't like being petted. Back in 1936, when I was a single man living with my parents, I used to milk Lollipop. She was young Lollipop then. And she was the best milker among our eighteen cows. Her milk was the richest in butterfat, too. Young Lollipop didn't like my father, and he didn't like Lollipop. They were both of the same high-strung nature. And when Pa asked Lollipop to stand still, if he raised his voice, she'd kick the bucket out of his hand. Many times I saw her wallop a big three-gallon bucket of milk. My father would get up from his milk stool, and what he said about Lollipop couldn't be quoted. Then Mom would rise up from her stool in defense of the cow. My father accused this young cow of being queen of the herd, because of her horns. And every year from 1936 until Mom's death in 1951, he threatened to have her de-horned. But there was sort of an unwritten law at our home that heifers and cows were allowed to keep their horns while steers and bulls must lose them. When my father talked about de-horning Lollipop, he met stiff opposition from my mother, even though it was true Lollipop used her horns as a two-pronged weapon to boss the herd.

Lollipop bossed all our steers, too. They followed her over the pasture as if she were their mother. Our big horses, Doc and Bess, never bothered her. When they got together in the barnlot on winter evenings, they often lay their ears back and ran at the cattle to frighten them. Once I saw Doc, who weighed exactly one ton, open his mouth, bare his teeth, and run toward Lollipop. She braced her feet, stuck her horns forward, and stood like a stone. Doc came up close and suddenly stopped himself, to avoid her horns. Then he turned and went in another direction. She was Queen of the Herd.

My father refused to milk Lollipop; he always by-passed her. She'd shake her head and horns at him. "I wouldn't have that cow," he said. "She's a good cow, all right, but she is dangerous with that pair of horns. She's such a disagreeable animal."

I learned the best way to milk Lollipop. It was a good idea not to set a bucket under her and milk with both hands, as I did the other cows. She was a one-hander and didn't like to be rushed. I also learned all animals, especially cows, have personalities just as people do. But I had never seen another cow with a personality like Old Lollipop's. No matter what extra rations Mom put into her feedbox, if a dog came close when I was milking she'd leave her feed and run after the dog. In those days we had Trusty Red Rusty, who had learned not to come close to Lollipop. Once she lifted him over the barn-lot fence with her horns. We had Sir Robert, who would go a mile into the pasture and bring the cows in at milking time. But he never got close to Lollipop. He brought all the other cows, and then Lollipop followed. Then, there was Jerry-B, who could whip any dog his size, kill a poisonous copperhead or a mountain rattler, but he too learned not to bother Lollipop. He once attacked her, and she pinned him to the ground with her horns.

My father made a rule at our home. Every one of us had to learn to milk a cow. My sisters and brother could milk. Each of them learned when he was big enough to sit upon a milk stool. Now two of my sisters were married and my father extended his rule to his grandchildren. When I married Naomi in 1939, one of the first questions my father asked about her was: "Jesse, can she milk a cow?" When I told him she couldn't he was disappointed. He wanted to teach her, but she refused.

When Naomi and I had our own home, I often went back to my parents' to help milk Lollipop. Old Lollipop's first two heifer calves had become cows. They were good cows, but neither daughter equaled her mother. People asked in advance for Lollipop's heifer calves. This pleased my father, for her bull calves brought very little on the market. Although we kept an excellent Hereford bull and all the other calves from our cows were well-marked, Lollipop's calves always looked like her. Not one ever showed any Hereford markings.

World War II came and we closed our house. We were

in Washington, D.C., for two years, but we never lost contact with Lollipop. My mother sent us golden butter made from her rich milk. When I went home on leave, I walked through the pasture fields on my way from the railway station. Each time I met some of the old cattle and some new ones. Old Lollipop always came within fifteen feet, stopped and looked at me with her wild eyes. She knew me, all right, but she wasn't as sentimental about my coming home like some of the cattle. Other cows tried to lick my face and hands with their scratchy tongues. And Doc and Bess put their chins over my shoulder and nibbled playfully at my ears. But when I walked on toward the house Old Lollipop was the only one to follow me, though she always stayed fifteen to twenty feet behind.

After the war was over and we went back to W-Hollow, my nephew and niece, Gene and Nancy Darby, went to live with my parents. Gene, though a very small boy, had taken over my job of milking Old Lollipop. My father was still complaining about her horns. One of the last journeys my mother ever made before she was taken in an ambulance to the hospital where she died was to get out of bed, go to the barn to see about Old Lollipop and her little heifer calf. On Christmas Eve, 1954, my father made his usual trip to the barn to see about Old Lollipop and his other animals. It was for the last time. This was the day of my father's death.

For the next month, Gene Darby took care of Lollipop. Then Gene was inducted into service. My brother-in-law sold all the cattle, except Old Lollipop and the horses, Doc and Bess. Old Lollipop was the only cow on our farm. She was lonely. She ran with Doc and Bess, always keeping her distance from the horses, whom she didn't like or trust. The feeling was mutual. Old Lollipop and the horses were given the range of four pastures. The gates were opened so they could go from pasture to pasture. The horses were turned out

213

on grass. Lollipop was turned dry, never to be milked again and never to have another calf. She was at least twenty-two years old, and maybe twenty-three or twenty-four.

In the summer of 1956, I bought forty head of yearling Hereford steers and three young bulls. I had to put cattle back on my pastures to keep them from growing up in grass and sprouts. Old Lollipop became Queen of the Herd immediately. When I walked up the valley to the pasture, I often saw her walking proudly in front leading the herd out to graze in the morning. In the afternoon, I saw her lead them back toward the salt blocks. Here they licked salt for a while before retiring for a night's rest under a grove of oaks near the barn.

In February 1957, an incredible thing happened. I found Old Lollipop in the pasture with a little newborn calf. I carried it to the barn to keep it from freezing. If my father and mother had been alive, they wouldn't have believed Lollipop could have another calf.

That summer Old Lollipop ran with the herd. Since no one milked her and she gave a great quantity of milk, we had a problem until we bought another young calf so she could suckle two. Two calves were hardly enough for this old cow. Although she liked the steers very much, when one came near either of her calves she would charge at him. He lost no time in getting away. In the autumn when I sold my herd, I sold Old Lollipop's two calves for baby beeves. Again Old Lollipop and the horses had the pasture all to themselves. I knew we would keep Lollipop as long as she lived. Several cattle buyers tried to purchase her for a "canner cow" to sell on the market for a small price. But I knew she would never go to a slaughterhouse. She would die a natural death here. And we would bury her in that spot of pasture over which she had walked so often. This was Lollipop's land, the land she loved.

But seeing her alone on the pastures, having outlived her owners and friends, hearing her lonesome bawls for those she must have remembered, cattle and people and the many calves she had had, I decided to put some cattle with her for company.

Now I was determined to get better cattle. So I bought a truckload of Hereford heifers. Then I bought a bull. Each Hereford I owned had a name as long as my arm. I was deeply impressed by the pedigrees of my cattle. When I said I had an old cow with horns that I wanted to let run with my herd, I was told it should not be done. But when I added that the cow was about twenty-five years old, they told me it wouldn't matter.

So I left Old Lollipop with my purebred cattle. And when heifers and bull went out into the pasture, they followed her. Again she was Queen and very happy.

In 1960, Naomi, Jane and I left for our stay in Cairo. I got reports on my animals and each time one of my heifers calved. Then I got a surprising letter from my brother-in-law, who had thought Old Lollipop dead. He searched over the 300 acres of pasture before he found her. She was in the most obscure part of the pasture, a dark woodland that was filled with deep ravines. The dense spring foliage was a green curtain behind which she was hidden.

"I've fixed a special stall for her in the barn," he wrote me. "She had a wonderful calf and she's so proud of her. This is one calf we are going to keep. She gives so much milk, I've had to buy another calf for her. How old is she, anyway?"

I couldn't tell him her exact age. I had milked her in 1936 and it was then 1961. She had to be twenty-seven years old at least and maybe more. I could hardly wait to get home from Egypt and see Old Lollipop with her new calf.

hot-collared mule

"Keep that mule a-goin'," Pa hollered as I passed by where he was sitting on a log under the shade fanning himself with sourwood leaves. "Run 'im until he's hot as blue blazes!"

I couldn't answer Pa. My tongue was out of my mouth and I was getting my breath hard. If you have never owned a cold-collared mule then you wouldn't understand what a job it is to run one long enough to get him hot so he'll work in the harness. What you do when you run him is put a collar on him and run along behind and slap him across the back with the lines when he begins to slow down.

The bad thing for Pa and me was, we had a mule we couldn't ride or work until we got his collar hot. Pa had tried to ride him. Pa went over his head when he bucked and came down belly-flat on the hard road in front of the mule, knocking all the wind out of him. When I had him galloping, he stopped suddenly with me. I bounced up in the air like a rubber ball. It was done so quickly I couldn't come down to the ground on my feet. I came down a-sittin' in the middle of the road. And I sat there seeing stars. Of all the trading Pa had done, he'd never got a mule like Rock.

"He's a-gettin' warmed up," I grunted to Pa as I passed him on the second lap.

"Fetch 'im around agin and I'll take 'im," Pa said. "Just be keerful and don't do any hollerin'."

If I had wanted to holler at Rock I couldn't, for I was so short of breath. I was running Rock up a logging-road to the turn of the hill; there we turned right up a cowpath that wound up the hill and connected with another logging-road which ran parallel to the one below and then turned perpendicular down the hill and connected with the first road. The circle of narrow road looked cool, for it was bordered by culled trees whose clouds of green leaves sagged in wilted pods. These leaves were so thick they not only obscured the sun but they kept out the little August breeze that idly swayed the wilted pods of leaves. It was a close smothery warmth down under the trees that heated up a man faster than it did a cold-collared mule.

"All right, Pa," I grunted as I came in on my last lap. "It's your time now."

"Hit'll be the last time one of us has to run this mule," Pa said as he took the lines.

I dropped down on the log where Pa was sitting and picked up the sourwood fan. Sweat ran from my face like little streams pour from the face of a hill after an April shower. I'd run Rock three laps around the circle. Now Pa would run him two. Pa couldn't run as well as I could, for he was older and his legs were stiffer and his breath came harder. While I sat fanning, I watched him go out of sight, running stiff-legged like a cold buck rabbit in the wintertime. The twist of burley leaf was jumping up and down in his hip pocket as he made the turn to climb the hill.

"Hit's a hard way to git a mule to work," Pa grunted as he passed me going into his second lap.

I was fanning fast as I could fan. I had cooled down some, but my clothes were as wet as if I had jumped into the river.

When Pa came around on his second lap, I didn't think he'd make it. But he did. His face was red as a sliced beet, and

217

his clothes were as wet as mine were. But a sweaty foam had gathered under Rock's flanks and his shoulders were wet around his collar.

"He's in shape to work now," Pa said as he dropped to the ground. "I'll wind a minute before we hitch 'im to the drag."

But Pa didn't wind very long. He sat there long enough to catch his second wind. We couldn't wait until Rock's shoulders cooled. We threw the gears over his back, hitched a trace chain to the singletree, and let him draw the log chain to the dead oak that Pa had chopped down for us to haul to the woodyard.

"When Cyrus sees my mule pull a log like this," Pa said as he wrapped the log chain around the log, "he'll swap that good mule o' his 'n and give me ten 'r fifteen dollars to boot! See, this log 's heavier than Rock. He'll be a-pullin' more than his weight on the ground," he went on as he fastened the log chain around the drag. "I'm a-goin' to ast 'im twenty-five dollars to boot. Then, maybe, I'll drop to fifteen dollars. Remember, I'm through runnin' a cold-collared mule. My ticker ain't good enough fer it and my legs won't stand."

"It's some job for a young man," I said

"All right, Rock," Pa said, slapping him with a line. "Git down and pull!"

Rock squatted, braced his feet, and pulled, shaking the big log from where it had indented the hard earth. Then, without Pa's telling him, Rock pulled again, and the big log started sliding along while sparks flew from his steel shoes.

"If he wuzn't cold-collared I wouldn't trade 'im fer any animal I ever laid eyes on," Pa said, holding the lines up from the briers.

I walked behind Pa as he drove Rock toward our woodyard.

Maybe our timing was just right. We pulled into our

woodyard under the sour-apple tree just as Cyrus Broadfoot rode his harnessed mule up and stopped.

"That's some log, Mick," he said.

"Well, it's purty good-sized," Pa said. "But Rock's pulled a lot bigger logs than this 'n. I'll pull 'im agin any mule of his pounds. Do you want to pull your mule agin 'im?"

"Not necessarily, Mick," Cyrus said, dismounting his mule.

"I thought if you wanted to hitch yer mule to my mule's singletree, we'd let 'em pull agin each other," Pa said as he unhitched the log chain from the drag. "If yer mule pulls mine backwards," Pa went on, "I'll give you my mule. If my mule pulls your mule backwards, then ye give me yer mule! That's fair enough!"

That was the way Pa always started a trade. He would always put the other fellow on the fence. He'd set a price, give or take. And he'd trade at sight unseen. That's how we'd got old Rock. He'd traded with Herb Coloney. Herb told Pa he had a mule that could pull his weight on the ground. That was enough. Pa traded him a two-year-old Jersey bull and got ten dollars to boot right there. Now he was going after Cyrus.

"I don't keer much about tradin' that way, Mick," Cyrus said, pulling a big knife from his pocket with one hand as he picked up a stick with the other.

"Yer mule's bigger 'n mine," Pa said.

"I know that," Cyrus said, whittling a big shaving. "But he ain't as old."

"How old is yer mule?" Pa asked.

"Rye's a-comin' five in the spring," Cyrus said, his words muffled as the sound of his voice was strained through his big mustache.

"Rock ain't but four," Pa bragged. "He ain't shed his colt's teeth yet."

219

Then Pa picked up a stick, pulled his knife from his pocket, and began to whittle. While Pa whittled big shavings from a poplar stick, Cyrus opened Rock's mouth and looked at his teeth.

"He's still got his colt's teeth all right," Cyrus said. "Don't ye want to look in my Rye's mouth, Mick?"

"I'll take your word fer his age, Cyrus," Pa said, whittling away. "Ye've allus been a good neighbor and a truthful man!"

Pa's words didn't please Cyrus. Maybe Cyrus was thinking about the last time he had traded with Pa. Pa had said these same words and patted Cyrus on the back when he sold three steers for a hundred and forty-three dollars. Cyrus kept them all that winter, put them on grass next spring and summer, and sold them late in the fall for a hundred forty-four dollars. He knew Pa was a good trader, the best among the hills.

"Jist how much boot are you a-goin' to ast me, Mick?" Cyrus asked.

"Tell you what I'll do, Cyrus," Pa said, laying his stick and knife down so he could pull his galluses out and let them fly back like he always did when he was trading. "Since it's you, I'll take twenty-five dollars to boot and trade."

"That's a lot of boot, Mick," he said.

"Won't take a cent less," Pa said.

"I won't give you a penny," Cyrus said, whittling a long shaving.

"I'll tell you what us do," Pa said. "Let's split the difference!"

"Okay," Cyrus said.

Cyrus pulled a ten-dollar bill, two ones, and a fifty-cent piece from a Bull Durham tobacco sack he was carrying in the little watch pocket on the bib of his overalls.

"Jist a minute," Pa said, before he took the money. "That means we're trading harness too!"

"Right," Cyrus said.

Then Pa took the money. I knew Pa had got a barg'in on the harness. Rock's harness was wrapped and tied in many places with ground hog-hide strings.

"You've got a pullin' mule," Pa said as Cyrus picked up the rope lines to drive Rock away. "He's the only mule in these parts that can pull his weight on the ground."

Then Pa looked at me and winked. I knew what Pa meant, for Cyrus didn't know how we had to run old Rock to get up steam. In a cold collar he wouldn't pull the hat off a man's head.

"I'm satisfied, Mick," were Cyrus's last words as he drove Rock up the hollow.

I wasn't sorry to see Rock go.

"Now we've got a mule," Pa said. "We'll hitch 'im to the express wagon and take that load of melons to town."

With all the confidence of a strutting turkey gobbler, Pa drove Rye to our express wagon. He was proud of his trade, and I was too. I never wanted to see another mule that I had to run to get steamed up like I had to run Rock. I never wanted to see another cold-collared mule.

Our express wagon was loaded with watermelons and parked under the shade of a white oak in our back yard. When Mom saw Pa backing the new mule between the shafts she came out at the door.

"I told ye, Sall, I'd have a new mule to take these melons to Greenup," Pa bragged. "I really set Cyrus on fire in that trade! I really give 'im a good burnin'. One he'll never forget!"

"I guess it's all right to do that, Mick," Mom said. "Men do such things. But one of these days you're goin' to get a good swindlin'."

"Not me," Pa said, laying the lines down and pulling at his galluses. "I've made you a good livin', ain't I?"

"Yes," Mom agreed by nodding her head.

"And I've done hit mostly by tradin', ain't I?" Pa went on bragging as I hitched the trace chains to the singletree.

"Yes, by cheating people," Mom said. "I feel bad about Cyrus Broadfoot's six little children. Never have a pair of shoes on their feet all winter!"

Then Mom turned around and went back into the house.

"Funny how softhearted wimmen are," Pa said as he fastened a chain through the loop while I fastened the other. "If wimmen had to make a livin' and men stay in the house, wouldn't that be funny? Could ye imagine yer Mom out a-mule-swappin'?"

Pa laughed at his own joke as he climbed upon the express seat and I climbed up beside him. With a light tap from the line, Rye moved the loaded express wagon across the yard and down the road toward Greenup. Pa sat straight as a young poplar with his whip across his shoulder and a chew of burley leaf under his sun-tanned beardy jaw.

As we drove down the sandy jolt-wagon road, I never heard such bragging as Pa did. He talked about the trades he had made in his lifetime, how he had cheated people from the time he began mule trading. That was when he was sixteen. He would tell about cheating people, then he would laugh. And when he spoke of how he had traded a cold-collared mule to Cyrus, he would bend over, slap his knees with his hands, and laugh until people walking along the road would stop and look at us.

"When old Cyrus starts runnin' Rock..." Pa would never be able to finish what he started out to say for laughing. He laughed until I had to take the lines and drive so he would have both hands free to slap his knees.

"Old Cyrus will get hot under the collar," Pa went on. "I can just see old Cyrus a-takin' off behind old Rock...."

The tears rolled from Pa's eyes down his sunburnt face.

"Wonder if he'll know what's the matter with..." and

Pa got down on the load of melons and rolled around like he was crazy.

At first it was a little funny, but after I thought about what Mom had told him I couldn't laugh any more. And I was ashamed of him the way he rolled over the watermelons, laughing. The people we passed would stop and look at him like he was out of his head. I'd never seen a man in my life enjoy a barg'in like Pa was enjoying his trade with Cyrus.

And Pa had made a barg'in, for Rye pulled the load easily and smoothly along the jolt-wagon road until we reached the turnpike. Now we were on the road to Greenup, where we would soon sell our melons. When we reached the turnpike where there were more people traveling, Pa got back on the seat beside of me, put a cigar between his beardy lips, and took the lines. He would never chew burley when we got near town. He would always light up a cigar, though Pa enjoyed a chew more than he did a smoke. He thought he looked more important with a cigar in his mouth.

Rye had pulled steadily along for three miles or more, and now I noticed there was foaming sweat dripping from his flanks and oozing from beneath his collar and dark shades of sweat on his sleek, currycombed and brushed brown hair over his ribs. Pa didn't notice the sweat on Rye. He just sat upon the high springboard seat with a whip over his shoulder that he carried for an ornament, a cigar in his mouth to make him look important, and looked down at everybody we passed.

"Pa, you'd better let Rye take it a little easy," I said. "He's gettin' pretty warm!"

"A mule can stand an awful lot of heat," Pa said, driving on.

But when we reached the Lottie Bates Hill, Rye braced his feet and wouldn't move a step.

"Wonder what's wrong with Rye?" Pa asked me.

"I don't know," I said.

"He needs a little ticklin' with the whip," Pa laughed,

223

pulling it from over his shoulder and tapping Rye on the back.

Then Rye started going backwards, shoving the express wagon zigzagging from one side of the road to the other.

"Slap on the brakes," Pa shouted to me.

I put on the brakes as quickly as I could and stopped the wagon. People passing us along the road started laughing. And Pa was really embarrassed. His sun-tanned face began to change color into a pawpaw-leaf crimson.

"He's a mule that goes backwards," a man said, laughing.

"Somethin's wrong with the harness," Pa said. "Here, take these lines. I'm gettin' down to see what's wrong."

I held the lines while he started to examine the backband and the trace chains. When Pa put his hand on the backband, Rye kicked up with both hind feet and squealed.

"What's the matter with that mule?" Pa said, jumpin' back in a hurry while the strangers walking home with loads on their backs stood at a safe distance and laughed. "He acts like he's crazy. I'm sure it's his harness hurtin' 'im or a blue-tailed fly on his belly."

"See if the bridle bit is cutting his tongue," I said.

When Pa started to open his mouth to look, Rye lunged forward with both front feet in the air and tried to hit Pa, but he side-stepped just in time.

"That mule's dangerous," Pa wailed. "Git this near town when we can see the smoke from the chimneys, then he acts up like this!"

The words weren't out of Pa's mouth when Rye lunged forward and I pulled back on the lines. Then he started going backwards and the express wagon started rolling down a little hill. The endboard came out and the melons rolled like apples from the wagon bed, down the hill into Town Branch.

"There goes our melons," Pa moaned.

Twenty people, who had stopped to enjoy our trouble,

all made a run for the melons that were broken and ruined. While all of them but one old beardy-faced man ran for the melons, Rye jumped forward again, veered to one side, and broke the shafts from the express.

"Hold 'im," Pa shouted.

"I'm doing my best," I said, rearing back on the lines until I brought the mule under control.

And now it worried me not so much that the people were eating our melons, but that I was providing entertainment for them while they ate. They could hardly eat our melons for laughing at us. But Pa puffed harder on his cigar and there was a worried look on his face.

"Say, stranger," the old man with the beardy face said as he slowly approached Pa, "I don't want to butt into yer affairs. But I'm an old mule skinner. I ust to drive a mule team when they had the furnaces back in this county. I drove mules fer forty-three years and hauled cordwood," he went on talking, "and I can tell ye what's the matter with that mule. I've seen four 'r five like 'im in my lifetime!"

"Hit must be his harness that's a hurtin' 'im, Dad," Pa apologized for Rye.

"Nope, that ain't it, stranger," the man said. "He's a hot-collared mule!"

"Never heard of a hot-collared mule," Pa said, throwing up both hands. "I've heard of a cold-collared mule!"

"Well, that's what he is, stranger," the old man said. "Somebody's give ye a good burnin'. He's sold ye a hot-collared mule. And this one is a dangerous animal!"

I looked at Pa and he looked at me.

"And I can prove to ye he's hot-collared," the old man said.

"How can ye do it?" Pa said, turning around to face the old man.

"Take this bucket and go down to the crick and get a bucket of cool water and throw hit over his shoulders," the

225

old man said, as he emptied his groceries so Pa could use it. "Ye'll see that he'll pull when he gits cool shoulders!"

"I'll try anything," Pa said. "I'd like to git my express wagon back home."

Thirty-five or forty people who had now gathered to eat our watermelons looked strangely at Pa when they saw him dip a bucket of water from the creek. They watched Pa carry the water up to the road and throw it on Rye's shoulder, while the mule stood perfectly still as if he enjoyed it.

"It'll take more water," the old man said.

While the people laughed at Pa carrying water to put on a mule's shoulders like he was trying to put out a fire, I thought of what Pa had said about Cyrus's having to run old Rock to get up steam. And the people with watermelon smeared on their faces laughed at Pa more than he had laughed at Cyrus. But after Pa had carried the tenth bucket of water the old man said, "That's enough now, stranger. Ye've put the fire out!"

And when the old man smiled I could see his discolored teeth through his thin dingy-white mustache.

"Now try to drive 'im, young man," the old man said to me.

"Get up, Rye," I said, touching his back lightly with the lines.

The mule moved gently away, pulling the express wagon with the broken shafts which made it zigzag from one side of the road to the other. And when I stopped the mule, Pa came up and said, "It's a new wrinkle on my horn. I never heard of a hot-collared mule but we've got one. We'll haf to wire up these shafts someway until we can git home. I'll haf to do some more swappin'. Yer mom was right."

the chase of the skittish heifer

Mules weren't the only animals that Pa thought he knew a lot about. He was also an expert on cattle. You take Jake Remines' heifer, for instance. . . . From early spring to late autumn, Pa carried salt to the hundred cattle in the big pasture. He'd carry seventy-five pounds at a load up the steep mountain to the long salt trough he'd made of hollow logs. He had cut down hollow trees and split them with wedges, trimmed each split log neatly with a double-bitted ax, and fastened them together. It was a long trough resting on foundation rocks so the cattle could stand side by side and lick salt.

This salting trough was the place where the cattle met in the big pasture field. It was where they got acquainted.

In early spring when Pa put strange cattle in the pasture he'd call to them to come and get salt. At first they didn't know his voice. But a few of our cattle did, and went running for salt when they heard his voice. The other cattle soon learned to follow.

At this meeting place Pa would count everybody's cattle that he was pasturing, to see if they were in the pasture. If one was missing, he

wouldn't stop till he found it. Pa soon learned every calf, cow, heifer, and steer in the pasture. All he had to do was look one over carefully and he never forgot it. He knew each of the hundred cattle in the big pasture where thirty belonged to us and seventy belonged to nine different people. He knew and could have called by name, if the cattle had been named, the hundred eighty-seven head of cattle he had in the other six pastures on our seven-hundred-eight-acre hill farm.

But when Pa called for the cattle to come to their salt in the big pasture, all would come but one. That was Jake Remines' heifer with the dots above her eyes. She would follow the other cattle near the salt trough. But she wouldn't come all the way. She'd come to within a couple of hundred yards. Then there she would stand and watch the other cattle lick salt. She'd watch them with her head high, her neck held stiff as a board, and her black eyes beaming in deep sockets as she looked at Pa. She would never come near him.

"That Remines heifer is a quare animal," Pa once said to me. "Cattle have always liked me. But not that one. She's the wildest thing I've ever seen. I've been a-tryin' to tame her since the day Jake fetched her here. But seems like she gets wilder all the time. Last April she didn't stand more than a hundred yards from the salt trough. Here it is August again and she stands two hundred yards away. Must be the fox hounds a-runnin' through here have made her nature wilder. But I will tame 'er and have her a-lickin' salt from my hands before Jake comes to get her."

That was what Pa thought. But in September the heifer would not come within three hundred yards of the salt trough.

"I can't understand it," Pa said. "That heifer must be a-goin' wild. Out here where she never sees anybody but me and the fox hunters. Out here where she hears fox horns a-blowin' and hound dogs a-barkin' and wind in the trees! I reckon that's enough to make a brute go wild!"

Among all the cattle Pa was pasturing for other people, cattle that would come and lick salt from his hand, Pa directed all his attention toward the heifer. "I'll tame her yet," he said. "I'll have her so tame that all Jake'll have to do when he comes to take his cattle home is to walk up to her and put his hand on her neck and lead her across the pasture. I've never seen one yet I couldn't tame. Something about me animals like. It hurts my feelings when a brute turns against me. Hurts me more than when a human being turns on me. I can't let Jake's heifer leave this pasture, without lickin' salt from my hand."

All through August and September Pa worked with Jake's heifer trying to tame her. When Pa would walk toward her, she'd bristle up like a doubtful dog and sniff the wind.

229

When he'd get within a hundred yards she'd take off, jumping like a deer, with her long tail floating on the wind.

Pa and I agreed we'd never seen a heifer that could run like that one. She'd leap over stumps, rocks, brier patches, and go to the tall timber where she'd disappear among the trees. We'd not see her until we went to salt the cattle again.

On the last day of October when Jake came to get his cattle, Pa told him about the heifer. Pa told Jake he'd not been able to get any closer than a hundred yards to her.

"She always had a wild nature," Jake told Pa. Jake pressed the long white beard down on his face. "But my heifer's not got a nature as wild as you say."

Jake paid Pa seventy dollars for pasturing his ten head of cattle for seven months. Jake bragged to Pa about how his cattle had grown. He said they'd put on about three hundred pounds of weight to the animal—all except the heifer. The heifer was standing so far away Jake couldn't see her too well.

But the other nine head of Jake's cattle stood close around us at the salt trough.

"Well, let's get her with the rest of my cattle," Jake said.

"I'll fetch her," Pa volunteered.

Pa wanted to show Jake what a man he was for his years. He wanted to show Jake how a lean, bony little man could run. Jake wasn't as old as Pa and the hair on his head was white as milkweed fuzz that the wind lifts from the pods and blows away in August. Pa's hair was still black as a charred stump in new ground. When Pa took off running to get on the far side of the heifer and drive her back toward us, he sailed over old stumps, rock piles, and brier patches like a scared fox.

"Look at that, won't you," Jake said as he watched Pa run. "Your father is a young man for his years. He's younger than you are. I'm an old man beside him."

230

But when the heifer saw Pa was trying to hem her up, she showed Pa how to run. She wheeled around on her hind feet in one whirl, and it looked to us like her feet were not touching the ground. Looked to us like she was stepping on the wind. Her legs moved like well-oiled pistons and her tail was riding on the October mountain wind like a kite. She was running toward the tall timber. The heifer outran Pa as easily as a fox outruns a slow hound, while we stood at the salt trough looking on. When Pa saw that the chase was useless, he put on brakes and skated like a young skater for a few feet on the damp dying October grass. There Pa stood and watched her disappear under the tall timber. I wanted to laugh, but I didn't. I knew who'd be running after her before we caught her for Jake Remines. Pa turned around and walked slowly and sadly back to us.

"You've done your best," Jake told Pa. "Honest, you can run like a greyhound. You stay in shape climbin' these mountains and carryin' salt to cattle. You can run like a hound dog yourself, but that heifer runs like a deer."

"Never saw anything like it," Pa said. "I can catch most any of 'em but her. Can't understand what has made her so wild."

"Never worry about it," Jake said. "I'll take these through the gate and drive 'em home. I'll be back tomorrow and get the heifer. I'll fetch my boys with me."

"And I'll come and bring Jesse and James," Pa told him. "We'll catch 'er, all right."

"Say, come to think of it, Mick," Jake said, pressing the white beard on his face again, "what will you give me for that heifer? I know you deal in cattle, and I do, too. Why not a little trade?"

"What'll you take for 'er?" Pa said in half words, for he was getting his breath hard. Pa's face changed. He smiled.

"She's a nice heifer, Mick," Jake said. "She's young and full of life."

"She's sure full of life, all right," Pa admitted.

"I think she's worth sixty dollars, Mick," Jake said, rubbing his cheek with his big hand.

"Too much, too much, Jake," Pa snapped. "She's not worth that. She's a troublesome brute."

"Well, I'm pricing 'er fifteen dollars cheaper to you than I would anybody else, Mick." Jake looked at the ground and kicked at the brown grass with the toe of his brogan shoe. "She's really worth seventy-five, the way cattle are selling at the market. Little hard to catch—that's the reason I priced 'er to you so cheap."

"That's too high, Jake." Pa turned to walk away.

"Not a cent cheaper," Jake said as he turned his cattle through the gate. "I'll be back to take her away tomorrow."

"We'll be here to help you," Pa said. I'd turned to watch Jake walk away behind his nine head of cattle. One of Jake's big steers turned his head and bawled to Pa as he went through the gate. All of them would lick salt from his hand.

As Pa and I walked along the path home, Pa walked in front. Now and then he let out a little wild laugh. That was the way he had done ever since I could remember, when he was thinking about a trade.

The very next day, Pa, James, and I met Jake and his sons, Dave and Bob, at the salt trough. All the cattle had been moved from the big pasture but Jake's heifer. We thought she'd be close to the salting place, but she wasn't.

"Heard her bawlin' out in the tall timber," Jake said "Out yander on that point."

"She's lonesome for the other cattle," Pa said. "Let's be after her."

Dave Remines was a long-legged young man about my age. Bob Remines was short and heavy. He was a thick young man with big arms and powerful legs. Brother James was six-feet-four and had always been a great runner.

"We'll get 'er now," Pa said. "My son Jesse used to be on

a high-school track team and he used to run long distances in college. James is a good runner, too. And I'm not so bad myself for a man my age."

"No, you're not, Mick," Jake bragged on Pa. "And I've got a couple of good runners here, too. Fox hunt every other night and climb these mountains. They'll be hard men to beat on a chase. I'm not a-sayin' this because they're my boys, either. Guess I'll be the slowest man among you."

James and I looked Bob and Dave over. I knew the thought that raced through my brother James' mind. He was goin' to try to show Bob and Dave Remines up on the chase after the heifer. We didn't have long to wait for the chase. We had just walked into the tall timber on the Hilton Point when Dave Remines spotted the heifer and we gave chase.

And that is a chase we will long remember. Pa started out leaping over logs and stumps. Dave Remines got the lead. His brother Bob was at his heels. James was third and I was fourth. Jake Remines trotted after me. Pa tried to skirt around all of us as the heifer took off like a young deer. She ran so fast we soon lost sight of her. We listened the way she went through the dry autumn leaves as long as we could and then we followed the way of the sound. And when we came to the place where we last heard the sound, all of us getting our breath hard, we picked up her tracks and took off again like a pack of hounds.

When we reached Coon Den Hollow, Pa and Jake were out of the chase. When we followed her tracks up the old log road to Seaton Ridge, Bob Remines fell down, holding his side with his hands.

"Can't go any farther, boys," he managed to grunt.

His brother Dave, who was now following my brother James, didn't say a word. He didn't have enough breath to spare. James was leading the chase and I was following. We had Dave between us.

"You boys are ridge-runners," he grunted in little half

233

breaths as we topped Seaton Ridge. In the distance we saw
the heifer running with all the ease in the world. She wasn't
tired.

Then across the open field where the land sloped gently,
James set a terrific pace with his long legs pulling against the
wind. Then I got closer on Dave's heels. I finally passed Dave,
and he was the third man. Dave didn't have much steam,
either—not enough for another three-mile circuit like the
heifer had just taken us. Before we reached Hilton Point
and the tall timber we met Pa and Jake coming on back.

"She's too much for us," Pa grunted. "We saw 'er but we
didn't give chase. She went over toward Howard Hollow."

James went in that direction and I followed. We never
saw Dave again—not on that chase. James went down into
Howard Hollow and I followed him. He found the track
again. We followed her tracks up the hill and over into Shingle Mill Hollow toward Coon Den Hollow again. I followed
James into Coon Den Hollow.

"Why run a heifer like this and kill ourselves?" James
asked, stopping suddenly. "We could run her all day and not
catch her. Run her till we have a heart attack. Run her for
what? What's this heifer to us?"

"Not anything," I agreed as the dry spittle flew from my
hot mouth. My tongue was dry. I was hot. I hardly had
enough breath to answer James. "Let's let 'er go."

Then James and I walked up the log road to Seaton
Ridge. When we got back to the salt trough Dave and Bob
Remines were stretched on the grass resting. Pa and Jake
were sitting on big stumps.

"Couldn't you get 'er?" Jake asked us.

"We can't do it," James said. "Never saw a heifer that
could take off like that one."

"See, I told you, Jake," Pa said. "Yesterday I would have
give you fifty for her. Today I won't. I wouldn't give you but
forty."

234

"Oh, that's not enough, Mick," Jake snapped. "I've just been out seven dollars to you for pasturing her this summer. Couldn't do that. We'll come and bring our shepherd."

"We'll be here," Pa said. "We'll ride mules. They'll be better for goin' under the brush."

So the next day we met again. Bob, Dave, and Jake Remines were in good saddles on three nice-looking saddle horses. They had brought their shepherd dog, Jolly. Pa was in the only saddle we had, astride our Barney mule. James was riding Dinah and I was riding Steve. We didn't have saddles. We brought with us our shepherd, old Bob. We were off, all of us riding toward Hilton Point. In the open space in a little hollow, and near the tall timber on Hilton Point, Pa saw the heifer.

"Yander she is, boys," he shouted. He pointed in the direction. We were off like a small cavalry, over the rocks, stumps, clusters of briers, and brush. The two dogs knew what we were after and they ran ahead of us. The heifer stood, sniffed the wind, and when Remines' shepherd, Jolly, ran up, she lunged through the air at him. All her feet were in the air when she pinned him against the ground and gored him with her sharp straight horns. Our shepherd, Bob, went the other way with his tail between his legs.

"She's killed Jolly," Jake Remines shouted. He was weeping when he stopped his horse and climbed from the saddle. He raced toward old Jolly who was lying there kicking and howling. All of us stopped our mules and horses and got down to look at Jolly while the heifer took her time trotting along toward the tall timber.

Jake felt of all the bones first in old Jolly to see if the heifer had crushed any. Then he examined the place where her horns had punctured his tough hide. The spot was bleeding, but not badly.

"He'll be all right," Jake said. "She just took the wind

out of 'im and skeered 'im half to death. He's never been after an animal like that one."

"The only way we'll ever take that heifer from this pasture is to take her dead," Bob Remines said. "If I had a gun I'd shoot 'er."

"Oh, no, never do that," Pa said. "She's not fat enough for beef. You'd lose a good animal."

"Come on, men," James said. "Let's be after her."

Old Jolly was up on his feet now, barking and howling and ready to follow. Old Bob had taken off toward home, after he had seen what the heifer had done to Jolly. Jake, Bob and Dave Remines, and Pa climbed back into their saddles. James and I leaped onto our barebacked mules. We followed the horses that took the lead. A wild grapevine caught Jake under the chin and lifted him from his saddle onto a bed of dry leaves. The branch of a tree that Dave let fly behind him slapped Pa across the face and eyes. We left Pa and Jake, scared but unhurt, and rode after the heifer. I thought somewhere ahead, I didn't know where, if a heifer could laugh, this heifer was laughing at us. We couldn't ride under the trees and through the brush and briers and undergrowth as fast as we could walk. Then a poplar limb with bark almost the color of the wind pulled Bob Remines from his saddle and his elbow hit a rock.

"No more of this for me," Bob said. "Let the heifer go. Shoot her."

We left Bob walking and leading his horse from the thicket. We went on until Dinah fell with James when she tried to leap the creek. James jumped to the ground and was safe. Steve was sure-footed and I stuck to his back. Dave Remines' horse slipped on a steep slope and pressed Dave against a tree. It took the breath from him just a minute. This was enough. We turned back while the heifer ran fleet-footed with the wind, over the dying grass and autumn leaves. She ran somewhere, we didn't know where. We managed to come back to the big grassfield in Shingle Mill Hollow and we mounted and rode toward the salt trough. We overtook Bob Remines on the way; he was still leading his horse.

"Think my elbow must be cracked," he said.

He had only a few more yards to walk to where Pa and Jake were sitting on their favorite stumps near the salt trough. Each of them was holding the bridle rein of his horse and mule.

"No, yesterday I would have given you forty, Jake," Pa said. "But not today. Not after I saw what that heifer did to old Jolly. I believe she's dangerous. I wouldn't give you a cent over thirty."

"Oh, I couldn't take that," Jake said.

"Take it, Pap," Bob Remines said, as he walked up leading his horse. "I've got a cracked elbow over that heifer."

"Take it, Pap," Dave Remines said. "I nearly got a panel of ribs busted when my horse slipped down against the side of a tree. Got the breath knocked out of me. Yesterday I ran after her until my heart nearly stopped. Take thirty bucks and let's get goin'."

"Boys, look what I've got in that red-blooded heifer," Jake said. "I can't take that. I'll take thirty-seven. That's just thirty dollars and the pasture money I paid out on her this summer. How about it, Mick?"

"Too much." Pa smiled as if he were in a position to set his own price. "I'll give you thirty."

"All right," Jake sighed at last.

"It's a bad deal, Pa," James said. "You'll be sorry you ever bought that heifer."

Bob and Dave Remines were pleased. Jake seemed pleased to be rid of the heifer. Pa paid him in cash right on the spot when he agreed to thirty.

Pa smiled as I never saw him smile before. I wondered what he was thinking.

237

Then Jake and Dave mounted their horses. James and I helped Bob into the saddle. They rode away with Jolly limping along behind them.

Then Pa climbed into the saddle and James and I leaped astride Steve and Dinah and we followed Pa toward home. Pa sat in the saddle laughing.

"What's so funny?" James asked. "Tell us and we'll laugh, too."

"I got a heifer that's worth a hundred dollars for thirty," Pa said. "Old Jake has always beat me on trading. Once he sold me a mule with the distemper for seventy-five. Mule wasn't worth ten to me. I've made it back in this trade."

"I wouldn't give you thirty for that heifer," James said. "He cheated you again. That heifer just never can be tamed."

"She'll be easy to tame," Pa said. "I wonder that Jake didn't think about it. Cattle often go wild. But there's a way to tame 'em."

"How, Pa?" I asked.

"Just leave 'em alone," Pa said. "Leave that heifer alone in this pasture until the first snow falls. She'll get hungry. And when she gets hungry, she'll be tame. She'll be lickin' salt out of my hand before December." Pa laughed as we rode toward home. "My hundred-dollar heifer won't be no trouble at all."

the old are valiant

"It's a good place for snakes out here," my father said as he stood leaning on his hoe handle. "I'm almost afraid to pull the weeds from around these potato vines. Afraid I'll put my hand down on a copperhead that's coolin' himself under a vine."

My father's breath came fast, for he had been digging hard with his hoe. Sweat popped out over his face, ran down the end of his nose, and dripped on the dusty mulch he had hilled around a potato vine.

"What do we care about snakes?" I told him. "We've got Jerry-B with us, and a snake won't have a chance. He's a young dog with good teeth and he's powerful."

Jerry-B was behind us, sniffing in the tall crabgrass.

"Jerry-B's got enough grit I reckon," my father admitted, "but he's not big enough. He won't weigh over eighteen pounds."

"Big enough to kill a snake," I said. "He's got a nose good enough to ferret all the snakes out of these weeds."

"I don't know about his smellin' a black snake," my father said. "But I can smell a copperhead myself. They're not hard to smell. One smells like hot cucumbers in the sun."

Jerry-B wiggled past us through the weeds.

His short legs moved cautiously. He sniffed as he moved along. His salt-and-pepper colored body was dotted with black. His half-curled hair bristled against the weeds as he snaked the potatoes for us.

We leaned on our hoe handles again and watched the dog until his short body was lost among the tall mass of weeds. We watched the weeds shake the way he had gone. Then we gripped our hoe handles and started digging again.

"We can't make much headway against this crabgrass," my father said. "We've worked two days and have hoed only twenty-four rows."

We stood under a sassafras bush at the end of our rows to shade a few minutes. We wiped sweat from our smarting eyes. We looked over the clean potato rows below and the weedy rows above us on the backbone of the ridge—a potato patch surrounded by thickets of wild gooseberries and huckleberries where the hot smelly wind was smothery to breathe.

My father mopped his wrinkled brow with his sweat-soaked bandanna.

"Believe I smell a copperhead," he said as he began to hoe another row across the field. "I smell some kind of a snake. It smells like sour dock."

"Look!" I shouted.

I pointed toward the snake. We took our hoes and ran toward the other end of the potato patch. Soon as we got near the big black snake he stopped to look at us with eyes that gleamed like small black agates in the sun.

"I'm goin' to kill him," I said. "I'm goin' to kill him with this gooseneck hoe! He's so big I might break my hoe handle when I hit 'im!"

"Don't do it," my father said, grabbing my hoe handle. "This snake reminds me of the snakes I used to see around this ridge when I was a young man. I could always tell when there was a snake sunnin' on a rock. My horse would rear up with me and stand on his hind feet and charge! I'd look around and see a big bull snake sunnin' on a rock in a huckleberry patch. I'd pull my .38 Special from the holster and feed him the hot lead. I've never liked a snake."

The big bull black snake lay with his head in one potato row, his body across two rows, and his tail in the fourth row. His body, in the largest part, was almost as large as the calf of my leg. His long body was slick as a peeled hickory tree and black as charcoal around a new-ground stump.

"That snake's long as a fence rail," I said.

"See, my nose didn't lie to me," my father told me. "I smelled that snake."

"Look, here comes Jerry-B," I said.

"He's trackin'," my father said. "Let him come up to him. See what the snake will do! I'll bet he'll put up a fight! He's an old residenter."

"Snake's almost big enough to swallow him," I sighed.

"But Jerry-B's tough," my father said. "He's been shot twice. The shots didn't kill him. Has been run over by a jolt wagon with two men in it. He got all right from that. He's a tough young dog. Now, let's see what he can do when he meets this old snake."

Jerry-B shook the tall weeds among the unhoed rows of potatoes as he tracked the snake toward our clean rows.

Jerry-B didn't look at us. He held his nose on the dry-parched earth where the black snake had left its broad trail across the dust. As soon as the bull black snake's lidless eyes saw Jerry-B sniffling the dust, he began to contract his big body from his head halfway down leaving his tail perfectly still.

"He's fought dogs before," my father said.

But Jerry-B sniffed, getting closer and closer as the bull black snake waited for him. Jerry-B came to the snake's tail that lay still as a wilted weed on the dusty ground. It was so still that Jerry-B Boneyard must have thought the snake was dead. He didn't look up, but his little hairy nose sniffled as he ran upon the snake's body without looking up. The big snake aimed at Jerry-B's head.

"Whow!" His powerful body shot forth with his big mouth open, and his iron lips hit Jerry-B between the eyes.

The force of the snake set Jerry-B back on his tail. He didn't whimper but jumped high in the air as the snake contracted to strike again. Jerry-B was now on his feet, and he was as mad as a wet hornet.

"He's one of the old residenter snakes that's come from one of the cliffs," my father bragged. "He might be one of the snakes I used to shoot at when I was a young man! That was fifty years ago."

Before he had finished his words, the snake struck half the length of his long body at Jerry-B.

"That snake's riled." My father stepped back to give them room to fight. "He knows how to fight."

"He's big enough to swallow Jerry-B," I said again.

"If that snake swallows him, he'll have a mess hard to digest," my father said, grinning. "Jerry-B won't lay very well on the snake's stummick. He never would lay any place very long."

Jerry-B ran in to bite the snake, but its neck was too big for his small mouth to cover, and its hide was too thick and tough for his small saw-brier-sharp teeth to penetrate. The snake contracted his body, catching Jerry-B in two coils, throwing him back into the next potato row.

"I've never seen anything like that," my father shouted. "It's the best fight I ever saw. I'll bet you Jerry-B can't kill that old residenter."

"I won't bet," I said.

Now Jerry-B was running at the snake, making him strike. When the snake struck, Jerry-B jumped back to let him strike the wind.

"He's tryin' to wear the snake out," my father said. "But he'll never do it. Not that old residenter."

242

No matter how often Jerry-B made him strike at the wind, the big bull snake didn't tire. He quit striking when he saw the tactics Jerry-B was using. He contracted to a half coil, stuck out his tongue, and waited for the dog to make the next move. Now, Jerry-B's tongue got thinner, and it was covered with flakes of spittle. Perspiration wet the whiskers around his mouth. Dust settled on his whiskers until there was a loblolly of mud around his mouth.

The potato vines around the snake and dog were mashed as flat against the dusty ground as dead autumn leaves weighted with snow. The leaves on the potato vines had been trampled by the dog's feet until they wilted in the blazing sun like the weeds we had cut with our hoes.

When Jerry-B learned how smart the snake was, he walked in for a rough-and-tumble fight. Before he reached the big black snake, he struck him on the jaw and set him back. Before he could come at the snake again, the bull black snake had re-coiled and struck him again and again. Jerry-B now dropped back the width of a potato row, lay flat on his stomach, and eyed the black snake.

"He's besiegin' the snake," my father laughed as he leaned on his hoe handle. "He doesn't want him to escape."

There was a distant growl of thunder in the sky far over Whetstone. In the hot sky above us, a few mares'-tail dingy-white clouds lay like potato ridges against the blue.

"That's the way the rains come," my father said. "How we need rain!"

Jerry-B lay flat on the ground watching the snake while the snake watched him. He panted harder than I had ever seen him. His sides moved in and out like a bee smoker. Spittle dripped from his muddy whiskers. His long barks were reduced to short grunts. His black eyes, under the long wisps of hair that dropped over them, danced with fire. He had found something he couldn't conquer. He couldn't pick this snake up and sling it in two as he had done all the other snakes he had found.

" 'Spect we'd better get back to our work," my father sighed. "I'd like to finish this patch before the rain."

"It's awful hot. And we're leavin' a good fight."

"I know the fight's not over."

As we spoke, the bull snake must have thought it was over, for he started crawling away, over a potato ridge toward Sulphur Spring Hollow. Slowly he crawled, with his forked tongue stuck out in the hot wind. Jerry-B jumped to his feet, ran around a potato vine and bit the snake. The snake stopped, coiled for another fight, but Jerry-B fell flat on his stomach, and the snake missed him.

"It's another siege," my father said. "But the snake has gained a row. He's makin' for that thicket, and if he gets to it, Jerry-B can't handle him."

Over Whetstone Creek, we could hear thunder. White thunderheads boiled upon the sky above the distant rim of the Whetstone ridges. We picked up our hoes, put them across our shoulders, and walked back to the end of the potato patch and started our rows.

"Six more rows. We ought to finish by five," my father said, leaning on his hoe handle and looking at his watch.

While we worked, Jerry-B growled like low thunder at the snake. He would try to crawl from one potato balk to the other, but Jerry-B would grab and try to hold on. The snake used both its mouth and its tail to drive him back two potato balks.

"That dog's got grit," my father bragged as we finished our rows and started back with two more. "He's the grittiest little dog I ever saw. But he's met his match."

"Look," I said as we hoed our rows out where the dog and snake were resting after another tussle. "The snake has gained six potato rows on Jerry-B."

"And look at our vines," he said.

The snake and dog had left a path of destruction across our potato patch where they had fought for every inch of ground. And the thunder was getting louder. A heavy cloud was hanging over Whetstone now.

"That's a rain cloud," my father said. "See how smooth and gray it is! Feel how much cooler the wind is. That wind is comin' from rain. We must hurry to finish before the rain!"

Before we had finished these rows, Jerry-B and the bull black snake tussled and rolled over more vines. They fought furiously to kill each other. We watched the potato vines fall as the snake and dog went end over end among them. When this fight stopped, Jerry-B lay flat on his belly on a clean balk and growled. He guarded the snake.

As we finished these two rows, the rain clouds were hanging over Sandy River. We could feel the rain in the wind. We could smell it. We knew it was coming. We worked hard and fast in the cooler wind as we started back in the last rows trying to beat the rain. Soon as we were back even with the dog and snake, we counted the rows they had fought over. They had smashed the vines in a strip across the patch broad as a jolt wagon road. They had fought over sixteen rows. Jerry-B was attacking furiously every time the snake tried to move.

In the distance, from our high hilltop, we could see the rain. It would soon be to the ridge top, but we would have our last rows hoed. Jerry-B was charging at the snake. We could see the snake striking back. He didn't strike with the same force he used at first. Both the snake and the dog were tiring. They were getting weak. We finished our rows and hurried across the potato patch to watch the finish. The lightning flashed around, and thunder roared over us like potato wagons across the skies.

The big snake was still trying to make it to the brush. He had only one more row to go. Jerry-B made a vicious

245

attack. The snake used new tactics on the tired dog. He didn't offer to fight back now but crawled toward the brush with Jerry-B's saw-brier teeth fastened in its skin holding with every ounce of strength he had. But the snake was so heavy he pulled the dog toward the brush.

"I'm goin' to kill that snake," I said, raising my hoe above my shoulder. "I'm not goin' to let him get away."

"No, you're not," my father said. "That snake deserves to live. He's a fighter. He's one of the few old residenters left. I don't like snakes, but I like him."

"If Jerry-B ever runs into this snake again, the fight will be renewed," I said. "My dog is a fighter too!"

As the snake reached the brush, with Jerry-B pulling back with all the strength in his tired body, it was not crawling much faster than a snail. Heavy torrents of rain began to fall. We started toward the tobacco barn as hard as we could go, for we were hot, and we didn't want to get too wet. Jerry-B gave his last pull in the rain, but the snake slipped from his mouth into the vast undergrowth that was its home.

This was the first time I had ever seen my father smile when a snake got away. This was the first time I'd ever seen him let a snake get away. It was the first time I'd ever seen him let anything trample his potato vines. But I didn't smile when I looked at Jerry-B walking beside us with his tongue almost touching the ground and his tail tucked between his legs. This was the first battle with a snake he had ever lost.

thanksgiving hunter

"Hold your rifle like this," Uncle Wash said, changing the position of my rifle. "When I throw this marble into the air, follow it with your bead; at the right time gently squeeze the trigger!"

Uncle Wash threw the marble high into the air and I lined my sights with the tiny moving marble, gently squeezing the trigger, timing the speed of my object until it slowed in the air ready to drop to earth again. Just as it reached its height, my rifle cracked and the marble was broken into tiny pieces.

Uncle Wash was a tall man with a hard leathery face, dark discolored teeth and blue eyes that had a faraway look in them. He hunted the year round; he violated all the hunting laws. He knew every path, creek, river and rock cliff within a radius of ten miles. Since he was a great hunter, he wanted to make a great hunter out of me. And tomorrow, Thanksgiving Day, would be the day for Uncle Wash to take me on my first hunt.

Uncle Wash woke me long before daylight.

"Oil your double-barrel," he said. "Oil it just like I've showed you."

I had to clean the barrels with an oily rag tied to a long string with a knot in the end. I dropped the heavy knot down the barrel and pulled the oily rag through the barrel. I did this many times to each barrel. Then I rubbed a meat-rind over both barrels and shined them with a dry rag. After this was done I polished the gunstock.

"Love the feel of your gun," Uncle Wash had often told me. "There's nothing like the feel of a gun. Know how far it will shoot. Know your gun better than you know your own self; know it and love it."

Before the sun had melted the frost from the multicolored trees and from the fields of stubble and dead grasses, we had cleaned our guns, had eaten our breakfasts and were on our way. Uncle Wash, Dave Pratt, Steve Blake walked ahead of me along the path and talked about the great hunts they had taken and the game they had killed. And while they talked, words that Uncle Wash had told me about loving the feel of a gun kept going through my head. Maybe it is because Uncle Wash speaks of a gun like it was a living person is why he is such a good marksman, I thought.

"This is the dove country," Uncle Wash said soon as we had reached the cattle barn on the west side of our farm. "Doves are feeding here. They nest in these pines and feed around this barn fall and winter. Plenty of wheat grains, rye grains, and timothy seed here for doves."

Uncle Wash is right about the doves, I thought. I had seen them fly in pairs all summer long into the pine grove that covered the knoll east of our barn. I had heard their mournful songs. I had seen them in early April carrying straws in their bills to build their nests; I had seen them flying through the blue spring air after each other; I had seen them in the summer carrying food in their bills for their tiny young. I had heard their young ones crying for more food from the nests among the pines when the winds didn't sough among the pine boughs to drown their sounds. And when the leaves started turning brown I had seen whole flocks of doves, young and old ones, fly down from the tall pines to our barnyard to pick up the wasted grain. I had seen them often

248

and been so close to them that they were no longer afraid of me.

"Doves are fat now," Uncle Wash said to Dave Pratt.

"Doves are wonderful to eat," Dave said.

And then I remembered when I had watched them in the spring and summer, I had never thought about killing and eating them. I had thought of them as birds that lived in the tops of pine trees and that hunted their food from the earth. I remembered their mournful songs that had often made me feel lonely when I worked in the cornfield near the barn. I had thought of them as flying over the deep hollows

249

in pairs in the bright sunlight air chasing each other as they flew toward their nests in pines.

"Now we must get good shooting into this flock of doves," Uncle Wash said to us, "before they get wild. They've not been shot among this season."

Then Uncle Wash, to show his skill in hunting, sent us in different directions so that when the doves flew up from our barn lot, they would have to fly over one of our guns. He gave us orders to close in toward the barn and when the doves saw us, they would take to the air and we would do our shooting.

"And if they get away," Uncle Wash said, "follow them up and talk to them in their own language."

Each of us went his separate way. I walked toward the pine grove, carrying my gun just as Uncle Wash had instructed me. I was ready to start shooting as soon as I heard the flutter of dove wings. I walked over the frosted white grass and the wheat stubble until I came to the fringe of pine woods. And when I walked slowly over the needles of pines that covered the autumn earth, I heard the flutter of many wings and the barking of guns. The doves didn't come my way. I saw many fall from the bright autumn air to the brown crabgrass-colored earth.

I saw these hunters pick up the doves they had killed and cram their limp, lifeless, bleeding bodies with tousled feathers into their brown hunting coats. They picked them up as fast as they could, trying to watch the way the doves went.

"Which way did they go, Wash?" Dave asked soon as he had picked up his kill.

"That way," Uncle Wash pointed to the low hill on the west.

"Let's be after 'em, men," Steve said.

The seasoned hunters hurried after their prey while I stood under a tall pine and kicked the toe of my brogan shoe against the brown pine needles that had carpeted the ground. I saw these men hurry over the hill, cross the ravine and climb the hill over which the doves had flown.

I watched them reach the summit of the hill, stop and call to the doves in tones not unlike the doves' own calling. I saw them with guns poised against the sky. Soon they had disappeared the way the doves had gone.

I sat down on the edge of a lichened rock that emerged from the rugged hill. I laid my double-barrel down beside me, and sunlight fingered through the pine boughs above me in pencil-sized streaks of light. And when one of these shifting pencil-sized streaks of light touched my gun barrels, they shone brightly in the light. My gun was cleaned and oiled and the little pine needles stuck to its meat-rind-greased barrels. Over my head the wind soughed lonely among the pine needles. And from under these pines I could see the vast open fields where the corn stubble stood knee high, where the wheat stubble would have shown plainly had it not been for the great growth of crabgrass after we had cut the wheat; crabgrass that had been blighted by autumn frost and shone brilliantly brown in the sun.

Even the air was cool to breathe into the lungs; I could feel it deep down when I breathed and it tasted of the green pine boughs that flavored it as it seethed through their thick tops. This was a clean cool autumn earth that both men and birds loved. And as I sat on the lichened rock with pine needles at my feet, with the soughing pine boughs above me, I thought the doves had chosen a fine place to find food, to nest and raise their young. But while I sat looking at the earth about me, I heard the thunder of the seasoned hunters' guns beyond the low ridge. I knew that they had talked to the doves until they had got close enough to shoot again.

As I sat on the rock, listening to the guns in the distance, I thought Uncle Wash might be right after all. It was better to shoot and kill with a gun than to kill with one's hands or with a club. I remembered the time I went over the hill to see how our young corn was growing after we had plowed it the last time. And while I stood looking over the corn whose long ears were in tender blisters, I watched a ground hog come from the edge of the woods, ride down a stalk of corn, and start eating a blister-ear. I found a dead sassafras stick near me, tiptoed quietly behind the ground hog and hit him over the head. I didn't finish him with that lick. It took many licks.

When I left the corn field, I left the ground hog dead beside his ear of corn. I couldn't forget killing the ground hog over an ear of corn and leaving him dead, his gray-furred clean body to waste on the lonely hill.

I can't disappoint Uncle Wash, I thought. He has trained me to shoot. He says that I will make a great hunter. He wants me to hunt like my father, cousins and uncles. He says that I will be the greatest marksman among them.

I thought about the way my people had hunted and how they had loved their guns. I thought about how Uncle Wash had taken care of his gun, how he had treated it like a living thing and how he had told me to love the feel of it. And now my gun lay beside me with pine needles sticking to it. If Uncle Wash were near he would make me pick the gun up, brush away the pine needles and wipe the gun barrels with my handkerchief. If I had lost my handkerchief, as I had seen Uncle Wash often do, he would make me pull out my shirt-tail to wipe my gun with it. Uncle Wash didn't object to wearing dirty clothes or to wiping his face with a dirty bandanna; he didn't mind living in a dirty house—but never, never would he allow a speck of rust or dirt on his gun.

It was comfortable to sit on the rock since the sun was directly above me. It warmed me with a glow of autumn. I felt the sun's rays against my face and the sun was good to feel. But the good fresh autumn air was no longer cool as the frost that covered the autumn grass that morning, nor could I

252

feel it go deep into my lungs; the autumn air was warmer and it was flavored more with the scent of pines.

Now that the shooting had long been over near our cattle barn, I heard the lazy murmur of the woodcock in the pine woods near by. Uncle Wash said woodcocks were game birds and he killed them wherever he found them. Once I thought I would follow the sound and kill the woodcock. I picked up my gun but laid it aside again. I wanted to kill something to show Uncle Wash. I didn't want him to be disappointed in me.

Instead of trying to find a rabbit sitting behind a broomsedge cluster or in a brier thicket as Uncle Wash had trained me to do, I felt relaxed and lazy in the autumn sun that had now penetrated the pine boughs from directly overhead. I looked over the brown vast autumn earth about me where I had worked when everything was green and growing, where birds sang in the spring air as they built their nests. I looked at the tops of barren trees and thought how a few months ago they were waving clouds of green. And now it was a sad world, a dying world. There was so much death in the world that I had known: flowers were dead, leaves were dead, and the frosted grass was lifeless in the wind. Everything was dead and dying but a few wild birds and rabbits. I had almost grown to the rock where I sat but I didn't want to stir. I wanted to glimpse the life about me before it all was covered with winter snows. I hated to think of killing in this autumn world. When I picked up my gun, I didn't feel life in it—I felt death.

I didn't hear the old hunters' guns now but I knew that, wherever they were, they were hunting for something to shoot. I thought they would return to the barn if the doves came back, as they surely would, for the pine grove where I sat was one place in this autumn world that was a home to the doves. And while I sat on the rock, I thought I would practice the dove whistle that Uncle Wash had taught me. I thought a dove would come close and I would shoot the dove so that I could go home with something in my hunting coat.

As I sat whistling a dove call, I heard the distant thunder of their guns beyond the low ridge. Then I knew they were coming back toward the cattle barn.

And, as I sat whistling my dove calls, I heard a dove answer me. I called gently to the dove. Again it answered. This time it was closer to me. I picked up my gun from the rock and gently brushed the pine needles from its stock and barrels. And as I did this, I called pensively to the dove and it answered plaintively.

I aimed my gun soon as I saw the dove walking toward me. When it walked toward my gun so unafraid, I thought it was a pet dove. I lowered my gun; laid it across my lap. Never had a dove come this close to me. When I called again, it answered at my feet. Then it fanned its wings and flew upon the rock beside me trying to reach the sound of my voice. It called, but I didn't answer. I looked at the dove when it turned its head to one side to try to see me. Its eye was gone, with the mark of a shot across its face. Then it turned the other side of its head toward me to try to see. The other eye was gone.

As I looked at the dove the shooting grew louder; the old hunters were getting closer. I heard the fanning of dove wings above the pines. And I heard doves batting their wings against the pine boughs. And the dove beside me called to them. It knew the sounds of their wings. Maybe it knows each dove by the sound of his wings, I thought. And then the dove spoke beside me. I was afraid to answer. I could have reached out my hand and picked this dove up from the rock. Though it was blind, I couldn't kill it, and yet I knew it would have a hard time to live.

When the dove beside me called again, I heard an answer from a pine bough near by. The dove beside me spoke and the dove in the pine bough answered. Soon they were talking to each other as the guns grew louder. Suddenly, the blind dove fluttered through the tree-tops, chirruping its plaintive melancholy notes, toward the sound of its mate's voice. I heard its wings batting the wind-shaken pine boughs as it ascended, struggling, toward the beckoning voice.

hummingbird

Hummingbird, there's no other bird like you! You are a jet and helicopter combined. But you have more maneuverability than either. You can fly forward, then rise from a flower and soar up through the windy skies toward a white cloud so fast that if you were not silhouetted against a patch of white clouds, we couldn't even see your flight.

Hummingbird, you can fly backwards just as fast. A jet can't do it. Maybe our engineers will learn to follow the design that the Creator of this universe used when he made you. You are the size of a man's thumb, with a pressurized body able to survive great speed, and you have such a tiny wingspread. Someday our planes may also have small wings. Maybe our engineers can discover how you can stand in the air like a helicopter while you use your bill, which is almost as long as your body, to draw sweet nectar from the flowers.

I stand here and watch you buzz down to the ground, close enough for a snake to get you, but a snake can't move quickly enough to bother you. You start on the lowest blossom of our larkspur and fly to each one until you reach the top. Then you move to another larkspur. And if you forget a blossom you back up and get it. I like to see you go into reverse and fly backwards.

Hummingbird, from the time I have been able

to walk I have admired you. I used to wish I could fly from flower to flower, gather my food like you, and then take off faster than an approaching storm. You are almost as fast as lightning. I have always liked the way you rise up and then swoop down to some place beyond like a long-projected artillery shell. I think the place you fly away to, that secret place, is your nest. Not many people ever find it.

Hummingbird, it fascinates me that the food that gives you the strength to soar is only the sweets from the wildwood flowers. It is such a little amount of sustenance. I wonder how it can give you such great speed and long endurance. You fly through the air with greater speed in proportion to your size than anything man has ever built. Our man-made planes must have the best fuel our technicians can make. They must be made of the strongest and most resistible metals that our earth can provide.

Another wonderful thing about you, hummingbird, is the way you take the pollen on your bill and carry it from male to female, providing a better production of fruit, berries, grain and vegetables! How wonderful you are to us on our farms. You fertilize plants we don't even know about. Maybe that is why the Great Creative Engineer invented you.

Hummingbird, I'd like to stand here and watch you fly to your nest. I wonder if you gather nectar from my flowers this morning to take home to little hummingbirds, high in the top of the tallest tree, out on a small swinging branch and under protective green leaves. Maybe there's not too much nectar to gather this morning, for it rained last night and some clear drops of water from the skies are probably lodged in the larkspur blossoms. Maybe you need both water and nectar for yourself and the young in your nest. How do you carry your load? In your long bill? If a storm should rise up, you can see it as you fly through the skies. And you can beat the storm to your nest and hover over your young birds.

Hummingbird, you're just a little larger than a bumble-bee. And you make more noise than a jet in proportion to your size. If the jet made as much noise as you do in proportion to its size, no city would want a jet base nearby. Vibrations from a jet can crack walls in houses, break windowpanes and lift roofs, but what damage would you do if you were the size of the jet? Houses would rise up and follow you in a wake of wind.

Hummingbird, I wonder where you go in the winter. If you do go away, it surely doesn't take you very long to reach your destination. We don't blame you for leaving because in winter we don't get many violets from under the snow nor many apple, plum, peach, dogwood and redbud blossoms. You have to go where you can eat. Do you go South to that vacationland where flowers bloom and the sun is always warm?

Do you know another country and its skies as you know my land and skies? Do you nest down there and raise your young and bring them up here with you when it's spring and summer here? When it's time for the last flowers to die here, when the last autumn flowers go, do you take your young and depart for that land? What a wonderful life, hummingbird! You have to go where you have food. And your method of travel is expensive.

Hummingbird, I wish you could speak. Before you finish the blue larkspur on the other side of this walk, I wish you could tell me more about yourself, for I am interested in you. I would like to know when you come in the spring. You arrive when there are many flowers and you are sure of nectar. You are sensible about the seasons. You don't come too early nor too late. Our beautiful flowers guide your destiny. We never know when you will arrive, but the best way for us to guess is to see the thousands of flower petals upon our warm spring earth and to smell their aroma upon the winds of spring. Then, if we look around for you, you will be here.

And in the autumn, when September days are still warm, you buzz to the farewell-to-summers, wild phlox, along the streams and to the sumac, daisy, ironweed, silkweed and queen-of-the-meadow. I see you enjoying early autumn just as much as I do. You are going to all the flowers and gathering nectar from their blossoms. You are flying over an earth that is beginning to change. You must see the few sassafras leaves that have turned red and fallen. You must observe very closely, for you don't stay long. But we never know when you leave. You go like a quiet spirit, much less conspicuously than an autumn brown leaf that the winds carry over the drying grass. But when you have left, in three days, often less, we can expect frost.

Hummingbird, who tells you about the seasons? Your judgment is canny. Are you a guiding spirit by instinct like a fresh spring wind? Do you plan your flights and carry a memorized chart in your little head? And what about your heart? How fast does it pump blood during your flight? I would like to feel its rhythmical beating.

Hummingbird, before you finish the last flower I have a few more thoughts. You are a spirit of beauty, living in an ethereal world except when you come down for food among the flowers. You live in the wind and sleep at night high on a swinging bough where only a few birds of the air can find you. If you fly at night, it's toward the moon and stars. In the morning you can fly and face the sun, and in the evening watch the sunset.

Your long bill gets gold-dusty with pollen and you ride the winds and feel the storms. You feast among the flowers. I wish it were possible to tell me the flower you like best. I think it's old-fashioned horsemint, and that is why I have planted it all over this yard. It is for you. I want you to come and visit me often. Don't be in such a hurry. I want to know

259

more about you. Hummingbird, yours is a world I love, too. Now you buzz backward, forward, up and down and you are off toward a lazy white cloud in the bright June sky. You go up and level off and as I see you, a little speck against the sky, I stand thinking of you and wondering where you have gone.

august

In the morning I went back to visit Anthill. Beside the lilac bush and under the shade of the big poplar, I found the city of ants very much alive. Here they had lived for a number of years, expanding from a few small hills into a large city of ants. They had carried up dirt from below until they had made a soft little hill. Now they were running in all directions in the morning sun.

I looked at their legion of guards. They were big strong black fellows, perhaps chosen especially for their size to protect their city. I watched them walking over their military roads. Other ants left the city and roamed over our back yard in search of food. Through the grass stubble, they dragged home worms, butterflies, moths, grasshoppers, katydids, cutworms, and bread crumbs our birds hadn't eaten. They dragged loads many times their own size long distances to Anthill.

Somewhere down in the underground chambers of Anthill were storage rooms for foods, depositories for ant eggs, nurseries for young ants. Somewhere down there sat the mayor, perhaps, directing the life of the city. I wondered what these inhabitants of Anthill would do in case of attack. What would happen if the guards found another race of ants on their premises ready to give them battle? It would be interesting to see if these industrious ants would fight for their city.

In the house I got three small white envelopes. Then I went back to the walk in front of the smokehouse, where dozens of large red ants were constantly running up and down and across the cement. I caught over one hundred large red ants and put them inside the three envelopes, which I had perforated with a pin. I sealed them and stuck them down in my shirt pocket. Then I took my red-ant troops to attack the city of Anthill.

When I opened the first envelope and dumped the red ants down on Anthill, as if they were paratroopers descending from the skies, the big black ant guards met them head-on to defend their city. Two black ants would grab a red ant, and they wouldn't stop pulling at him until he was finished. If they happened to be pulling in different ways, they would often pull the red ant in two. Then each made off with a portion of the body to a cemetery or a storehouse below. In a very few minutes these big guards had polished off the first company of red ants I had dumped down on Anthill.

Now the word had spread through all Anthill, and troubled citizens came running to the surface from all directions, obviously excited over what had happened. Since they were running wildly over Anthill seemingly in search of more red ants to conquer, I obliged them by dumping two more companies of paratroopers from the low skies over Anthill. At first the black ants went after them one for one. The red ants didn't know exactly who their attackers were or how they got there, but they knew they were in a position where they were compelled to fight. And being a brave species—as are all ants, large or small, that I have watched—many waged a brilliant battle. But most of them wanted to get away. They weren't in their home territory. This strange land was more than fifty feet away, over the close-cut back-yard grass, from their native area of our yard. Many tried to escape on the military roads but were met by strong detachments of black ants which immediately gave battle. Ants died on both sides, but more red than black. I watched red ants being carried downstairs in Anthill while they were still alive and kicking.

Now the red ants were outnumbered two to one, for dozens of black ants had swarmed up on the hill from their underground city. More quickly than I thought possible, they subdued the three companies of red ants. Not one escaped that I could see to carry the sad news back to the packs of wild red ants that roamed over our back yard. The excited black ants ran all over Anthill until sundown. They seemed to be hunting for more red ants to pull apart and take downstairs. They ran out into the stubbled grass, and they climbed the soft ridges that old mole had made with his long snoot and his strong forepaws. They ran in widening circles around Anthill looking for these enemies until the shades of the lilac and the poplar lengthened over the yard. They had tasted victory and found it sweet.

Yesterday morning I thought I would balance the scales. The black ants were still strong. They hadn't lost nearly so heavily as the red ants. If I was going to promote an insect war, at least I should give each side an equal chance. Before breakfast I put bread crumbs on the walk in front of my writing room. I don't know where all the red ants came from. They must have smelled the bread crumbs, or maybe the first ants to the crumbs hurried back to tell others. I put thirty to forty ants in each envelope. I spent most of the morning gathering hundreds of red ants for the afternoon assault on Anthill. These were big strong country ants that didn't like to be confined in these small envelopes. I let them grow restless and heard them scratching on the stiff paper. I didn't care if they got a little mad and overanxious for their moment of battle to come.

At noon the first company of red ants fell from the skies upon Anthill. They were immediately met by the guards. Big black ants swarmed up from underground to overwhelm the already outnumbered red ants. But the battle wasn't going to be so onesided today. Hastily I reached for my envelopes and emptied one after the other onto Anthill. The red and the black mingled in combat. It was hard to see the ground under them. There were dead ants everywhere, and living ants heaving their carcasses along the military roads. When the black ants, perhaps because they were fighting for their home, again seemed about to get the upper hand, I emptied my last two envelopes of reserve troops. Red ants went tumbling down through the skies.

More black ants came up to meet them, not the big, strong guardian blacks any more, but smaller artisan ants. But the reds, in equal battle at last, were no longer seeking routes of escape. They stuck it out, killing and being killed. Not a single black ant that I saw deserted his home. Now both red and black ants were being carried downstairs. I suddenly wondered what would happen if the red ants were victorious. Would they migrate from their distant part of the yard and take over Anthill? As the minutes passed into an hour, there were fewer and fewer able-bodied ants of either color left on Anthill. It was hard to tell which side had won.

I waited until this afternoon, the third day of battle, to find out. I thought that probably the black ants would have had time to recuperate and to finish off the last invader. I waited until I thought Anthill would be a place of activity again, as it had always been in spring, summer, and early autumn throughout the years.

Crossing the domain of the red ants near the kitchen, I was surprised to see only a very few scattered here and there. When I reached Anthill, I didn't see a guard on top of this city of ants. There was not a single ant crawling on the roads, the small and big turnpikes, which led to Anthill.

Anthill was quiet for the first time in three years. The big heap of soft dirt looked strangely empty. It was hard for me to believe there weren't any ants on Anthill under the lilac bush. So I picked up a stick under the big poplar and went back to Anthill and carefully removed some of the dirt. The ground beneath was honeycombed by small entrances.

In one place I found small ants' eggs. In another I found dead worms, bugs, a cricket, two grasshoppers, and crumbs of cornbread. After a little more prodding with the poplar branch, I knew the reason why there wasn't any activity. I came upon dead black ants, dozens of them. Whether these had been buried or had crept below to die, I don't know. Then I found dozens of red ants, too, killed in the battle for Anthill and dragged below.

As far as I could tell they had fought to the last ant. Not a single black ant had deserted his city. At least I couldn't find a trace of one in the grass nearby. And there was not a living ant, red or black, in all of Anthill.

Now I had a depressed feeling about my black ants. I knew that I would miss them. I had carried them crumbs. I had made old mole crawl under their city once, something he would never do a second time. I had fed these ants grain that the birds hadn't eaten. My original question, Would the black ants defend their city? was answered. Now I wished that I had let it go unanswered, for I was lonely for them.

cities that vanish
in the sky

I looked at the steep hill where I set my orchard of
wild peach trees. The spiders had pitched their
pup tents everywhere. This hill seemed to be a
favorite place for spiders. When I saw all of these
white webs, now filled with morning mists, I
wanted to walk out into their fragile world. I knew
so little about spiders, for I had never read anything about them. All I knew was what I had observed through my own eyes. I didn't know where
they went in winter although I thought they were
in semi-hibernation in holes in the ground, under
old trees, and in cracks and crevices. On warmer
winter days they were out looking over the earth. I
knew how they got into houses and spun their
webs. There were dozens of various kinds of spiders. The only creature I had ever seen that would
eat a spider was a mud-dauber. He relished them.
He paralyzed them with his sting, then kept them
alive and fresh in the mud-daubers' nest where
they were stored to feed their young.

After breakfast, I walked up W-Hollow. Bright
rays of the morning sun were slanting down
over the east wall into the valley. Where this
bright light touched the dew-laden spider webs,

millions of dewdrops sparkled like diamonds. This was something I never tired of seeing. And it was the reason why I had come this morning. I couldn't stay home when a warm wind blew toward the south, making it just warm enough for pleasant walking.

How can a little spider have the intuitive instinct to design a web like this one, I thought as I stopped beside the road. Here a spider had spun his web by anchoring it to the two branches of a water-birch that weaved to and fro in the early morning wind. How can he know so much plane geometry when so many intelligent youths find this a most difficult high school subject?

This particular web was round like a wagon wheel. Spokes went from the rim into the center hub. These wagon-wheel spokes would have been too long and too fragile if this spider hadn't clearly known before he began what he was going to do. He had attached threads of support, beginning near the rim. Then he went all around making a circle that was practically equidistant to the outer rim.

Next he moved closer toward the hub with another thread that went around in a perfect circle embracing the spokes. He continued forming the web in this manner, keeping these threads equidistant all the way up to the hub. His designs and patterns had worked perfectly. The web was filled with drops of dew clinging to the threads, drops that would vanish into a little cloud of mist in the morning sun.

No two spiders build their houses the same way. Each spider works in his own fashion; each creates a different design. Spiders are not assemblyline workers. Each is an artist and an individual. If a community government existed for a village of spiders, it would be most difficult to find a spider who could serve to please the others.

There were many small fields of white where webs were spun close to each other up this valley. I could see white villages up the ravines on the pasture slope shining in the

267

morning sun. They were everywhere. Spiders had come from a hidden place where they remained in bad weather, to build their cities over the land. Perhaps they were making their webs to trap the last flies before winter. I hadn't seen any spiders in the webs. They had built their homes, then deserted them.

The strange thing about all of this was that when the sun evaporated the dewdrops the wind would blow these artistic houses away. Not one would be left if the wind became very strong. I had seen this happen before. When the weight of the dewdrops was lifted up into white cloud mists, the framework of gossamer threads, unraveled by industrious spiders, was carried away by the surging puffs of wind. By sunset, the many cities I observed in the morning would have vanished.

I walked on into the broomsedge in the pasture fields. Here I found few villages of spiders. They had built their webs in open places where leaves, sticks and grass lay flat against the earth. The broomsedge stood up, bending down when the wind blew, rising again after it passed over. There were many webs down near the dwindling stream. I wondered if spiders liked to live near water. I thought the dew would supply sufficient drinking water for the needs of their tiny bodies. I walked through the dry fluffy broomsedge, watching it bend and rise like a field of ripening wheat in July. I liked to walk over this rugged terrain. I liked the stiff sounds of the broomsedge restraining the wind. A little tired of walking, I lay down flat on my back on the dry broomsedge. I looked up through the branches of a locust shade tree.

While I lay there, I watched the small white clouds rise up over the land toward the sky. Perhaps I went to sleep, for time passed I did not remember later. When I rose from my bed of broomsedge, poking my head into a brisk wind, there weren't any small white clouds rising from the valley and the pasture field. Down in the ravines I didn't see a single spider web left. Everything was different.

The world I had seen this morning had completely vanished. Those white, magnificent, spider-homes made of gossamer threads lasted only a few hours. But where had they gone? I didn't know. I sat upright where the sunny-dry broomsedge crackled stiffly around my ears. Then I looked up toward the sun that was climbing high in the afternoon sky.

I saw a spider anchor his thread, travel downward and suddenly stop, suspended. Then he moved off, unraveling his thread in another direction. The strand of web wasn't anchored any place. It was free to the wind. It rose from the broomsedge very slowly with a small spider on it. It went higher until it touched a twig on the locust tree. But the wind pulled it loose. I watched the silver strand, bearing a lone spider, rise up between me and the sun. It drifted out of sight on a south wind. Here was one way for a spider to hibernate during the winter, and a wonderful way to see the world. I wondered how many spiders were in the south winds going places. I wondered where they would travel. This was nature's way of spreading them over the world, maybe for thousands of miles. Slowly I arose, and reluctantly walked away from the world where so many small white cities had vanished.

night and the whippoorwill

The whippoorwill woke me at five one April morning. He was in the back yard not too far from my bed. I think he must have been sitting upon the kitchen roof. I never heard such singing! The energy he expounded in that love song to his mate! And somewhere, far away, I heard his mate returning her affections with a love song. I lay in bed and listened.

To hear a whippoorwill in the spring brings back memories. The whippoorwill has always impressed me. I associate it with the milkgap and my mother milking a cow. I used to fetch the cow and often got her to the milkgap after the stars were in the sky and the moon was up. Then the whippoorwills started to sing. One often came close to where Mom was milking and sat on a limb in the white oak and sang. The whippoorwill close by was always answered by one far away. And the mournful song impressed me the first time I heard it. I have always thought the whippoorwill was a lonely bird. I cannot recall ever hearing one sing a happy song like the redbird or the pewee.

The whippoorwills used to perch upon the hill and sing when Mom and Dad sat in the yard with their children around them. My parents listened to the mournful bird in silence and never had to tell us to keep quiet. There was something romantic about the whippoorwill. It has a quality no other bird posseses. Also, we didn't have any kind of music in our home. All the music we heard was played by the old-time musicians who came on holidays and performed on the courthouse square in our county seat, Greenup. So there was something extra special for us about the whippoorwill's singing. It was a sad, mournful plaintive music akin to the death and sadness in our old mountain ballads.

In the evenings, after work, when the stars and moon were in the sky, and my time was my own to run and play, the singing whippoorwills entertained me. I heard as many as eight singing at one time. Those were great evenings and I have wonderful memories of them. The singing whippoorwills, and the small gold specks of light that were the fireflies above the meadows, are associated in my mind with home and happy childhood.

Hearing the whippoorwill this morning brings back a scene—a group of us are walking to Plum Grove Church. Someone in the group has a harmonica. He walks over a path in the white moonlight, playing some old, sad melody. The whippoorwills are singing and fireflies are lighting the way through the velvety darkness.

I learned how the whippoorwills built their nests. Actually, the whippoorwills don't bother to gather straws and leaves and build a nest above the ground. This is too much work. They are lazy birds. The mother whippoorwill lays a few eggs on a fallen leaf, sits on the ground, and hatches her eggs. The whippoorwills expend their energies singing their lonesome ballads of love and death in the night. They love to sing their lonesome songs to each other, from hill to hill.

It's amazing that the whippoorwills have survived foxes, cats and snakes. They are rather gullible and easily caught. I like to remember the nights when the moon was shining on the summer dew, enlarging the sumac leaves beside the road until they looked like silver palm leaves. Often, when Naomi

271

and I drove home at night, the whippoorwills shone like fiery little red balls when our car lights flashed on them sitting beside the road. Many a night our car barely missed a whippoorwill. If we had been driving fast, we would have killed many of these awkward birds.

This morning when I heard the first whippoorwill my mind was so filled with memories I couldn't go back to sleep. I thought of the many superstitions connected with the whippoorwills. If one flies inside the house, there will be a death in the family within twenty-four hours. If one lights on the porch and sings, it is a song of death. If one keeps coming back to the yard, it is the sign of illness in the family. Whippoorwills are mentioned in songs and are always spoken of with affection in this country. It is regarded as a sin to kill a whippoorwill, for he is considered a sort of sacred bird in these hills.

The whippoorwill nearly always lights upon something

above the earth and sings, but when he sleeps during the day
he sits on the ground. This morning's arrival sang until 5:30;
then daylight came, and he stopped and descended for his
day's rest, and I wrote this little poem before I got out of
bed.

> This night has ended
> For the whippoorwill
> Has now descended
> And all is still.

or they perish

The study of the survival of wildlife through rugged winters in America should be quite enlightening for those of us who live in heated houses, sleep in warm beds under electric blankets and eat three warm, satisfying meals a day. How the warm-blooded birds and animals survive in nature's housing, on such scanty fare as can be found above and under the snow, is something of a miracle.

A bird so small that it can be covered by a woman's hand, can sleep in a fodder shock, a clump of grass or on a branch of a tree on a winter night when it is 20 degrees below zero, fly away at daybreak and find itself a breakfast of frozen weed seeds. What kind of circulatory system does it have when flesh, blood, feathers, and bone and beak together don't weigh even eight ounces? What sort of digestive system enables it to gain complete sustenance from a spoonful of frozen seeds?

More amazing than the bird is the possum. In winter, he lies on a bed of leaves in a hole in the ground, under a cliff, in a hollow tree or log. But when he gets really hungry and has to go in search of food, those little ears of his, so thin they are almost transparent, never freeze in subzero weather. I used to hunt possums when I was a boy; now, I let them live under my floor and sleep by the warm water pipes and feed them in my yard. During an unusually cold winter, I found one eating dirt near a creek bank. I took him to the house, fed him and kept him until spring. Because of the wildness inherent in the possum's nature, I never attempted to pet him. He wouldn't have let me.

Then there are the ground squirrels and ground hogs who go into holes and sleep most of the winter. Sometimes they get restless and stir. Once my dog treed what I was sure was an opossum. It was a big ball of fur up high in a leafless December tree. Then I shook the tree and the animal fell out, he was a big ground hog. I didn't bother him but let him go back to his hibernation den, his sleep and winter dream. Then, of course, wasps, hornets, yellow jackets and mud-daubers prefer holes in logs or trees and places under bark, boards, and planks for their semi-hibernation.

The cold-blooded living creatures, snakes, terrapins, turtles, frogs, salamanders and lizards, that hibernate and sleep, forget all about food for the winter. They go, with the exception of the lizard, into the rind of earth where they sleep until the warm spring rains seep down, warming and wakening them. Their lives are resurrected into a new world and a new season. Such is the dream of humanity, for another life, a new world, a new hope. Our cold-blooded friends on the earth around us fulfill our wish every year.

But what interests me most are the winter survival problems of the warm-blooded creatures who don't hibernate— both animals and birds. They must have food, water and housing. Wild deer often come and eat with my cattle and share the saltblocks with them. There was a time when my father and I worried what to do about wild honeysuckle. When birds ate the seeds and deposited them over the ground, honeysuckle began to grow everywhere. It climbed, smothered and dwarfed trees. We knew birds needed the seeds in winter, but we thought such an abundance of wild honeysuckle was harmful and tried to exterminate it—an impossible task.

Then we fenced the woodland areas where it grew and made a winter pasture for our sheep. Wild honeysuckle makes wonderful winter forage for deer. It also provides warm cover for roosting quail and it is even a good place for snakes to hibernate.

Since our fruit is imported and few people have orchards, there are no frozen apples under the leaves for the rabbits and possums. Orchards were once a great reservoir of food for wildlife. And since we are paid not to farm our cornland and no longer cut and shock corn in the valley and on the slope, another supply of food is practically gone. Some seasons the young persimmons freeze. And persimmons are a delicacy for most wild animals, especially possums, rabbits and foxes. So the food for wildlife becomes scarcer and scarcer, and unless farmers plant grain for animals and species of birds that remain in winter, our wildlife is in great danger of starvation.

People know more today about our wildlife and its struggle for survival than ever before. The possums often get so hungry they come into homes and pilfer from the garbage cans. The wild rabbits venture into yards where green grass lies under the snow. On our farm we have grasses that remain green all winter. Here I have tracked rabbits in the snow and found where they have pawed down to the grass.

In this area we have helped our wildlife through the rugged winters so much that they have become very dependent upon us. I now wonder how long it will be until wildlife will cease to be wild and become tame.

Like my father and his father before him, I used to be a good hunter. But then I found I could no longer kill. My farm became a game reserve. I fed all forms of wildlife, and animals that would come to my yard in winter. I bought fats and grain for them and fed them scraps from the table. Even the rare redheaded woodpeckers come to my feedboxes to eat grain. Now I feed wildlife all year round.

I want no copperheads about, so I encourage the black snakes to stay close. I don't feed them but let them forage. The creatures of nature can keep their own balance of power better than I can. And what a pleasure it is to have wildlife around.

If we do not feed our wildlife now, many species will become extinct. Some species will disappear if we continue to hunt and kill as we have in the past. And the saddest and loneliest countries in the world are those without wildlife.

about the author

Jesse Stuart—poet, short-story writer and novelist—is one of America's best-known and best-loved regional writers. He has written over twenty books, all of which are set in his native Kentucky hill country. He has taught and lectured extensively. One of his most famous novels, *Taps for Private Tussie*, was a Book-of-the-Month Club selection. *Save Every Lamb* is his seventh volume of collected pieces.

Jesse Stuart lives on his Kentucky farm near Riverton with his wife Naomi. The Stuarts have a daughter, Jane.